THE GREAT PERHAPS

THE GREAT PERHAPS

God as a Question

Burton F. Porter

ROWMAN & LITTLEFIELD
Lanham • Boulder • New York • London

Published by Rowman & Littlefield
A wholly owned subsidiary of The Rowman & Littlefield Publishing Group,
Inc.
4501 Forbes Boulevard, Suite 200, Lanham, Maryland 20706
www.rowman.com

Unit A, Whitacre Mews, 26-34 Stannary Street, London SE11 4AB

British Library Cataloguing in Publication Information Available

Library of Congress Cataloging-in-Publication Data

Porter, Burton F., author.
The Great Perhaps : God as a Question / Burton F. Porter.
pages cm
Includes bibliographical references and index.
ISBN 978-1-4422-4721-5 (cloth : alk. paper) -- ISBN 978-1-4422-4722-2 (electronic)
1. God. 2. Religion. I. Title.
BL473.P67 2015
212--dc23
2014048216

∞™ The paper used in this publication meets the minimum requirements of
American National Standard for Information Sciences Permanence of Paper
for Printed Library Materials, ANSI/NISO Z39.48-1992.

Printed in the United States of America

To refer all questions to science is like losing your keys on a dark road, then walking to a street light to look for them. That is, science cannot shed light on all questions. But what do we do with the issues that science, or even logic, cannot address? Are they still valid, or are they illegitimate concerns? Are there keys on the road, in the dark?

To Barbara,
who makes me grow younger,
like Indian summer when time flows backwards

CONTENTS

INTRODUCTION

What Has Athens to Do with Jerusalem?

Religion is of universal interest, a worldwide phenomenon from the beginning of the human race. But we are not content simply to believe; at times, we ask questions about the truth of what we believe. Those with faith in God want assurance that their worship is justified, and atheists want confirmation that God is nowhere to be found.

In short, we are intrigued by religion, at times obsessed by it. Religion seems to represent the deepest yearnings of the human heart, but we do not want to believe in a fairy tale. We search for the reasons for belief in God rather than living in a fool's paradise; we want our beliefs to be more than a comforting delusion. And if we use God for what we do not know, then the more we know, the less room there is for God; he is edged out of the universe. We certainly do not always act in terms of religion in our everyday lives. Bankers do not grant loans to "whoever asketh of thee," insurance companies do not offer lower rates to people who pray, and if our nation is attacked, we do not turn the other cheek. In an age of science, will religion persist or become outmoded as a historical curiosity?

In the West we particularly wonder about the God of the Judeo-Christian tradition—his wisdom, power, and goodness. We ask about his relationship to the world, why a loving and almighty Father would allow his children to suffer. What could justify earthquakes, hurricanes, tornadoes, and tsunamis, an innocent child contracting leukemia, and why would a benevolent God make Monet go blind, Beethoven go deaf? What would life after death be like, the survival of our soul after the disintegration of our body? Why does Freud dismiss religion as an infantile neurosis, and Marx regard it as the opiate of the masses? And do miracles happen, are prayers answered, and how can we tell? We also wonder whether we can even pose such questions, whether religion is simply a matter of faith. One theologian was asked, "What was God doing with himself before he created heaven and earth?" He answered, "Creating a hell for people who ask questions like that."

In this book we will explore such issues in a way sympathetic to the spirit of religion—its remarkably rich music, painting, and architecture, its multiple forms of worship that have persisted from the beginning of civilization. We appear to have a basic need for meaning in the world, a desperation for things to make sense, especially through a God who gives purpose to our lives. At the same time we want to be critical of spiritual claims, demanding reasoned argument to prove they are true. The desire to believe in a supernatural order is so strong that it could induce us to accept ideas we would otherwise dismiss as far-fetched. For most of us, our religious beliefs were acquired during childhood, and absorbed without question, perhaps because they calmed our fears about the wider world. As Voltaire said, "If there were no God, it would be necessary to invent him." The wit says that God created man in his own image; did man return the compliment? If triangles had a god, it would have three sides.

The reasoned approach is to be open to religion in the light of the role it has played in human history and in the human heart, while at the same time maintaining a critical distance. We should bring a sympathetic intelligence to bear on the religious dimension of our lives. This seems the only viable approach, even though it carries a risk of losing something precious. Even if the truth would kill our faith, that does not justify killing the truth.

This book, therefore, is not an evangelical tract or an atheistic rant. Rather, we start with minimum assumptions and maximum objectivity, trying to decide whether the worldview of religion does, in fact, diagram reality. We begin with questions rather than answers, asking whether God is an actual being, personal and fundamental, or simply an imaginative construct that personifies our hunger for purpose and immortality. Clerics are already committed to worshipping God, and they look for the foundation that lies within; they want to interpret, elaborate, and refine the structure of theological ideas. A more neutral approach is to start with few presuppositions. The committed will pray, "Dear God in heaven," whereas the critic says "Dear God, if there be a God, in heaven, if there be a heaven."

We will therefore tread the line between belief and skepticism. The religious person assumes that everything happens for the best in a world governed by a benevolent God, but the nonreligious person thinks that sometimes things work out well, at other times badly. And when illness strikes, the religious person asks, "Why me?" trying to understand his or her place in the scheme of things, whereas the nonreligious person says, "Why not me? I'm as likely to get sick as anyone else."

The aim is to engage you, the reader, in a thoughtful exploration of religion, beyond the attitude that "it's all a matter of faith." For not only is this a rational argument against the use of reason, and therefore self-contradictory, but it offers no protection against delusions. If we all thought like this, we would have no way of separating true beliefs from false ones; each person could claim that his or her position is based on faith and beyond all criticism. That way lies massacres, crusades, and jihads. What's more, we would have a welter of different beliefs, many inconsistent with one another, with each claiming to be the last word. Each would be immune from attack, and yet they could not all be true. Obviously, this is an impossible situation. Perhaps we may never reach certain answers to religious questions, but that does not mean religion's answers may never be questioned. We can at least dismiss absurd ideas, close some doors, and leave a residue of sound possibilities. As a contemporary philosopher, Daniel Dennett, writes, "Before you appeal to faith when reason has you backed into a corner, think about whether you want to abandon reason when reason is on your side."

Although the relation between faith and reason is very complex, many theologians and philosophers have held that logical thought has a legitimate role in religion. They have offered rational arguments as proof of a religious reality. Although they are unwilling to abandon their faith when their arguments are criticized, they do attempt to justify their belief.

Here we will push logic to the extreme to determine if there are good reasons for faith. This means we cannot go against logic just because logic goes against us. That would be like playing chess, and when our opponent says "check," we kick over the chessboard.

I

WHEN RELIGION FIRST TREMBLED INTO EXPRESSION

Primitive religion is the name for beliefs and practices of isolated, preliterate cultures that have not become technologically advanced civilizations. These cultures may not be "barbaric" or "pagan," but they are less complex and sophisticated than the developed societies of the world.

Some social scientists quibble with the label "primitive." They charge that such judgments are patronizing and only reflect a Eurocentric bias, a cultural bigotry. So-called primitive societies may produce cruder tools and artifacts, but they are sophisticated in other ways. Some early cultures had knowledge of healing herbs and possessed high-level hunting skills; the Maori in New Zealand, for example, were far ahead in their understanding of the stars and ocean currents. Therefore, it is argued, we should call such cultures "preliterate," or "hunter-gatherers," or "tribal societies of indigenous peoples."

Now although we want to be open-minded and tolerant, the more developed cultures do appear further ahead in a number of respects. They seem more advanced in governance, communication, agriculture, economics, transportation, politics, science, business, education, technology, housing, law, social services, medicine, commerce, literature, the arts, and, of course, religion.

In any case, the phrase "primitive religion" was applied first to the "primal" forms of prehistory in the Paleolithic, Mesolithic, and Neolithic eras. The Neanderthals buried their dead and prepared them for the afterlife; perhaps they thought the spirit departed when the body went limp. More often it refers to cultures such as the Australian aborigines, the natives of New Guinea, the jungle tribes of India and Southeast Asia, the Indians of the Upper Amazon and the Americas, village societies of Africa, such as the pygmies in the Congo, and so forth.

Within the academic world, the first scholarly theories about primitive religion and its origins were formulated by the cultural evolutionist Edward Tylor, in *Primitive Culture*, who proposed that belief in souls led to belief in gods, and by the social anthropologist James Frazer, in *The Golden Bough*, who found religion to be based on magic. Other prominent names in the field include E. E. Evans-Pritchard, Herbert Spencer, and Wilhelm Schmidt, and, more recently, Mircea Eliade and Joseph Campbell. Each had a different interpretation about the start of religion, and since they were speculating about prehistory, they could only offer hypotheses, using artifacts as empirical proof. Anthropologists still debate the question of what constitutes religion, especially compared to magic and science.

Nevertheless, there is some rough agreement. Each commentator believes that early religion (or prereligion) served a necessary function in early societies. It enabled people to face the terrifying and mysterious forces of nature that confronted them, and to feel some measure of control. Typhoons, earthquakes, and volcanoes destroyed their houses; droughts and insects ruined their crops; savage animals crippled and killed them; and sickness and death devastated their families. The world appeared chaotic, hostile, and unpredictable.

But perhaps it could be managed. For the power of nature seemed more than physical; it also had a spiritual dimension. Things happened in accordance with hidden purposes, for uncanny reasons. By believing in such powers, primitive peoples made sense of their world and felt some measure of control over the events surrounding them. Spiritual forces were personal and could be influenced for protection from danger. The physical and the spiritual were inseparable, indeed, the natural and the supernatural worlds were the same.

This union became a part of primitive culture, and the fusion conferred a degree of power over a hostile environment, especially the threat of injury. What mystified people was made understandable, safety could be achieved, and meaning could be found in every phase of their lives. This included the mystery of birth and death, which paralleled the cycle of new growth in the spring and the withering of vegetation in the fall. Furthermore, the common beliefs promoted solidarity within the group. There is comfort in obeying the ancient customs, and in following the moral rules of the tribe against such things as cheating and stealing. In fact, the world was maintained in being by the rituals that were practiced, hallowed by ancestors and tradition. The order of the world could be preserved through ceremonies and by storytellers who kept alive the tribal lore, repeating the myth of the tribe's creation and its importance. Above all, divine forces could be summoned that ensured the group's safety. The environment became less frightening, and people could feel that they belonged within a larger, spiritual world.

UNCANNY FORCES AND MORTAL DANGERS: *MANA* AND TABOO

When people first became conscious of religious powers, and translated this awareness into words, they referred to a force called *mana* that permeated their surroundings. *Mana* can be defined as supernatural energy resident within objects, individuals, or animals that makes them excellent in their own special qualities and enhances their strengths. It can be found in anything, which does not mean it is contained in everything. A spear with *mana* will fly straighter and hit its target more often; a field with *mana* will be fertile and grow richer crops; a boat with *mana* will be swift and stable; and if the fisherman's net catches a lot of fish, then it too possesses *mana*. A knife with *mana* will penetrate well, giving its user uncanny skill in hunting; wearing an animal skin imbued with *mana* will make it warm; and a house containing *mana* will be dry and comfortable, capable of withstanding high winds.

If an ancient Hawaiian finds an unusually shaped rock, he will bury it in his garden, and if good crops grow, he will know he was right: it had potency. In the same way, if he carries that rock with him while hunting and makes a kill, he will be sure to take the rock with him whenever he goes hunting again.

Objects such as charms, pendants, amulets, talismans, and fetishes also contain *mana*; they ward off evil. Our contemporary belief in the power of images, statues, or relics of saints might be a carryover of this early belief, because these things are attributed with an uncanny power akin to *mana*. Holy altars, priest's vestments, or sacred scripture might also fall into this category, and the Bible (or the U.S. flag) must not touch the ground. If you have ever used a particular pen for an exam, or used a special bat, racquet, or golf club, you have assumed that objects can possess extraordinary powers.

Particular foods can also possess *mana*, and since it is assumed that we are what we eat, consuming such foods can impart unusual powers to us. Bread is sacred in various cultures, and on Good Friday we bake hot cross buns, originally representing the four phases of the moon. Soma, a drink of fermented honey or flowers, is a ceremonial offering by Hindus along with clarified butter (ghee); milk is poured on Shiva linga in Taoist temples. We know that offerings of grape wine and beer were made 10,000 years ago, and mead, distilled from honey, appears in both the Bible and the Rig-Veda, a book of ancient Indian scripture. The coca shrub in Peru and hallucinogenic mushrooms in Mexico are natural drugs containing obvious power. Eggs, of course, represent fertility and rebirth, and are prominent at Easter—from chocolate eggs to jeweled eggs by Fabergé. Beans are thrown at Khmer weddings, rice at Western ones. Water too has special powers and can cleanse and purify like fire, whether in the Ganges or as holy water in a font. All foods nourish our bodies, but some feed our spirit—and serve as the ambrosia and nectar of humans.

When applied to people, *mana* denotes those of high prestige and importance. Their *mana* is obtained through birth, skill, or warfare. *Mana* dwells in the heads of chiefs and tribal elders, such as medicine men, giving them authority and status. It is also present in fierce warriors, skilled hunters, outstanding craftsmen, and gifted storytellers.

Mana is more of a noun than a verb, perhaps a quality. Whenever someone distinguishes himself or is exceptional in a field, that shows he possesses *mana*—something we might feel when confronted with remarkable artists or athletes. It provokes wonder, as if such people had uncanny powers. You may have had this sense in the presence of an extraordinary football or basketball player, a singer, dancer, or writer. Genius seems to be redolent with *mana*.

Women have naturally high *mana* because of their ability to reproduce; they are the dark, earthy half of nature. However, men usually have greater *mana* and may not eat with women for fear of contamination and the reduction of their power. Sometimes, though, they will have low *mana* and need to undergo purification or increase ceremonies, especially before a battle. But whether *mana* is natural or acquired, male or female it can be passed on to apprentices or to children. Also, by keeping objects together, *mana* can be transmitted; it will flow freely between things.

The word *mana* comes from the South Seas, where the belief was most prevalent. It was a feature of the primitive religion of Polynesia, which includes Hawaii, New Zealand, Samoa, and Melanesia, which includes New Guinea, Fiji, and the Solomon Islands. According to recent research, *mana* may not be universal but it is widespread, with parallels in the Egyptian *ka*, the Greek *ichon*, the Roman *numen*, the *wakan* of the Dakotas, and the word "Manitou" of the Algonquin. In North Africa the term is "baraka," and it applies to the sea, the moon and the stars, horses, twins, children, the blind, and the insane. All of these cultures treat *mana* as an internal force, more like electricity than gunpowder, a life-energy that makes our implements unique, spiritualizes our food, and enables people to transcend themselves.

Mana itself, as an impersonal force, is neither good nor bad, but it can be dangerous. This dark side of *mana* appears in the notion of *taboo*, tabu, or tapu. An object becomes taboo because it contains a high degree of *mana* and is therefore prohibited to those with less. The same prohibition could apply to persons where there is an inequality in the degree of *mana*. Captain Cook in *A Voyage to the Pacific Ocean* describes it as "consecrated, inviolable, forbidden, unclean, or cursed." For example, it is taboo for a commoner to have his head higher than the chief, or to walk in his footprint or his shadow; he could reduce the chief's *mana* and be snuffed out as if struck by lightning. For the same reason, a barber's hands must be purified when he cuts the chief's hair, and any food left over from the chief's meals must be buried. Likewise, no one can use the chief's furniture, his mat, or his fire. If these taboos are violated, banishment or death could follow. There are even recorded instances of people dying of dread after committing these offenses.

Ritualistic objects, ceremonial clothing, or, in later religion, sacred books, chalices, and altars contain *mana* and must be handled delicately and with reverence. Some objects cannot even be approached or mentioned by laypeople, much less touched. The situation may be compared to curse words, which should not be said, or fire, which has obvious power and is prohibited to children. The figure Uzzah in the Old Testament reached out to steady the Ark of the Covenant, and because it was taboo to him, he was struck dead. Pork is taboo to Jews and Muslims, beef to Hindus, and Adam and Eve were forbidden to eat of the Tree of Life. Burial grounds and sacred mountains, the onset of adolescence, marriages, and births are all surrounded by high *mana* and have taboos connected to them. During periods of change or when "the times are out of joint" and everyone is apprehensive, we need to tread very carefully. Taboo shows people the right and the wrong path, relieving some of the anxiety. Don't touch a corpse, hold your breath when passing a cemetery, and the groom must not see the bride before the wedding.

In Hawaii, during the reign of King Kamehameha II, the islands became practically uninhabitable because no one could even walk where his highness had walked; the king had to be carried about on a litter. Finally, defying all taboos, Kamehameha and his people sat down together for a communal meal, and when nothing happened, many of the taboos were abandoned. It was a brave move, similar to lighting the fuse of a bomb and hoping it would not go off.

Mana and taboo, like other primitive forms, explain the otherwise inexplicable, and by following the rules, unity and solidarity are achieved. If everyone does his part, knows his place, and respects the customs, then the world is maintained in balance. On the other hand, if taboos are violated, the world order could become askew, and everyone would suffer.

THE SPIRIT WITHIN AND OUR ANIMAL ANCESTORS: ANIMISM AND TOTEMISM

Animism is a term first used by Edward Tylor, referring to belief in spirits that inhabit plants, animals, and all natural objects, the way our soul resides within our body. The Latin *anima* means "spirit" or "soul." It may be the oldest belief, and can refer to breath, shadow, or life itself as "animating" every natural object—rivers, lakes, waterfalls, woods, mountains, animals, fish, flowers, grass, birds. Human beings are the model, because our body is thought to contain our soul; we are both physical and spiritual. What we do is directed from inside, reflecting the inner person. Even the involuntary beating of our heart, the flow of our blood, and the contraction of our eye reflects the spirit within.

Unlike pantheism, which holds that everything is spiritually united in a binding, universal force, animism maintains that distinct spirits dwell in each individual object. The natural world is animate and innately alive, not filled with gods as in polytheism but with "shades" of a spiritual kind that live within oceans and animals, sticks and stones. And unlike *mana*, these spirits have personality, emotion, will, and reactions.

According to Tylor, animism was the beginning of religion. Indigenous peoples recognized a spirit within everything that surrounded them. All natural objects led a life of their own because of an indwelling soul. Tylor dismisses animism, explains it away as a childish mentality or "cognitive underdevelopment," an early groping for religious understanding. He thinks the mistake lies in assuming that everything resembles animals that do things deliberately. The psychologist Jean Piaget also sees a parallel with children, who attribute all events to consciousness and intention. To the child, there are no accidents; every happening has a reason, including sickness and injury. This tendency can persist into adulthood if we try to make sense of each event, looking for meaning in whatever occurs. In times of disaster, we can even search our own souls, wondering what we did to deserve such punishment; we can assume that we ourselves are responsible for a natural catastrophe.

Trees are a prime example of animism because they contain a spirit that is sometimes revered. As Frazer put it, "the spirit is viewed as incorporate in the tree; it animates the tree and must suffer and die with it." The trunk and branches are either the spirit's body or its abode. Trees can be humanized to the point where they have voices, which can be heard in rustling leaves, and if a flood washes away a great tree, "the spirit of the tree cries." They can also be identified as either male or female. A Hindu farmer might splice trees, "marrying" a mango tree to a jasmine, and a tree in blossom is like a pregnant woman—it must be carefully tended. The Wamka of East Africa say of the coconut tree that it "gives them nourishment as a mother does a child." All fruit trees, especially the date palm, apple, and peach, have sacred meaning because they provide life.

Other types of trees also provoke feelings of awe, such as the baobab, holly, willow, redwood, and ash; in Celtic lore, the oak is the abode of fairies. The Christmas tree is part of Germanic folk tales; the papal and banyan trees are holy to Hindus; and the bo, bodhi, and fig tree are sacred to Buddhists. In villages in India, the ashoka tree is believed to have an indwelling female spirit. Worshippers offer flower garlands and circle the tree, paying out a spool of thread. Trees are holy objects because their roots and branches unite earth and heaven, and their decay and fresh growth is a metaphor for resurrection. The loss and renewal of foliage suggests immortality.

Animals likewise are sometimes thought to have a spiritual life; pastoral and hunting communities held different animals as sacred. The animal itself was not revered but rather what it manifested. The creature's strength, speed, agility, and so forth signified an inner spirit that was powerful and worthy of worship.

The ancient Egyptians celebrated the falcon, the eagle, and the ibis, and had a cult of the bull (Apis). In Greek culture, girls danced as bears in honor of Artemis, goddess of wild nature, and the satyr figure, representing male potency, had the hooves, horns, and beard of a goat. The temple of Apollo and Aphrodite contained pools of sacred fish. In China, tigers are one of the twelve zodiac animals, and there are tiger dances and charms with images of tigers that will keep the wearer safe. India has traditionally revered the cow, the monkey, and the snake, especially the hooded cobra. In Africa, it is the python, in Thailand and Cambodia the elephant has sacred status, feted in life and mourned in death. Germany has revered the bear; Mongolia, the wolf; the Inuit, the crow; and the Aztecs, the Quetzalcoatl bird.

Before a tree is cut down or an animal killed, the believer apologizes for doing so, explaining that he had to gather lumber for his house, or needed meat to survive. He might pray beforehand, showing deference and respect. In Borneo, when crocodiles are captured, the hunter expresses regret and lets the crocodile die on its own rather than kill it. When the Eastern Crees hunt bear, they are careful not to insult him; they return his skull to the forest, honoring his soul.

According to Tylor, belief in an inner spirit was satisfying to early peoples because it explained dreams and visions. The soul departs on journeys while the body sleeps, wandering freely. It encounters friends and dead relatives, fights battles, and performs heroic deeds. Some Native Americans hesitate to wake people too abruptly because the soul may not be able to return in time. When apparitions are seen, they could be the spirits of those who are asleep, their ghosts wandering abroad. Above all, the idea of a spirit explained the difference between being alive and being dead. In death the soul frees itself, leaving only the empty shell of the body behind. The person is alive but his mortal remains decay. When we view a dead person, it is natural to think that they themselves are not there; their essence has departed.

On this view, the human soul survives and goes on to a peaceful world, a place of bliss or tranquility, perhaps spiritual ecstasy. This can lead to ancestor worship and rites of mourning, because the dead need to be remembered in order to continue to be. People may have to offer prayers, light candles, leave messages, or perform rites to sustain their soul. Or the departed spirits may wander the earth, and the actions of the living may be necessary to complete their passage to the other world. People may even fear the ghost of a relative, and want to assuage his anger so he does not harm them. They are expected to offer food or money, even sacrifices of blood to support the shade of the beloved. In Borneo, the person's slaves were killed to accompany their master to the afterlife; in India, a man's widow was thrown on the funeral pyre; the Pawnee used to slaughter the man's horse; the Arabs killed his camel at the gravesite.

According to one theory, belief in God arose this way, along with the rituals and ceremonies that accompany worship. Once the soul is separated from the body, it is an easy step to conceive of a universal spirit who resembles us, one who has an ideal nature and is present everywhere and always.

New Age religion is decidedly animistic, stressing the supernatural force inherent in all things and our relatedness to other biological forms. We must respect the natural world because it is alive like us. And neopagans call for a new identification between spirit and matter, the sacred and the profane.

Totemism stands for belief in a mystical kinship between a clan on the one hand, and an animal or even a plant on the other. As defined by Frazer, "A totem is a class of material objects which a savage regards with superstitious respect, believing that there exists between him and every member of the class an intimate and altogether special relationship."

The French sociologist Émile Durkheim did the most extensive research on totemism and concluded that it was "the primal religion." He found totemism widespread among Native Americans in the Pacific Northwest and Alaska, and even among the Bushmen in Australia. The word "totem" originated in the Ojibwe language (a dialect of the Algonquins), but totemic belief exists on practically every continent.

In totemism a clan will believe it has a unique connection with some animal or plant, and will even adopt its name, for example, the bear or kangaroo clan, the wolf or turtle clan. It will also claim to be descended from the totem animal, that the first member of the clan was born from a snake, a cougar, or a lizard. Sometimes, the reverse claim is made: that the totem animal was born from a member of the tribe. In either case, a spiritual affinity exists between the two such that the group embodies the creature's characteristics. Particular reverence must be shown to the animal as an ancestor, the core of the clan's identity, and everyone within the totem culture is a kinsman or brother.

Perhaps a kind of reincarnation took place whereby the spirit of the animal assumed human form, or the clan regards itself as endowed with the traits of their totem. Some tribes had personal and clan totems, and the individual could exhibit physical or psychological similarities to his totem creature.

Theories abound as to the origin of totems. For example, Herbert Spencer argued that totemism began in the Native Americans' custom of naming their children after animals—Little Beaver, Standing Coyote, and so on, depending on the nature of the child. They then confounded these metaphorical names with real objects. Frazer, on the other hand, speculated that it began in "ignorance of paternity." That is, primitive peoples did not see any causal connection between sex acts and the birth of a child, so they assumed the real father was a totem. Both theories have insufficient evidence. However, it does seem reasonable to think that totemism marked a stage from hunting to domestication, and it declined as tribes began to raise animals for food. When wild creatures were tamed and bred, they lost their mystique, and totemism collapsed.

Usually, members of the clan were "exogamous," that is, they had to marry someone of another totem; this ensured a certain genetic diversity and avoided incest. Also, they could not kill or eat their own totem animal except during religious festivals. At such times there were "increase ceremonies" to replenish the species, which was reciprocated by other totem clans. Tribal histories and tales were told of the spiritual connection, and there were dramatic performances of the totem myth, reaffirming the clan's identity with the guardian, protective spirit. Dancers moved like the totem animal, often uttering its cries and wearing its skin. In the eyes of the tribe, they became the actual animal rather than imitating it, the way an idol can become the thing it represents.

Totem poles are the most conspicuous example of totemism, but anthropologists treat them more as monuments than religious artifacts. They did incorporate some totemic beliefs, and displayed frogs and birds, arms and wings, but mostly totem poles commemorated notable events or the lineage of the tribe and displayed the crests of the chiefs. They were mainly works of art, carved from tall cedar trees. And contrary to common opinion, totem poles were never worshipped and the figures were not arranged in order of importance; being "high on the totem pole" did not indicate a superior rank.

Altogether, totemism showed a spiritual connection with an animal, more mystical than symbolic. It was a means for human beings to relate to the natural world and to invite nature into society. People assumed their place as incarnations of one of nature's creatures, and after death they would go to the totem home. According to Durkheim, it brought discipline, coherence, vitality, and euphoria (contentment) to the group, even more than other early beliefs.

We have a secular version of totemism today in emblems, heraldic badges, ensigns, and crests. Canada's coat of arms shows a lion and a unicorn; the great seal of the United States features an eagle—noble, fierce, and majestic. Family crests have stags or stallions to indicate nobility. Even our sports teams identify with animals, calling themselves the Colts, Panthers, Penguins, Cardinals, Blue Jays, Rays, Falcons, Dolphins, Seahawks, Cubs, Marlins, and so forth. We also hear echoes of totemism in Boy Scout packs and dens named for tigers, wolves, and bears, with Eagle Scout as the highest rank. In addition, cars can have animal names, such as Mustang, Ram, Jaguar, Impala, Lynx, Hornet, Firebird, Skylark, Rabbit, Spider, and Beetle. Obviously these are not totems in the religious sense but symbols that retain a vestige of their tribal meaning, connoting the qualities of the animals.

BLACK AND WHITE MAGIC: FORMULAS, SPELLS, AND MEDICINES

In primitive cultures, *magic* means the use of formulas, materials, and techniques to gain control over nature beyond what is physically possible. More generally, it stands for the attempt to make an event happen by means of spells and medicines that invoke ethereal powers.

One of the classic differences between religion and magic is that religion appeals to a god through prayer, trying to persuade the deity to act, whereas magic compels spiritual forces to do what the person wishes. If prayers are not answered, the worshipper concludes that God knows best, but if the magic does not work, then the magician assumes the methods were faulty: an unclean person performed the rite, newt's blood was not used, it should have been done at midnight, and so forth.

Magic is more mechanical than religion, as though invisible wires were connected to the supernatural, forcing some effect. If a person pulls the right levers, an event has to occur. In this respect, magic is closer to science, which also compels an outcome. In chemistry, for example, if an experiment does not produce the expected result, the student does not question scientific method. Rather, he or she attributes the failure to mistakes in performing the experiment: the beaker was contaminated with ammonia, the formula was incorrect, sulfuric acid should have been used rather than hydrochloric. In the same way, if a patient dies unexpectedly, the doctor wonders whether he made the right diagnosis, or prescribed the right drugs, but he does not doubt the efficacy of medicine. Similarly, if magic does not work, that is not considered the fault of magic.

However, in another respect, magic is closer to religion because it draws on supernatural powers. It goes beyond the natural world in a way that science does not. The magician hardly appeals to God but he taps into spiritual forces nonetheless, and he trusts them as a chemist or physician trusts natural law. One anthropologist, Evans-Pritchard, claims that magic does not replace cause and effect but explains good and bad fortune. Other anthropologists take it further and maintain that magic substitutes the transcendent for all causal explanations.

Obviously, magic does not have the rigor or exactitude that science requires. In science, physical proof is demanded, predictability, and the ability to replicate the results. In addition, vagueness, ambiguity, and contradiction are not tolerated. Magic, on the other hand, is a looser system that does not demand lucid explanations, and it leaps to conclusions without ruling out other possibilities. If inconsistencies arise, further explanations are introduced to account for the discrepancy. If the various parts do not mesh with one another, that does not trouble the magician because he does not use logic; a coherent system is not necessary, only a satisfying one.

According to Frazer, magic follows two principles: *the law of similarity* and *the law of contagion*. The law of similarity is homeopathic magic, which assumes that whatever is alike is the same. For example, if an image or fetish of a person is made, such as a voodoo doll, then magic can be worked against the person through that figure. He can then be injured or killed, made affectionate or kind by manipulating the image. It can be stabbed with a knife, buried to rot, roasted over a fire, sprinkled with pepper, or stuck with pins for shooting pains. On the positive side, the image can be bathed with a love potion, or herbal remedies can be applied to cure an illness.

The figure must be as lifelike as possible, and contain something of the person—a hair, nail cutting, partially eaten food, or even an article of clothing. A mirror or a picture can capture a person's likeness, perhaps their spirit, which is why tribal peoples are wary of cameras. In one instance, a Blackfoot Indian placed a hair of the woman he loved on her image, and she followed him around for days.

Even knowing a person's name confers power over the person, so that in some primitive cultures people are given two names: their real name, known only by their parents and the medicine man, and the name they go by. An enemy can only harm them if he knows their real name.

The identification between a person and that person's name seems very common, and persists to the present day. Some sociologists speculate that when a woman marries and assumes her husband's name it symbolizes a partial change in her identity. And as a person grows, and Chuck becomes Charles, Meg becomes Margaret, and Bill becomes William, that indicates the emergence of a different, mature individual. More significantly, the biblical prohibition against taking the name of the Lord in vain may be rooted in this concept. Conservative Jews will not write the full name of God, or Jehovah.

The law of contagion, on the other hand, states that things that were once in contact tend to remain connected. For instance, if someone is hurt in battle, his wound is treated, but so is the arrow that caused the wound. If the arrow is broken and fixed, then the person is likely to recover. Meanwhile, the enemy will keep his bow near the fire to cause fever in his victim, and he will twang the string occasionally to prolong the pain. He will also drink spicy liquids because that too will raise his enemy's temperature. Because of contagion, spitting is dangerous for magic and can be sent back along the trail to the person. For the same reason, you must be careful about your shadow and your footprint; if your enemy steps on your shadow, you could fall ill, and if sharp stones are put in your footprint, you could become lame. The Australia Bushmen used this technique to slow down kangaroos in the hunt. In East Africa the Nandi cut off some of their captive's hair; then they cannot escape.

Black magic, of course, is considered Satanic because it seeks to do evil. The prime example in more modern times is the Black Mass, which is a ceremony designed to bring about someone's death. The mass is said backwards at night in a deserted church, beginning at 11:00 p.m. and ending at midnight. A black host is used, and rather than wine, some water from a well—preferably one in which an unbaptized infant has been thrown. The sign of the cross is made, not in the air with the right hand but on the ground with the left foot. Then the name of the victim is pronounced, who immediately dies.

Witchcraft, which generally uses black magic, occurred particularly in Europe, between the fourteenth and eighteenth centuries, and is associated with devil worship and demonology. Americans are familiar with the Salem witch trials in 1692, in which 150 men and women were arrested and 19 hanged; it is widely taken as a cautionary tale about the dangers of religious extremism. The witch was accused of using magical powers, mainly to inflict harm, (bad witchcraft) and secondarily for healing and love magic (good witchcraft). In sub-Saharan Africa, witchcraft tends to persist today, and if people are accused of witchcraft, they can be imprisoned or executed. In Kenya in 2008, eleven people were burned by a mob as witches; in Tanzania in 2006, twenty-five Albinos were killed; in Nigeria in 2008, a thousand children were murdered as witches.

Witchcraft can be considered a cult, meaning a form of religious devotion by a relatively small number of worshippers that is regarded as strange or sinister by the majority. The cynic questions this definition, of course, and says a cult is a religion without political power, just as a language is a dialect with an army. But witchcraft can be a genuinely depraved practice.

White magic is beneficial, and may be best seen in fertility rites. A stone, bone, or wooden phallus is carved, which represents the erect male organ and symbolizes the generation of children. Less often, the female genitals are depicted, standing for reproduction. Ceremonies and rituals then take place in which these figures are central. Pillars, obelisks, and towers have been erected as phallic objects, and in India the *lingam* along with the female *yoni* was revered for its generative power; this worship also occurred in Egypt, Greece, and Rome. The Willendorf Venus, a rotund, devotional figure with heavy breasts and thighs, dates from 22,000 b.c. and was revered as symbolizing fertility and abundance. A pregnant woman who walks through a field will ensure rich crops, just as pouring water on the ground from a gourd will bring rain. In medieval Europe, candles were used as protective magic—slim, red candles during childbirth to guard against demons, large, blessed candles to ward off evil spirits. Are these powerful male symbols?

Our oldest art, the Paleolithic cave painting done around 32,000 years ago and the recently discovered cave paintings in Indonesia, shows evidence of belief in magic. In 350 caves in France and Spain, especially Altamira and Lascaux, we see paintings of animals with spears or arrows in their flanks. Presumably, the Stone Age hunter is gaining power over the animal. These representations of bison, horses, and deer are not intended as art since they are found in some of the darkest, most remote crevices of the caves, but were probably meant as hunting magic.

We know that primitive people believed that we took on the characteristics of the animals we ate in a magical transference. In order to be a fast runner you had to eat agile animals, such as monkeys, birds, deer, and fish, and to avoid sluggish beasts, such as cattle, swine, and sheep. Eating rabbits would make you timid but leopards or wolves promoted bravery, especially if you ate their heart and drank their blood. For a long life, you should consume a tortoise; a crow will make you wise; and a kangaroo will help you jump higher. Consuming an owl enables you to see in the dark, and eating birds' tongues can make you eloquent. Cannibals believe that if they eat an enemy who was brave, they will absorb his courage, intelligence, and strength.

To quote Frazer's *The Golden Bough*, "The savage commonly believes that by eating the flesh of an animal or man he acquires . . . the characteristics of that animal or man; so when the creature is deemed divine, our simple savage naturally expects to absorb a portion of its divinity along with its natural substance." Frazer draws the analogy with the sacrament of communion, which he traces to homeopathic magic. Symbolically absorbing the body and blood of Christ, or actual transubstantiation, can guarantee eternal life.

All of these forms tend to overlap—*mana*, taboo, animism, totemism, and magic—so that the lines are difficult to draw. *Mana*, for example, has been called "the stuff from which magic is made." Today, they are all regarded as superstitions, defined as "widely held but unjustified beliefs in supernatural causation." But such superstitions have remarkable staying power, permeating our culture: don't let a black cat cross your path, shoes on the bed mean a death in the family, or walking under a ladder is bad luck (maybe because you could be covered with paint). Some people even accept omens such as "if a cat sneezes, licks its face, or sleeps with its back to the fireplace, it is sure to rain."

In any case, these forms of belief did serve a useful function within early cultures; they can be called beneficial myths. The members of the tribe feel more in control of their lives and believe they are connected to the world. They have an explanation as to why things happen, and they know what to do and what not to do. When they practice hunting magic, game is in fact killed at some point; they avoid taboos, and nothing awful happens for a while; they honor the totem animal, and no animals attack them, at least not often; and if they perform a rain dance, it does rain eventually. Failures are soon forgotten, successes are remembered, and the belief assures the tribe of safety, power, and cohesion. To the civilized mind, timing has a great deal to do with the success of a rain dance.

From a philosophic standpoint, some primitive thinking commits the fallacy called *post hoc ergo propter hoc*. That is, it is a logical mistake to assume that because one event preceded another the first event caused the second to happen. Even though a rooster crowed before the sun rose, that does not mean the sun rose because the rooster crowed. A subsequent event should not be confused with a consequent one; the first is temporal, the second causal. We make the same *post hoc* mistake if we argue that hospitals kill people because people have died after being admitted to hospitals. People do die in hospitals, despite what medicine can do to save them; the hospital does not kill them (at least not usually). Allowances must be made for alternative explanations besides the preceding event.

With regard to magic, people can become sick if black magic is used against them, which, some claim, proves that it works. But people only become sick if they know magic is being aimed at them. This shows the power of the mind over the body, not the reality of magic.

2

NATIONAL RELIGIONS OF THE ANCIENTS

Apart from Asian cultures, Egypt, Greece, and Rome are the best-known civilizations of the ancient world, and each had a rich religious tradition. Their belief systems have been reconstructed by archaeologists and anthropologists who have unearthed temples, altars, ceremonial objects, and written documents describing the gods and the rituals of worship. Their religions were more sophisticated than those of primitive cultures but still crude by later standards. Furthermore, their gods were highly anthropomorphic, resembling strong, wise, idealized people who lived forever in a timeless realm. Compared to the gods of the world religions that followed, they lacked the transcendence and superiority that separates gods from mortals.

THE HUMAN-ANIMAL GODS OF EGYPT

By all indications, the ancient Egyptians were deeply religious, and their beliefs were not abstract but literal and clear, like their art. From 3000 to 800 b.c. artists created line drawings with the figures shown in their best aspects, the shoulders square, the face, hands, and feet in profile. They were, in fact, illustrations more than art, lacking perspective or depth. The pyramids too were straightforward and obvious, geometric with planes like shafts of sunlight, and Egyptian writing did not consist of letters but hieroglyphics. These word-pictures made it difficult to express abstract ideas. Similarly, when portraying the gods, the Egyptian passion for clarity prevailed; they created unambiguous forms. Just as life can imitate art, their art reflected their life; the influence flowed both ways. Every aspect of belief was lucid and practical, without imagination or subtlety.

Perhaps human beings need a concrete illustration of an idea rather than an abstraction in order to fully grasp it. As one critic remarked, dance is for people who cannot understand music without seeing it.

Some scholars have speculated that the Egyptians were incapable of philosophic thinking, that they only understood the visible and concrete; they disliked questions that had more than one answer. But whether by nature or by choice, the Egyptians created a world in which everything was taken at face value, even if the parts did not fit together neatly. The priests of Heliopolis or Thebes were never troubled by contradictions in their theology; that simply did not matter. If ideas appeared obvious, they were accepted, whether they were inconsistent or not.

This attitude produced a conservatism that is a major characteristic of Egyptian religion. Throughout the centuries, the Egyptian vehemently resisted change. Every idea was retained and nothing discarded. Gods might be added to the pantheon but none were eliminated, because that could entail awful consequences. The Egyptian therefore trailed after himself the deities of his ancestors, building an elaborate polytheism by "syncretizing." As one commentator, George Moor, put it, "The Egyptians of later ages could learn but not forget—the most fatal of all disqualifications for progress." For this reason, when we read the history of Egyptian religion, we can see at the end what was thought at the beginning.

According to the earliest records, each Egyptian "nome," or town and surrounding area, had a prince and a god of its own. This system is called "kathenotheism." The god was a simple, geographical deity, jealously guarded as the protecting divinity of a people. Some gods were so local that they had no name other than the nome to which they belonged, such as "He of Edfu," "She of Elkab." Approximately 2,000 gods and goddesses have been identified, each with a temple as a dwelling place for the patron deity of the nome.

Gradually, however, gods of surrounding areas were added, either through conquest, absorption, or because they appeared powerful. The existence of the previous deity was not denied, but rather the new god was attached to the name of the old, a mingling of divinities. Also, the regional gods eventually became departmental gods, in charge of some aspect of nature. For example, Amen, the god of Thebes, came to be regarded as the deity of fertility. The Egyptians also worshipped the heavenly bodies, the Nile River, trees, piles of stones, and their kings or pharaohs. The pharaoh was considered a god, or an intermediary between the people and the gods, sometimes both.

Another distinctive feature of Egyptian religion was the reverence for animals—animals that were believed to be tokens of holiness. The jackal protected royal tombs and conducted the dead to the afterlife; the hawk was a powerful hunter that saw everything and swooped down silently on prey; the mongoose robbed nests and ate predatory creatures; and cats watched for the sun while keeping down the head of the serpent of darkness. Some creatures were admired for their strength, such as the crocodile and the hippopotamus, and the delicate ibis was revered because it killed the land snakes and devoured crocodile eggs. The beetle was pictured in the solar boat, "the boat of millions of years," frogs and toads brought fertility, and locusts consumed crops. The bull represented power and masculinity, but the cow displayed gentle, feminine virtues, sustaining life with her milk. Every animal had its place, from the goat to the fish to the praying mantis. In fact, some historians say that animal worship was more prevalent in ancient Egypt than at any other time, dominating the thinking of the people. When the Romans occupied Egypt, one of the legionnaires was torn to bits by a crowd for accidentally killing a cat.

But some historians question whether the animals themselves were worshipped or the gods they represented. The animal may have been regarded as a vessel or living image of the god. Apis, the god of Memphis, was a bull; Thoth, the god of Hermopolis, was a baboon; and Apophis was the world serpent, but each may have been considered a manifestation of the deity. Although the Greeks ridiculed the Egyptians for their reverence toward animals, perhaps the worship was not literal but symbolic, the way that carved images represent saints in shrines. If the figures themselves were worshipped, that would be idolatry, and sometimes it is difficult to make the mental separation.

In any case, the animals did become symbols after a time, and many of the gods were depicted in human form with animal parts that indicated the god's signatures. Curiously, the gods were shown as chimeras with human bodies and animal heads, or sometimes (more rarely) the reverse. The god Khnum appears as a man with a ram's features; Hekt was depicted as a woman with the head of a frog; Bastet had the ears of a cat; and Anubis peers out from the head of a jackal. The famous example of a human head with an animal body is the Sphinx, a figure with the face of a man and the body of a recumbent lioness; it represented Harmachis, the rising sun. (In Greek mythology, the sphinx had the head and breasts of a woman, the body of a lioness, and wings.)

Finally, the gods became completely human, but because of Egyptian conservatism, they retained vestiges of the animal that is their emblem. Hathor, for example, is a complete woman, but she has a crown of cow horns on her head; Selkhet wears a scorpion, without its sting; Amen-Ra is a male figure, but he retains two long feathers and a pair of ram's horns. He also holds a scepter and an ankh, the key of life. The ankh is shaped like a cross but with a loop at the top, probably representing the sun, rising above the crossbar of the horizon. A disk symbolizing the sun appears above the heads of many gods, as halos do above saints.

The tendency toward retaining the past and assimilating former gods affected Egyptian theology in significant ways. For instance, when the position of supreme god was conferred upon Ra, the previous gods were identified with him in both name and attributes. For this reason hyphenated labels were created, such as Ra-Horus and Ra-Amen. In fact, triads of gods were formed, and enneads (clusters of nine), many of them family groupings with one god supreme. In Thebes, there was Amen the father, Mut the mother, and Montu the son; in Memphis, it was Ptah, Sekhmet, and Imhotep; at Abydis, Osiris, Isis, and Horus.

In the associated mythologies, the son inherits his father's authority and becomes his mother's husband—a plot that Sophocles used effectively in *Oedipus Rex*, which is set in Thebes. Incest was the limit of horror to the Greeks, and it is a widespread taboo in societies, but the Egyptians accepted it for the gods and for dynastic succession of the royal family.

Although the gods were not arranged in a hierarchy but prominent at different historical periods, several divinities seem to have dominated. The god Ra, previously mentioned, is highly important as the incarnation of the sun. He is the sun-god, and he first appeared at Heliopolis with the head of a falcon, holding the Uraeus serpent as a symbol of authority. Throughout the religious history, Ra is a powerful deity—the Egyptian sun in its full heat and light. Another high god was Amen, the presiding deity of Thebes, who was often pictured as a he-goat or a bearded man. For a time, as Amen-Ra, he was the national god of Egypt.

Still another major deity is Aton, who at one period actually became the only god of Egypt. The pharaoh Amenhotep IV instigated his worship, calling himself "Ikhnaton," or "Spirit of Aton." He did not add other gods but demanded universal worship for Aton as the sole god. The priests would chant verses, such as

> How manifold are thy works!
> They are hidden before men,
> O sole God, beside whom there is no other.
> Thou didst create the earth according to thy heart.
> Thou didst make the distant sky in order to rise therein,
> In order to behold all that thou hast made,
> While thou wast yet alone
> Shining in thy form as living Aton.

This was the first monotheism, but it was short lived. Ikhnaton died before he was thirty after a reign of just seventeen years, and after his death the people quickly reverted to their traditional polytheism. Apparently, Ikhnaton was a colorful figure, somewhat intolerant and obstinate as a ruler, but he has been called "the great idealist" and "the original revolutionary" because he first conceived of one supreme god—and in 1375 b.c.

In addition to Ra, Amen, and Aton, the god Osiris was one of the most prominent divinities, pictured as holding the hook and flail to symbolize his authority. At first he was the personification of the Nile, representing the birth and death of vegetation as the Nile flooded and receded from the land. Later, as the Egyptians became preoccupied with the afterlife, Osiris became highly important as the god of the dead.

Perhaps the overriding feature of Egyptian religion was its obsession with individual immortality. They were preoccupied with life after death, more than any other culture in history. Some historians attribute this to the extremely dry climate that preserves everything from decay. The Egyptians may have extended this principle to human life, reasoning that if the body lasted forever, assisted by various burial rites, then so might the soul. In fact, it became an article of faith that the person would exist eternally if their body survived intact. Hence the process of mummification, its placement in a heavy coffin, and the elaborate tombs and sealed pyramids that were designed to withstand the ravages of time.

When a man died, professional embalmers would remove his entrails and immerse the rest of the body in salt water treated with natron and bitumen, a mineral tar. The abdominal cavity was stuffed with linen, sawdust, cushions, and resin, and the entire body was rolled in bandages with jewelry and amulets between the layers. The mummy was then placed in a wooden or stone sarcophagus in the shape of a man, decorated with magical symbols. Food and drink were left at the site along with games, which would be useful in the next life. Doors were painted on the coffin to allow the dead man easy passage in and out, and eyes were inserted at the head end to enable the man to see the rising sun. The inside of the coffin and the mummy's chest were inscribed with texts pertaining to the afterlife, mainly from *The Book of the Dead* and *The Pyramid Texts*; the latter is our oldest collection of religious spells, dating from 2400 b.c. Finally, the coffins were laid in modest tombs for the poor, imposing tombs for the wealthy, and in massive pyramids for pharaohs or kings. Some of the tombs had provisions of wine, dates, grain, and cakes; some contained chariots, boats, and wooden figures of servants. The great Pyramid at Giza, one of the wonders of the world, was built like all Egyptian architecture on massive lines, designed to last forever, along with the pharaohs they protected.

Osiris sits in judgment on the souls of the dead, while the god Thoth conducts the "Weighing of the Soul," questioning the person about his earthly deeds. After this trial, the individual is admitted to the Osirian fields or consigned to "the Devouress." To pass on, the person must recite a list of offenses that he has *not* committed: "I have not killed men or women"; "I have not committed robbery or violence"; "I have not committed adultery, I have not lain with men"; "I have not made deceit"; "I have not angered"; "I have not blasphemed"; and so forth. The list, of course, reflects their value system. The sins or "shalt nots" are twenty-one in number, and since people would be lying if they deny all of them, magic formulas are used to blind Thoth as he weighs their soul against a feather. The soul consists of several parts, and it is the *ka*, or "life force," that is judged rather than the *ba*, which is akin to personality.

If the dead are judged worthy, they are then free to continue living but in a transformed state. The contemplatives could regard truth and justice for all eternity; royalty could travel with Ra across the sky; others could return to earth and participate in human affairs, including intervention in the lives of relatives. These relatives, of course, did not always welcome visits from the mummies. In earlier beliefs, all souls were able to live among the gods, climbing a ladder in the west (if the *ka* knew the magic formula). Death was a passage to a better existence, and an inordinate amount of Egyptian life consisted of preparation for this transition to the next life.

Egyptian religion is foreign to our minds but, at the same time, familiar and accessible. We can identify traits from primitive religion, especially animism and magic, but other elements, such as the minimalism in the art and architecture, seem almost modern. The human forms of the gods, the halo like the sun, the shepherd's crook of authority, the ankh like a cross, the emphasis on burial rituals—all have their counterparts today. And, of course, the triads of gods resemble the Christian trinity. (Maybe we tend to arrange our experience in threes: mind, body, spirit; executive, legislative, judicial; Id, Ego, Superego.) Perhaps the Egyptian concern with death and immortality is characteristic of religion in general, and it makes people who lived 5,000 years ago seem like our contemporaries.

GREEK DIVINITIES AND THEIR MYTHOLOGIES

We know relatively little about pre-Homeric religion in Greece, that is, the beliefs prior to the eight century b.c., but we have uncovered a great deal about its later forms. We do know that the early deities were nature gods, that the Greeks believed in an afterlife, and that religious festivals were held at the changing of the seasons. In particular, spring was a celebration of fresh growth and rebirth, the renewal of fertility, and the winter solstice merited a feast because, thereafter, daylight lasted longer. It was always a celebration when the sun did not continue to disappear lower on the horizon. Their beliefs too were polytheistic, and each *polis* had its god who brought sunlight, thunder, and rain. There was a goddess who was Mother Earth, and one who was the queen of the chase; there was a shepherd god, a god of the fire, and a spirit of the sea. Knowledge of later, classical Greek religion is contained in Hesiod's *Theogony*, Ovid's *Metamorphosis,* the *Odes* of Pindar, and, of course, Homer's epic poems, *The Iliad* and *The Odyssey*.

The physical geography of Greece played a significant role in the country's development, because the land is separated into valleys divided by inlets and mountainous terrain. Therefore, the various communities were isolated from one another, which fostered independence, pride, and a religious parochialism. One feature of local worship was the communal meal in which the citizens of the *polis* and the gods of the pantheon were thought to come together, renewing their mutual bond. The *polis*, or "city-states," did eventually merge into a nation, but Greek history is that of both division and unification—and Greek religion is no exception.

Zeus was the overarching god and the major deity throughout Greece. He was the supreme ruler, a celestial being who controlled the sun, lightning, thunder, and rain, symbolized by the eagle. Zeus was "the father of gods and men," the designer and savior of creation, but also "lord of justice," peacemaker, guardian of political freedom, the protector of civil society. He is usually portrayed as a bearded, middle-aged man with a youthful body, looking powerful and majestic. Like all Greek sculptures, he is shown as an idealized human being, larger than life. Even the Greeks did not look like the Greeks.

According to the mythology, Zeus's father, Cronus, was warned that one of his children would depose him, and to prevent this, he swallowed his newborns: Demeter, Hera, Hestia, Hades, and Poseidon—all except Zeus. To save him, his mother, Gaia, wrapped a stone in swaddling clothes, which Cronus then swallowed, and Zeus was spirited to Mount Dicte, where he was raised in a cave. When he returned as a young man, he overthrew his father and his dynasty, and forced Cronus to regurgitate his children. The universe was then divided among them— Poseidon was given the sea, Hades the underworld, and Zeus took the heavens for himself.

Like most of the Greek gods, Zeus was not a moral being, much less a deity of infinite goodness. He was "deathless," all-seeing, wise, and extremely powerful, all of which made him a god. Although he bled a special blood called *ichor*, he could not die of his wounds. Zeus is admirable not for his virtue but for his magnificence and extraordinary might. He does not consume bread and wine like mortals but exists on ambrosia and nectar, which bring eternal youth. He lives on Mount Olympus, hurls thunderbolts at his enemies, and is invincible. He is not limited by moral principles but commits acts of incest and rape with impunity. Zeus is also capable of theft and deception, of quarreling and feuding, of petty jealousies and anger at insults. As a god he is neither good nor evil, but mighty, men must placate his anger. Humans mock him at their peril. For the Greeks, sin did not consist in violating ethical rules but in *hubris*, aspiring to be equal to the gods. One must not be so arrogant as to transgress the boundaries of human understanding or, like Icarus, who flew too high, one would be dashed to earth.

Zeus does behave capriciously and immorally, especially in making love to goddesses and mortals as his whims take him. His "gold-throned" queen, Hera, bore him such deities as Athena, Ares, and Hephaestus, but he also seduced numerous mortals, often in disguise. He attracted Leda in the form of a swan, producing two sets of twins, Castor and Pollux, and Clytemnestra and Helen of Troy. As a shower of gold he enticed Princess Danae; abducted Europa as a bull; appeared as an eagle to the Trojan prince Ganymede; and used thunder to appeal to Semele, the sound acting as an aphrodisiac. His liaisons produced numerous offspring, such as Perseus, Dionysus, the nine Muses, the three Fates, and the three Graces. For his potency, philandering, and cleverness, the Greeks found Zeus admirable, even though he broke the laws of Greek society, such as the prohibition against incest; for example, his wife, Hera, was also his sister. But his lust was interpreted as an exuberance for life that reflected and enhanced the Greeks' own vitality.

Other gods were also worshipped, mainly as departmental deities in charge of different aspects of life. Aphrodite was the goddess of love, beauty, and sensuality. According to Hesiod, she was born from the sea foam, and Botticelli painted her as Venus standing on a giant scallop shell. Her attractiveness caused jealousy among the gods, so Zeus married her to Hephaestus, the homely, lame, smith-god, but it did not help. In fact, Hephaestus rendered her irresistible by making lavish jewelry for her and a girdle of wrought gold with magic woven into the filigree. Even Zeus succumbed to her powers, fathering Eros the winged infant, who had a quiver of love arrows that always hit their target. Her other lovers included Adonis, the handsome youth, born from a myrrha tree that cracked open, and Ares, the god of warfare, "piercer of shields," perhaps a commentary that love and war are not opposites. Aphrodite represents the power of beauty but an untamed beauty that is free and can bring pain. Her emblems were the dove, the apple, the shell, and, significantly, the mirror.

Apollo is another major deity, a son of Zeus and Leto, with a twin brother, Artemis. When Hera learned of Leto's pregnancy, she jealously forbade her to give birth on stable land, so Apollo was born on the floating island of Delos, encircled by a flock of swans. The swan became sacred to him, along with the wolf and dolphin, but he is usually pictured with a laurel crown, a bow and arrow, and a lyre (*cithara*). Apollo was, in fact, the god of music, directing the choir of the Muses, as well as the god of prophecy, archery, medicine, poetry, dance, and contemplation. Moreover, he was identified with light as Phoebus Apollo, the deity of radiance and sunshine. In one of his exploits, he killed Python, who had spread destruction in Delphi, sacking villages, destroying crops, and polluting streams.

Delphi became a sanctuary where a priestess issued oracular pronouncements, seated over a grate in the temple floor, breathing vapors from hallucinogenic mushrooms. The Greek oracles, at sites such as Delphi or Dodona, were thought to be in contact with the gods or to act as interpreters of their signs. Although the Greeks knew the oracles were hallucinating, they assumed the gods could only be accessed in this way, not under an ordinary state of consciousness. It is an open question whether extraordinary states such as this, induced by alcohol or drugs, music, dancing, hunger or pain, will distort our awareness or bring us closer to spiritual reality.

Artemis is the goddess of the wilderness, "delighting in wild boars and hinds." She is queen of the hunt, and of wild animals, who paradoxically takes life and protects it. Death makes way for new birth, so several gods in world religions, such as Shiva in Hinduism, are both creators and destroyers. Artemis is a chaste goddess who roams the forest with her virgin nymphs hunting lions, deer, and panthers. This "mistress of wild animals," as Homer calls her, is also patroness of young children and protectress of women's fertility, but her shafts can bring instant death in childbirth. A crescent moon appears above her head, showing her association with Selene, goddess of the moon.

Above all, Artemis is associated with chastity, which was imposed upon her by her father, Zeus, and she punished women who were impure or men who defiled her person. The huntsman Actaeon, for example, stumbled upon Artemis bathing in a forest pool surrounded by her nymphs, so she turned him into a stag and had her hounds chase and slaughter him: "she refused to let any mortal say he had seen Artemis naked." Similarly, the hunter Orion tried to rape the virgin goddess, so she killed him and his dog, using a scorpion, or perhaps an arrow. Orion became a constellation, and his dog became Sirius, the Dog Star. Young girls were often initiated into the cult of Artemis, but when they married they had to lay the symbols of their innocence on the altar: toys, dolls, and a lock of hair.

Other gods and goddesses fulfilled different roles, and the mythology surrounding them shows the charm and grace of the Greek mind as well as their psychological insight into human relationships. Poseidon was the god of water, horses, and earthquakes, and Hermes was the winged messenger and herald of Zeus, governing roads, travel, and trade, "the heavenly guide." Demeter was the goddess of agriculture, bringing forth the fruits of the earth, especially grains, and the gray-eyed Athena was the goddess of wisdom, justice, and the arts, the patroness of Athens and all of civilization. Each of the deities had its place in Greek life, functioning as familiar gods who received sacrifices, libations, and a companionable devotion.

However, toward the latter part of the Hellenic age, the Greeks grew restless with these gods of the state. Worship became too formalized, belief too doctrinaire. Although the gods were personal and explained events, the people wanted more immediate religious experience.

In response, various cults from the north began to appear and to attract the populace—cults such as the worship of Dionysus as the bull, a god incarnate. Dionysus was the deity of wine and passion, and his worship was orgiastic, with women going to glades at night and dancing to cymbals, flutes, and drums by the light of torches. The women worked themselves into a religious ecstasy, all to be free from the restraints of life and to achieve communion with the god. Sometimes snakes were fondled, and animals were torn to pieces and eaten raw.

Another cult, that of Demeter and Persephone, celebrated the rebirth of crops in spring, which emulated the resurrection of the soul.

Persephone, Demeter's daughter, was abducted by Hades, and because she ate six seeds in the nether world, she had to remain there six months of the year. During this time, Demeter wept and the earth languished, bringing people to near famine. When Persephone returned in the spring, the earth became fertile once again, which was cause for riotous celebration. The myth formed part of what was called the Eleusinian mysteries, and it satisfied its devotees that there would be new life after death in an eternal cycle.

Another cult that seized the Greek imagination was the Orphic Brotherhood, centering around Orpheus, the sweet singer, who could charm wild beasts with his music and even move stones. According to the *Odes* of Pindar, he wandered into the mountains while grieving for his wife and suffered a terrible death. His worship stressed his resurrection and that of anyone who could separate himself from sin. The body was "the prison house of the soul," but salvation could be achieved through leading a righteous life and practicing mystical rites. The soul had to be liberated from the body, mainly through discipline and ascetic living. The phrase "austerities of the Orphic life" became proverbial. However, sacraments, ritual, and personal faith became more important than moral behavior, although there were prohibitions against homicide and suicide. The worshippers of Orpheus, dressed in white, were preoccupied with their divine origin and their divine destiny, and they strove for eternal life. Their beliefs obviously influenced the development of Christianity.

The Greeks were far more philosophic than the Egyptians and produced thinkers such as Socrates, Plato, and Aristotle, but more than anything else their religion expressed a joy in living. The Egyptians seemed death-centered by comparison, but the Greeks embraced life, and this was reflected in their gods. They were not oppressed by feelings of sin, or prone to melancholy about mortality or the brevity of their existence, or distressed by warfare, which must be met bravely. Rather, their religious, social, and political forms show an energy that is life-enhancing. Death was omnipresent, and regarded as horrible and menacing; sacrifices must be made against it in temples. Chthonia dwells in nether-earth, and men are chilled when her shadow falls across them. But meanwhile, there are stately temples and sculptures, the pleasure of conversation, plays at the amphitheater, spoken poetry, delicious figs and fish and honey cakes, the effulgent sun, and "the wine-dark sea."

ROME: BORROWINGS AND ADAPTATIONS

As is commonly known, the Romans were not an imaginative people but an intensely practical one. They did not have much patience with mythology, an eye for beauty, or an ear for music, and their minds did not run to philosophic speculation. Instead, they were superb warriors with a genius for organization, law, government, and conquest, a pragmatic people who judged things by their usefulness. They built roads and aqueducts and coliseums, but their art was derivative and their gods were forgeries of the Greeks.

The early religion of Rome contained deities that had power, but fragmented power, each in charge of a small segment of life. For example, the infant was guarded by the god Cumina, the toddler by Statina, and by Locutius when he began to speak. Seia took charge of the corn before it sprouted, Septia when it was fully grown, and Nodotus when the straw was knotted. Vesta was guardian of the hearth, and the Penates protected the storeroom. There was a god for the door, the hinge, and the threshold, and a god of the pestle and of the broom. In addition, each sex had a protective divinity of its own, Genius for the man, Juno for the woman. Overall, it was a polytheistic, family religion, which the Romans accepted without much question.

The *pater familias* acted as the priest of the household, assisted by his wife and children. The father made sure that a fire burned continually in the hearth for the continuity of the family line, and that offerings were made to ancestors to ensure their happiness. Each household also had a shrine, which constituted the center of family worship.

Gradually religion became more of a state affair, organized under a Minister of Religion, who made sure the rituals were performed properly, in large temples. The worship would only work if it were done with the closest attention to detail, otherwise the ceremony had to be repeated. An official religion was established, incorporating various Etruscan beliefs in addition to cults brought back by the legions and standardized throughout the empire. Above all, the state religion borrowed and adapted the Greek deities. When the Romans invaded Greece in about

200 b.c., they appropriated all of their gods, along with other features of Greek culture, giving them Latin names. As is often said, Rome defeated Greece, but then Greece returned the favor and conquered Rome— *Graecia capta ferum victorem cepit*.

In the high temple were housed the Sibylline Books, holy books containing secrets that were prohibited to laypeople and were only opened to determine important matters, such as the reason for crop failure. Oddly enough, whenever the priests consulted the books, they recommended that various Greek deities be added to the pantheon. In this way, through the sanction of the state, each of the gods of Greece found their way into Roman worship.

The high god Zeus became Jupiter; his wife, Hera, was Juno; Ares, the god of war, became Mars; and Hermes was identified as Mercury. Artemis became Diana; Athena became Minerva; Poseidon became Neptune; Demeter became Ceres; Dionysus became Liber; and Aphrodite was given the Latin name of Venus. The Roman gods were, in fact, fused with those of Greece, and the result was almost a parody of Greek worship. But rather than having personalities and adventures, the gods were formalized entities, and rather than being loved, they were feared.

During the later years of the Roman Empire, the emperors themselves were worshipped as divinities incarnate, usually after they died, which did not make other gods more human but the emperors more transcendent. A temple inscription read, "Divine Augustus Caesar, son of a god, imperator of land and sea." Some of the emperors were benevolent, some were brutal, but few were worthy of being called holy. Nero, for example, loved music and massacres. And as one historian said, "[Emperors] had a job for life but that life could always be shortened. Assassination was an occupational hazard." Of course, a succession of immortal emperors does raise questions.

In addition to displaying their religion publicly, the Romans were also extremely superstitious and moved by signs and omens that could be read through divination. In augury, flights of birds were noted, their height, direction, and quadrant of the sky, all of which foretold the future. And in ritualistic sacrifice, when animals were offered along with milk, fruit, and cheese, their entrails were examined to read the mind of the heavens. The liver, in particular, was thought to contain the secrets of the gods, but the gall, heart, and lungs could also tell tales; their markings, size, shape, and color were revealing. The animal that was ritually slaughtered depended on the god: for Janus, a ram, for Jupiter, a heifer. The gladiatorial games may have originated in the practice of religious sacrifice, only applied to the slaughter of slaves.

Dreams were also important signs, and werewolves, vampires, and shape-shifters were believed to be real. One should never enter a house with the wrong foot (*sinistra*, left, rather than *dextera*, right), and if a cock crows during a dinner party, the food must be discarded. One should be vigilant against the evil eye, but amulets and charms will afford protection. In addition, animism was part of their belief system, so they saw spirits in stones, trees, caves, lakes, mountains, and stormy seas. Offerings were made to the beings resident in nature, "whether you be god or goddess."

In general, Roman religion was not a spiritual experience but a contract between heaven and earth: a familiar expression was *do ut des*, "I give so you will give." It was a system of reciprocity, one hand washing the other. The Romans honored their ancestors, maintained the fire, held festivals, offered sacrifices, worshipped the gods, and revered the emperor—mainly as a guarantee of safety. If they gave praise, they would be blessed, and if they acted wrongly, they would be punished. It is questionable whether this kind of bargain—to believe in order to receive—is religious.

It was a sensible arrangement, suited to a militaristic people, who for over five centuries invaded and ruled the nations surrounding the Mediterranean; they called the waters *mare nostrum*, "our sea." At its height, the Roman Empire controlled more than 4 million miles of territory, from England to Africa, and from Syria to Spain, which meant the rulers were conquerors rather than tender-minded poets. The material world mattered far more than the spiritual one, a tangible world of violent sports, brutal warfare, and iron rule. One of history's ironies is that the spread of Christianity, a religion of love, contributed to Rome's downfall. Ultimately, spirit conquered matter, faith overcame physical force. A well-known Japanese haiku reads, "A great warrior. / And what will make him / get off of his horse? / Cherry blossoms will."

3

THE NATURE OF THE WESTERN GOD

When we come to the Western, monotheistic tradition we are in a more disciplined place that gains in consistency but loses the charm and immediacy of nature gods. We may be closer to the truth but without the delightful "just so" stories of how things came to be. Compared to the Greeks, enchantment is absent in Western theology, and we enter a serious world of creeds and edicts, sin, redemption, commands, and salvation. It is an open question whether the believer is happier in this mental world, but that may not be the point.

Judaism, Christianity, and Islam are the great world religions, and they are all monotheistic. Our emphasis will be on the attributes of the God worshipped by these religions, especially Christianity, the predominant religion in this country. The Bible, of course, contains the sacred writings of the West, but it does not list God's attributes per se, and they are not contained in revelations. Theology infers these attributes from scripture and through reflection, meditation, and prayers, which are taken to be divinely inspired. The attributes do change over time because they are responses to questions, and each age asks its own questions.

A WHOLLY GOOD, WISE, AND ALMIGHTY BEING

To call God *wholly good* is axiomatic, because within Western religion we would not call a being God unless he were entirely good and devoid of evil. Unlike earlier concepts of the divine, which had to do with strength and immortality, goodness is an essential attribute of the Judeo-Christian God. An evil Lord is a self-contradiction, just as a square circle would be. His goodness is simply a necessary part of his nature. If God is not good, then he is not God.

In the Old Testament, God's goodness is shown mainly in justice and fairness, whereas in the New Testament it centers on love, mercy, and forgiveness. The parallel distinction for human beings has to do with our reaction to wrongdoing: we can respond with either love or justice. Should we return good for evil or should awful action be properly punished? We want to be better than those who harm us, but when we forgive them and refuse to retaliate in kind, we may be encouraging evil by default.

One major philosophic problem that is generated by ascribing goodness to God has to do with the existence of natural evils on earth—things or events that bring suffering to human beings. Why would a loving God, who wants the best for his creatures, design a world that contains catastrophes and disasters, such as hurricanes, earthquakes, and tsunamis; sickness and diseases, such as cholera, malaria, and cancer; hostile environments, such as deserts, jungles, and Arctic wastes; dangerous animals, such as lions, cobras, and sharks; and the degeneration of old age, followed by death? More specifically, why create carnivorous animals when having all herbivores could eliminate so much pain in the world, and why visit suffering on innocent infants and children? This issue is called "the problem of evil," which does not concern man's inhumanity to man but the nature of the world that human beings were given.

The question is why would God freely choose to inflict pain on people, or why wouldn't he intervene when, say, the devil causes human suffering? This problem has traditionally been the greatest stumbling block to faith. It assumes that God, in his omniscience, is aware of the misery on earth; through his power, is able to prevent it; and as a benevolent father, would want his children happy. Why, then, do we have the world we do? An ancillary question is why a God of forgiveness would condemn people to eternal punishment in hell.

God is also defined as *omniscient*, that is, all-knowing and perfectly wise. He is aware of everything in heaven and on earth, in this world and the next. Nothing we create is new, since it was already present in

God's mind; human beings discover truths rather than invent them. God is never surprised, he would never change his mind, he does not take any risks, and he never makes mistakes. He possesses complete knowledge, which, significantly, includes foreknowledge. That is, he knows the past, the present, and the future. He is conscious of whatever is happening, remembers everything that has occurred, and foresees all events that are to come.

As stated in the Bible, God has "perfect knowledge" (Job 37:16), "knows everything" (1 John 3:20), "his understanding has no limits" (Ps. 147:5), and "not one [sparrow] will fall to the ground" without his awareness, "And even the very hairs of your head are numbered." One theologian, William Lane Craig, goes so far as to say that because of God's complete knowledge, those ignorant of Christ can be condemned to hell, because God knows which ones, if presented with the doctrine, would reject it.

However, this concept of omniscience also involves certain philosophic puzzles, mainly about foreknowledge. The chief problem is that if God knows everything that will occur, then those events must happen as they do, otherwise he could not foresee them. That is, nothing can occur other than what God foresees, which makes all acts unavoidable. Why be angry with man, then, for sinning when God knows in advance that he will succumb to temptation, especially that he would commit the original sin of Adam and Eve?

That is, if God is all-knowing, then people do not have freedom of choice. If divine omniscience entails knowledge of all future actions, people must perform those acts that God predicts. Everything has to happen as God knows it will happen, and human actions are not free. For example, if God knows that I will steal, then I must steal and cannot be blamed for stealing; I had no choice. So human beings have the illusion of being free but not the reality, and they should never feel guilty or responsible for their conduct. Everything is already fixed, otherwise it could not be foreseen.

But couldn't God know what we will do without forcing us to do it? Couldn't he know the free choices people will make? If you have a friend, you might know that he hates cats and you can predict that he would never own one, but you are not forcing him to avoid cats; you only know that he will never choose a cat as a pet. That is, you know what he would do, not what he must do.

That seems reasonable, except that if you absolutely know what your friend will do, then something is compelling him to do it. Since God in his wisdom can predict the actions people will take, without exception, their actions must be unavoidable, otherwise he could not know what their conduct will be. That is, God himself may not force our behavior, but he could not know our behavior unless the future were predetermined. He either wrote the plot or saw the film, including all the action and the ending, or he would have no knowledge of what the future holds. Simply put, if God knows what we will do, then we are not free to do otherwise; on the other hand, if we are free to do otherwise, then God does not know what we will do and is not omniscient.

This is a significant criticism because being free is a prime component of humanness and the fundamental basis of our moral responsibility. If we lack free will, we cannot be praised for our decisions and rewarded with heaven, or blamed and sent to hell. But if God knows whatever choices we will make, the future is already written, and we have no free choice or accountability.

Some theologians, such as Martin Luther and John Calvin, have taken this approach, denying free will in order to give God maximum power, especially the power to confer grace. Martin Luther, for example, said, "man like a beast of burden, can be ridden by God or Satan but cannot decide what to do himself." John Calvin preached, "Predestination is the eternal decree of God." According to Calvinism, "eternal life is foreordained for some, and eternal damnation for others" (nevertheless, oddly enough, people are still responsible for their "voluntary" deeds). But most denominations ascribe free will to human beings, and this becomes questionable if God is all-knowing.

A literary rendering of this dilemma appears in *Penguin Island*, by Anatole France. Here God says:

> My foreknowledge must not be allowed to interfere with their free will. So as not to limit human freedom, I hereby assume ignorance of what I know. I wind tightly over my eyes the veils which I have seen through, and in my blind clairvoyance, I allow myself to be surprised by what I have foreseen.

God is also conceived as *omnipotent*, almighty, or all-powerful. According to the liturgy, the Lord is a mighty fortress, a bulwark never failing, an absolute force that acts without limitations. He possesses infinite ability, which enabled him to create the universe. He produced all of reality and sustains everything that exists, and he has the power to intervene in the lives of individuals and in human history. He is the source of every blessing, he responds to all prayers, and exacts retribution for sin, as in the Flood and in Sodom and Gomorrah. He answers our pleas for help with a strength no earthly obstacle can resist. "With God all things are possible," as scripture says, since God is the almighty ruler of the universe.

But again certain philosophic puzzles begin to arise from this description. If God is omnipotent, could he create the world and not create the world at the same time, or is that impossible even for an omnipotent God? Could he make a statement both true and false, or create a figure that is both square and round at the same time? Could he make the right wrong and the wrong right if he wanted to do so, turning values inside out, like a glove? Because he is almighty he could certainly perform miracles, enable the blind to see and raise the dead, make snakes, bushes, and donkeys talk, and he would be able to suspend the laws of physics so that the sun could stand still in the Valley of Ajalon. But could he violate the rules of logic and make $2 + 2 = 5$ if he so chose? The preeminent Catholic theologian St. Thomas Aquinas asks whether God could "create a triangle with internal angles that do not add up to 180 degrees."

An old philosophic chestnut, called "the paradox of the stone," highlights this apparent contradiction: Can an omnipotent God create a rock so large that he could not lift it? The obvious dilemma is that if we say yes, then he is not omnipotent because he cannot lift the rock; if we say no, then he is not omnipotent because he cannot create such a rock. Another iteration of the problem is to ask whether an omnipotent being can create a task he cannot perform, or pose a question he cannot answer. Whether we respond positively or negatively we find ourselves faced with an impossibility.

Because of such problems, some theologians such as Aquinas have suggested that even an omnipotent God cannot do what is self-contradictory; he cannot violate logic, doing what is rationally impossible. He is only able to "bring about every absolutely possible state of affairs." For instance, he cannot make a sound that is both loud and not loud, at least not in the same respect. A pin drop may be loud to an ant but soft to a person, but it cannot be both loud and soft to the ant, or loud and soft to a person. According to a basic law of thought, we cannot contradict ourselves, saying that something *is* and *is not* simultaneously, or we are not making sense. The same principle applies to God. Although he is omnipotent, that omnipotence is circumscribed by reason; he cannot do what is logically impossible.

One suggestion is that God's omnipotence does not extend to violating his own nature, or to doing anything that would make God less than God. Lying, for example, would be intrinsically impossible for him, and he cannot sin because of his moral perfection. In the same way, he is unable to alter history, erasing the fall of Rome or the rise of Napoleon, because that would make something false that is true. He certainly cannot reject his omnipotence in order to prove his absolute power. As one wit put it, "Even God cannot change the past, although historians can."

Now, it seems plausible to limit God's omnipotence by saying he cannot violate logic or his own nature, but at the same time we wonder how omnipotence can have boundaries. Are there degrees of all-powerfulness? The seventeenth-century philosopher René Descartes claimed that God must exceed the laws of logic or he is not God. And theologians such as St. Augustine have argued that God can do whatever he chooses to do, voluntarily limiting himself: "[God] is called omnipotent on account of his doing what he wills." Perhaps God has the greatest range of power that any being can have. But the question still remains whether any limitations are consistent with omnipotence. In short, the issue ultimately remains unresolved.

A simpler question to answer is this: If God does not possess any evil, ignorance, or weakness, then isn't he lacking something and therefore imperfect? No, because these are negatives not positives. If he were weak, ignorant, or evil to any degree, that would create gaps in his being, making him less than perfect. If God cannot sin, that is to his credit.

WHO EXISTS EVERYWHERE AND ALWAYS

The Western God is also considered *eternal*, which translates to being infinite, having an endless past and an unending future. He is the "everlasting God" (Gen. 21:33), "the eternal God [who is] thy refuge" (Deut.

33:27), to whom we should give "honour and glory forever and ever" (1 Tim. 1:17). And because he is eternal, he knows what the future holds as well as the frozen past.

But eternality can mean two things: that he exists outside time altogether, or that he exists for all time, that he is the beginning and end of time, the alpha and the omega. That is, he is either a timeless being, occupying a realm beyond time, or he exists for all time and will never grow old, much less die. Both meanings have been held, but they raise different puzzles. For example, if God lives outside time, how could he enter the temporal world through his Son? And if God experiences all time, then in some sense he must exist within it, enclosed by time and perhaps be subject to change.

God is also thought to possess the attribute of impassibility or immutability, which means permanence, not subject to change. He is always the same, constant, dependable, and faithful. Everything on earth changes, from flowing rivers and oceans to mountains that thrust up by temperature and pressure and are worn down by weathering and erosion, as well as entire continents that shift on their tectonic plates. God, however, is unchanging. He is not in the process of becoming but is a state of complete being.

But some argue that change must take place in time, and if God is timeless, he is unable to change. Others argue that God's nature cannot change because change implies imperfection. Others point out that by performing actions he must at least move, and movement means change from one position to another. Presumably God reaches out to human beings out of love or in response to their pain, and that means movement. Such puzzles occupy the philosopher and theologian but seem moot to most people.

In addition, God is thought to be *transcendent* in that he is "wholly other," existing far above us, beyond our comprehension and, in the end, unknowable. He is "the infinite mystery of wideness," or "a circle whose center is everywhere and circumference nowhere." Removed from the world, he exceeds our intellect and comprehension. Unlike human beings, he is pure and perfect, separate from the physical realm and outside our understanding. "As the heavens are higher than the earth, so are my ways higher than your ways and my thoughts than your thoughts" (Isa. 55:8–9). The first astronaut in space, Yuri Gagarin, reported that he did not see God anywhere, but no one was surprised; he is not a visible being.

The prohibition against idols probably stems from fear of contaminating the divine realm by taking the image for the supernatural object that it stands for. Generally, the Catholic Church favors images—statues, icons, crucifixes, paintings, and figures in stained glass, whereas Judaism and the lower Protestant denominations oppose representations because of the danger of idolatry. Islam in particular regards pictures of God as blasphemy.

Some theologians are so impressed with God's difference from humans that they claim nothing can ever be said about him: "Those who say, don't know; those who know, don't say." He is fundamentally unknowable, and we can only "negate the opposite." That is, to say God exists means he is *not* a fiction; omniscience means that he is *not* ignorant; and loving, that *nothing* about him involves hate. We can state what God isn't but not what he is, because his positive qualities exceed our understanding. Some claim we cannot even know God's name—not Lord, Jehovah, or Yahweh, but *Qui Est*, "He Who Is." Most theologians do not go so far as to think that God is unutterable and a complete mystery, but they still see him as having a different order of existence altogether.

But if we cannot articulate God's nature, how do we know we have grasped him? Perhaps we know things we cannot express, truths deeper than words, but they could also be illusions we only think we know. If something is beyond language, ineffable and inexpressible, how can we be sure there is something we cannot understand? Belief in astrology and Tarot cards has also claimed a higher status, somewhere beyond language and immune from logical criticism. However, such claims cannot be proven or disproven, and perhaps we are hearing the clang of the escape hatch.

At the same time that God is considered transcendent, he is also thought *immanent*, meaning resident in the world, an all-pervading presence suffusing time and space. He is omnipresent, existing everywhere and always, and especially within us. Our soul has been termed God, our essential identity, the divine spark animating us, or that still, small voice of conscience. The Zoroastrianism of Persia held that light (order) lives within us and should be resistant to darkness (chaos); Quakers believe "a part of God's spirit . . . dwells in every human soul."

Mystics, in particular, speak of God as internal, known through meditation more than revelation from outside ourselves.

These two attributes of transcendence and immanence pose an obvious conflict: God cannot be both beyond the universe and resident within it, surpassing creation but permeating its very fabric. In fact, the two attributes seem to vary inversely. As transcendence is highlighted, immanence is put in the shadows, and vice versa; majesty and intimacy operate in a see-saw relation. Also, if God's transcendence is emphasized, that could imply deism, whereas an immanent God is often associated with pantheism.

THE DIVINE CREATOR, PERSONAL, AND SIMPLE

Genesis, the first book of the Bible, opens with the words "In the beginning God created the heavens and the earth" (Gen. 1:1), clearly identifying God as the *creator*. The Nicene Creed and Apostle's Creed also refer to God as originating everything. He made all things from nothing, *ex nihilo*, including his favored creature, human beings. He conferred the gift of life and a multitude of blessings on humanity. Genesis describes how each element of the world originated through God's agency:

> And God said, "Let there be light," and there was light . . . and he separated the light from the darkness . . . And God said, "Let the water under the sky be gathered to one place, and let dry ground appear". . . And God said, "Let the land produce vegetation; seed-bearing plants and trees on the land that bear fruit with seed". . . And God made two great lights—the greater light to govern the day and the lesser light to govern the night . . . And God said, "Let the water teem with living creatures, and let birds fly above the earth across the expanse of the sky" . . . And God said, "Let the land produce living creatures according to their kinds: livestock, creatures that move along the ground, and wild animals" . . . Then God said, "Let us make man in our image, in our likeness, and let them rule over the fish of the sea and the birds of the air and over every living creatures" . . . God saw all that he had made, and it was very good.

The Gospel of John reinforces God as creator but emphasizes the "word," or *logos*:

> In the beginning was the Word, and the Word was with God, and the Word was God. He was in the beginning with God. All things came into being through Him, and apart from him nothing came into being that has come into being . . . And the Word became flesh, and dwelt among us, and we saw His glory.

Logos is a highly ambiguous term, translated as "word," "order," "knowledge," "speech," or "reason," or perhaps it is the animating principle. Its meaning is so varied that Christ can be referred to as the incarnation of *logos*. To translate it as "word" could indicate the creative force of language. The prohibition in the Bible against taking the name of God in vain suggests that God's own name might be too holy for ordinary human use. This harks back to early magical belief.

Stories that explain how the world came into existence are commonly referred to as "creation myths." This phrase does not necessarily imply a fiction but a tale that is part of the folklore of a people, an oral or written legend about the tribe's origin. It can be compared to a nonrepresentational work of art that does not faithfully copy its subject but can still be profound; it is not lifelike but true to life. Creation myths can carry the same symbolic significance. They are very prevalent in cultures throughout the world, explaining how everything came to be.

In the ancient Chinese account, the beginning was "featureless yet complete, born before heaven and earth; Silent—amorphous—it stood alone and unchanging." In the Inca version, the earth was first covered with darkness, then the god Con Tiqui Viracocha emerged from the Collasuyu Lake (modern Titicaca) and created the sun, the moon, and stars to light the world. Norse mythology refers to a great void, all ice and mist, then a separation of north and south by Odin; he also created heaven and earth and man, giving him a soul. The Zulu myth cites Umkilunkulu, the Ancient One, who grew on a reed in the swamp and brought forth people and cattle, mountains and streams; he taught humans how to hunt, to make fire and grow food. To the Aborigines the earth was originally a bare plain, without life or death; the sun and stars slept beneath the earth along with all creatures. When the ancestors arose in the Dreamtime they wandered the earth, and finding people in shapeless bundles, they carved them into human figures with heads, arms, and legs.

Although creation myths lack common elements, they do have similar features. Most describe the world as an undifferentiated, primordial chaos without form or parts, and covered with darkness. The dark is then separated from the light, night is divided from day. Alternatively, an expanse of water covers the earth, sometimes from a flood, and land must be brought to the surface. A pair of cosmic parents, the Sky Father and the Earth Mother, are responsible for the emergence of plants, animals, and people, and their thoughts and desires bring life into the world—sometimes from a cosmic egg. But the world has imperfections because of man's transgressions, which must be punished. Sacrifices are needed to reduce the suffering on earth, conquer death, and live eternally.

The similarities to the biblical account are obvious, and Genesis cannot be taken as literally true. Like other creation myths, it appears to be the invention of a people imagining their beginnings. When viewed in this perspective, we see the Western deity functioning in a traditional, creator role along with the gods of other cultures. The belief in spontaneous creation could be equated with the scientific view that the universe began with the explosion of the primal atom. According to some astronomers, time itself began with a big bang. But whether Genesis can be reconciled with a big bang is an open question. It seems metaphorical at best, and cannot be regarded as truth.

God is also regarded as *personal* or anthropomorphic, meaning a human-like being. This God possesses a personality and a character just as we do, being alternately stern, forgiving, jealous, merciful, angry, caring, just, and so forth. We even refer to God with the personal pronoun "he" (or "she"), and as "God the father." In Christianity, he is human enough to have a son. The Father is "ungenerated," the Son is formed by the Father, and the Holy Spirit from the Father through the Son; it is a triangle rather than a line. Strictly speaking, the term "father" does not have a gender connotation but is meant as "fathering forth," the source of all creation.

Both men and women were created in the image of God. According to different passages in Genesis, either Adam and Eve were made simultaneously, or Eve was produced from a rib of Adam. Feminists obviously prefer the former passage because it implies equality; it also speaks of a direct creation, not a derivative one.

Being "created in God's likeness" also refers to having a personal nature and the ability to think and choose, that is, to use our intellect and to exercise our free will. As mentioned, the skeptic charges that God created man in his own image and man returned the compliment: "If triangles had a God, He'd have three sides." On the other hand, Martin Buber, the twentieth-century Jewish theologian, maintains that God and human beings must meet in full personal relationship, as "I–Thou" rather than "I–It." Because of his personhood, we can relate to him and feel an emotional rapport. He is not Truth, Love, or Wisdom, but King, Judge, Lord.

In addition, this theistic God is *holy* or sacred and must be approached with a sense of awe and mystery. "Holy, holy, holy is the Lord of hosts; the whole earth is full of his glory" (Isa. 6:3). He is not the same as natural laws, such as gravity or electromagnetism, and he is not a physical force or abstract power. Rather, he is a sanctified presence that inspires us to reverence and solemn worship. A person can never be holy in the way that God is holy. The term "glorious" is often used of him, which means having splendor and eminence, evoking wonder and praise.

Finally, the Judeo-Christian God is *simple*. The characteristic of simplicity means unified and complete, without any difference between attributes and being. With regard to a lion, for example, we can separate its existence from its strength, fierceness, color, and so forth, but with God no such differentiation is possible. As St. Thomas Aquinas puts it, "The reason why a nature is called simple is . . . that there is no difference between what it *is* and what it *has*." In other words, the questions "Does God exist?" and "What is God?" are the same. Of course, one of the logician's quibbles is that if God is identical with his properties, then he is a property, and God as a being is absent.

The Trinity, of course, is the dogmatic heart of Christianity, the doctrine of three persons in one, and this has been challenged as violating the idea of simplicity. Can three persons be one substance or are we really in the realm of polytheism? Is the Holy Spirit a person? And if the Trinity is not mentioned in the Bible, is it a legitimate concept?

Obviously, the Christian answer is that the Trinity is real. To explain the parts of the Trinity, certain words are used: "different facets," "dimensions," "essences," "aspects," "manifestations," and "personalities" that are "inseparable," "interdependent," "co-equal," "co-eternal," and "threefold." The assumption is that there is unity in diversity, and each person of the Trinity is distinct but joined in one divine being, separable but one. The Muslims, of course, find the Trinity a heresy, especially the idea of Jesus being the son of God. In the Koran it states, "They say the God of mercy has gotten to himself a son. Now have ye uttered a grievous thing . . . It is not meet for God to have children."

From a rational standpoint, for three to equal one is a mathematical impossibility, so here we enter the realm of Christian mysticism. It may be a matter of faith to accept an irrational idea, but how can we separate a paradox that expresses a higher truth from a self-contradiction that is an absurdity? The issue of the Trinity and simplicity raises that question.

At a deeper level, the issue concerns the limits of reason, especially with regard to religion. It is dangerous to accept a belief that it is incoherent. We then open the door to ridiculous things, and we are forced to accept the reality of *mana, taboo, animism, totemism,* and *magic.* They could also be called a mystery, beyond our understanding. On the other hand, we do not want to limit a deity by circumscribing him with logic, saying this is impossible even for God. The border might be permeable. How, then, do we differentiate good sense from nonsense in searching for beliefs we can trust? The remainder of the book will attempt to shed light on that question.

4

AN ARRAY OF ALTERNATIVE BELIEFS

THEISM, OR THE TRADITIONAL GOD, AND DEISM, OR THE ABSENTEE LANDLORD VIEW

In classical terms, *theism* means the belief in one God, the transcendent creator and ruler of the universe. It is synonymous with *monotheism* and refers to the single deity of Judaism, Christianity, and Islam. The Old Testament declares, "Hear, O Israel, the Lord our God, the Lord is One," and the New Testament states, "there is one God, the Father, from whom are all things." As we have seen, the Christian doctrine of the trinity does not mean three gods but three aspects of one god. The Koran, which is the sacred scripture of Islam, repeatedly declares that "God is one God"; he has ninety-nine most beautiful names, including the sovereign of heaven and earth, the ruler of life and death, he who holds dominion, the eternal refuge, the just and merciful, the benevolent one who is terrible in his wrath.

Theism includes faith in a personal deity who governs the universe, interacts with human beings, and is the foundation of all that it contains. This includes the earth and its animate forms, especially human beings, but also the sun, the moon, and the stars, the mountains, forests, lakes, and oceans, and all manner of living plants and animals.

To the theist, God creates human life and imbues it with purpose, so that we live our lives against a cosmic backdrop, as a spiritual drama. He makes our time on earth meaningful and gives our history a narrative. Each star that shines and every sparrow that falls is known to him, and all things happen for some end. We have a *raison d'être*, a reason for being. Everything works out for the best in accordance with an over-arching divine design. The world is warm, personal, and just, not cold, factual, and indifferent. A supreme being is in charge of our lives, and we can appeal to him for mercy and help. He intervenes in human affairs out of justice and love, and he will hear our prayers of praise, confession, worship, supplication, and guidance. Through him we can hope for eternal life.

As we have so far discussed, the Western God possesses various attributes to a superlative degree. Human beings possess a certain amount of strength, but God is *omnipotent*, or "almighty"; we have partial understanding, but he is *omniscient*, or "all-knowing"; and we have limited *goodness*, he is a name for love itself. In fact, theism comes from the Greek word *theos*, "god." We reify our best qualities in a divine being.

In addition, God is transcendent, which means wholly other, beyond the range of human experience, existing in a higher, spiritual realm. He is not subject to the limitations of the physical universe, and he sur-passes our understanding. At the same time, he is immanent, which means existing within all things, particularly inside human beings. This immanence is sometimes interpreted as our inner conscience or soul, a spark of the divine. "Eternality" is another divine attribute, and it means existing forever, without beginning or end. Here God is thought to persist throughout time or outside of time. This eternality has been compared to truth itself, which is everlasting, or to mathematical rela-tions, or perhaps moral values. Eternality often includes the quality of *immutability*, which means remaining in an unchanged state, having the same nature for all eternity.

Furthermore, God is considered to be the creator of heaven and earth, the ground of all being, and specifically responsible for the exis-tence of human life. He is also considered personal, that is, a deity who resembles human beings but with qualities far surpassing us, magnified to cosmic dimensions. This anthropomorphic view enables human be-ings to relate to God who, in Christianity, is even considered a Father with a Son, but he is so far superior to people as to be worshipped in his perfection. In addition, he is set apart by being *holy*, which means sacred. Unlike physical laws, God is a being who inspires reverence and confers blessings. We bend our knee or bow our head in worship, far removed from the scientific world of the microscope or the telescope.

A final attribute is *simplicity*. We normally differentiate between an existent thing and its characteristics, for example, people themselves as distinguished from their kindness, intelligence, skills, attractiveness, and so forth. In God, no such separation exists. He is assumed to be a unified being whose qualities cannot be separated from his existence.

In brief, theism ascribes every excellence and ideal to God. He is omnipotent, omniscient, and wholly good, eternal, immutable, transcendent, immanent, personal, holy, and simple. As a complete being he lacks nothing, which justifies his sovereignty. God is not considered perfect in the way that an apple can be judged perfect, with ideal taste, form, and color, or the way that a racehorse can be called perfect, with speed, style, and stamina, but a being that possesses excellence in all positive qualities.

This is the God preached by Moses Maimonides and Mohammed, by the classic Christian theologians St. Augustine, St. Thomas Aquinas, and St. Anselm in the Middle Ages, and by John Calvin, Martin Luther, and John Wesley during the Reformation. He is the complete God of the Judeo-Christian tradition.

By contrast, *deism* affirms belief in a God who created the universe, set it in motion, but chose not to be involved in its ongoing operation. He regards the world with a benign indifference. He is a God who made a tree, not one who makes trees, the creator of Adam and Eve but not all humankind. He flicked the first domino, which tipped over the rest. He was the initial thrust that started the ball of the universe rolling, and then withdrew, not participating in its day-to-day operations.

This deistic God is the originator of physical laws *ex nihilo*. He designed its structure and processes and foresaw how they would play out, but he did not interfere with its unfolding. He is the spark for the "big bang," building into the primal explosion all the potential for the actualization of the universe. The cynic sees deism as an "absentee landlord" view of God, a being who began the universe then sat back paring his fingernails. A positive interpretation is that he is the *primum mobile*, or "prime mover" of the natural world. Obviously, we cannot worship the law of gravity, but we can praise a god who enacted the law and enabled our world to exist.

One major premise of deism is that religious understanding can be achieved by reason alone without benefit of faith or mysteries, of prophecies, scripture, or revelation. By observing the natural world, we can see the work of a creator and evidence of the plan he initiated. Belief need not depend on miracles that suspend natural law, or on prayers directed to a supreme being who participates in worldly events. To the deist, God is transcendent, more of a mathematician (a geometer) than a counselor. Deism is a cerebral creed rather than a mystical communion with the supernatural.

During the Age of Enlightenment, deism was a prominent feature of religion in Great Britain, its American colonies, and France. The movement began in the seventeenth century as a result of the scientific revolution, particularly in the writings of Nicolaus Copernicus, Johannes Kepler, and Galileo Galilei. They all demonstrated that the universe is far larger than we ever imagined, and that the earth is not the center of the solar system. This placed man on the fringe, not at the center, of creation. Thereafter, the Bible lost some of its authority on factual matters, and it began to be viewed more as a source of inspiration and ethics. If science presented an accurate picture of reality, it seemed reasonable to think of God as the cause of the physical laws of the universe.

During the freethinking of the eighteenth century, deism continued to influence religious ideas, particularly through Matthew Tindale's *Christianity as Old as the Creation,* the deist's bible. Tindale believed religion should be based on rational understanding, and he rejected the notion that "we must adore what we cannot comprehend." Thomas Jefferson's book *The Life and Morals of Jesus of Nazareth*, called "The Jefferson Bible," also preached a deistic doctrine, which saw God in the natural order of things. God is knowable and can be grasped. People have been given reason along with emotion, and our mind is adequate to "apprehend, judge, and infer" God as the creative force of the universe.

In England, the philosophers John Locke and David Hume were major influences; in France, Maximilien Robespierre was a prominent deist, as was Jean-Jacques Rousseau; and in America, the Founding Fathers were strongly deistic, especially Jefferson, Ben Franklin, James Madison, and John Adams. Also included in the ranks of deists were Alexander Hamilton, Ethan Allen, Thomas Paine, and, perhaps, George

Washington. Madison and Adams, in particular, inveighed against theism. Madison wrote, "What have been [its] fruits? More or less in all places, pride and indolence in the clergy, ignorance and servility in the laity; in both, superstition, bigotry, and persecution." And Adams wrote in a letter to Thomas Jefferson, "The question before the human race is, whether the God of nature shall govern the world by his own laws, or whether priests and kings shall rule it by fictitious miracles."

Today deism is on the rise, but it is sometimes regarded as "rationalism with a nostalgia for religion." In many ways, deism seems more intellectual than spiritual, and it does not appeal to people's yearning for union with a loving Father. Perhaps it is atheism in religious clothing, because God is identified as starting the universe but not operating in it. Many believers doubt that a loving God would abandon the world, leaving it to gravity, electromagnetism, the law of motion, and weak and strong forces. Nevertheless, an increasing number of people think deism presents a more realistic picture of reality. Perhaps something divine precipitated the flower in the crannied wall, and the universe in a grain of sand.

POLYTHEISM, OR MULTIPLE DEITIES, AND PANTHEISM, OR NATURE AS DIVINE

If multiple gods are worshipped rather than one, this is termed *polytheism*—a belief in any number of deities arranged in a divine pantheon with varying degrees of stature and power. Sometimes goddesses and gods are specified; at other times, the term "god" embraces goddesses, the way that mankind can include women. These deities are strongly anthropomorphic, possessing greater power than people; they are wiser and live forever but also share human faults and weaknesses. In this way, they are more approachable than a perfect God. We have already seen examples of polytheistic worship in Egypt, Greece, and Rome.

One tension in religion is that if the gods are considered pure and abstract, then they are inaccessible, too far above human beings to be worshipped, but if they are too like us, then they are unworthy of worship.

A mythology always accompanies a polytheistic system—a mythology in which the deities are the main actors, constantly intervening in human affairs. These mythologies tell stories of sky gods, visible in sunlight and thunderstorm, gods of death and the underworld, mother goddesses and love goddesses. They each have separate skills, and depending on the occasion, appeals are made to different ones. There are deities that guarantee good crops, good hunting, and good children, there are those of the hearth, of battle, and of birth, in fact, there may be a god governing every aspect of life, as in Roman religion. Very often there are families of gods, sometimes strung together with hyphens, and sometimes the relationships are incestuous; both features occurred in ancient Egypt. The gods can change the outcome of a hunt, mate with mortals, make rain, or bring locusts that devastate a crop. They are embodiments of natural phenomena, beginning as spirits or demons of nature, then personified in humanlike form.

In the variety called *kathenotheism*, which is belief in regional gods, they have power over a clan, a village, or a people, even drawing their name from the location. If one tribe defeats another, that shows their god is more powerful, and he could be adopted by the conquered tribe. In *henotheism*, which is belief in departmental gods, different deities are worshipped at different times, without discarding the others. In Greece, Zeus is the highest god, but Poseidon is the god of the sea, Athena of civilization, Aphrodite of fertility. A gracious goddess in Indian lore is Ushas, the goddess of dawn; men awaken when she touches their eyes. The Bible refers to polytheism obliquely in the special, covenant relation between Yahweh and the Hebrew peoples. One of the commandments is this: "Thou shalt have no other gods before me." That suggests polytheism was present in ancient Judea, and a temptation to the Hebrew people.

When Catholics pray to patron saints that are in charge of different parts of life, this may be a carryover of henotheism; for example, St. Catherine of Bologna for art, Agatha for nursing, Vitus for animals, and Elegius for mechanics; and more exotic saints, such as St. Adrian of Nicomedia for arms dealers, Dymphna for sleepwalkers, Erasmus for abdominal pains, and Claire of Assisi, the patron saint of television. And although Christianity is monotheistic, the three aspects of the godhead might suggest an earlier polytheism.

In some polytheistic systems, the power of the gods is compromised by fate or destiny, which is more powerful than any deity. In the early Vedic faith of India, Rita has final say and dictates the order of the universe, including the seasons and the daily passage of the sun. In Greek religion, Moira is higher than Zeus, compelling all events to occur as they must. This is depicted in the Theban plays of Sophocles— *Oedipus Rex*, *Oedipus at Colonus*, and *Antigone*. For Oedipus in particular, whatever he does to avoid his fate is fate's means of fulfilling the dictates of fate.

Just as deism emphasizes transcendence, *pantheism* stresses the immanence of the divine. According to pantheism, God is identical with nature or the universe. It is not that nature expresses God's spirit or represents his form, but that the forces and laws and body of nature are God. Nature is more of an organism than a machine, an organism animated by spirit. The pantheist rejects the view of God as an external, personal being, and rejects worship, prayer, miracles, and any inherent purpose for humankind. There are neither rewards nor punishments, only consequences. Nature itself is sacred, without a mind behind it responsible for its creation: "God is everything, and everything is God."

To the pantheist, nature is our only paradise, the only source of our salvation, and there is no imaginary "beyond." The universe itself can inspire feelings of reverence at its grandeur; we do not need a supernatural being who created it. Looking at the stars at night, we experience a sense of awe and solemnity, just as we do at the advent of spring or the birth of new life. "There is no divinity other than the universe," the pantheist Paul Harrison wrote, so we must "revere and care for nature [and] joyously accept this life as our only life."

Some pantheists emphasize natural law, and claim that science, not revelation, shows nature's complexity, uncovers her secrets. The physicist Steven Hawking once said that he is a believer if by God is meant "the embodiment of the laws of the universe." Similarly, the astronomer Carl Sagan remarked, "The idea that God is an oversized white male with a flowing beard who sits in the sky and tallies the fall of every sparrow is ludicrous. But if by God one means the set of physical laws that govern the universe, then clearly there is such a God." However, he added, "This God is emotionally unsatisfying . . . it does not make much sense to pray to a natural law."

Historically, the Greek philosophers Heraclitus and Anaximander are credited as the founders of pantheism, followed by the Roman Stoics, especially Zeno and Emperor Marcus Aurelius (featured in *Gladiator*). In the Middle Ages, the friar Giordano Bruno was burned at the stake for this "heresy." In the seventeenth century, Benedict de Spinoza mounted a complete defense of pantheism in his *Ethics*, and John Toland wrote his definitive *Pantheisticon*. In more recent times, the English poets William Wordsworth and Samuel Coleridge embraced pantheism, as did the American transcendentalists Walt Whitman, Ralph Waldo Emerson, and Henry David Thoreau.

At the same time, institutional religions, and Catholicism especially, have been hostile to pantheism, regarding it as a threat to orthodox belief—if not atheism pure and simple. If God is a name for nature, then how is that different from secularism, where the scientist devotes himself to investigating the natural world? God then becomes superfluous. Pope Pius IX condemned pantheism in his *Syllabus of Errors*, it was criticized by Pope Benedict XVI in his 2009 encyclical, and excoriated by the Vatican in the New Year's Day statement of 2010. Many traditionalists regard pantheist as "a term of theological abuse," but *pan* means "all," and *theos* means "god," so to the pantheist, the whole of reality is divine. That suggests reverence rather than atheism.

The current movement of ecology or environmentalism emphasizes respect for the natural world, a respect that borders on religion. Rather than having "dominion" over the "fish of the sea, and over the birds of the air" and "over all the earth," as Genesis declares, the environmentalist believes we should be stewards, caretakers, and managers of the land, entrusted to protect the planet. God and the natural world can be considered one, and we have an obligation to safeguard God's physical manifestation. The Endangered Species Act may be taken as expressing this attitude, and a billion people in 190 countries celebrated Earth Day recently. Environmentalism, in fact, may be a type of pantheism.

AGNOSTICISM, OR WE CANNOT KNOW IF GOD EXISTS, AND ATHEISM, OR THERE IS NO GOD

Agnosticism, a word invented by T. H. Huxley, is the theory that God's existence can neither be proven nor disproven. This is because (1) there is not enough evidence either way, or (2) because such matters are beyond our understanding. That is, the divine is either unknown or unknowable. The agnostic does not deny God, but sees no grounds for accepting him either.

What's more, the agnostic is unsure how to approach the question of God's existence, that is, what arguments would be relevant or what kind of evidence is admissible. He wonders whether any proof is possible, and whether we will ever be able to reach a sound conclusion, much less certainty. We know how to solve a problem in mathematics or chemistry, and how to go about settling a dispute in law, but what would establish the reality of a god? The agnostic's position is that, without an adequate foundation for knowing, the only honest response is to suspend belief. When the agnostic Bertrand Russell was asked what he would say to God if they ever met face to face, he replied, "not enough evidence, Lord, not enough evidence."

Agnosticism is basically a theory of knowledge: that we can only be sure of what we rationally understand or experience through our senses. This is the scientific perspective, which holds that we are unable to decide questions of religion, conscience, beauty, value, or the soul; they are all beyond empirical measurement. Such matters cannot be tested in the lab or in the field, by research or experimentation, therefore it is pointless to pursue them. As for the orderliness of the world, that is hardly evidence. It can be attributed to natural forces, discovered by the hard sciences. Furthermore, the world also exhibits disharmony and randomness amidst the order.

Agnosticism can take the form of a general skepticism that doubts every claim of knowledge; its opposite is dogmatic certainty. At the extreme, skeptics even doubt the existence of the external world and of themselves as actors in it. A solipsist says only he exists, but no one else does. Of course, a thoroughgoing skepticism undermines itself, because if all claims are questionable, then the claim "All claims are questionable" is itself questionable. As commonly put, we cannot say we know nothing, since that at least is something we know. Similarly, a solipsist cannot communicate his ideas because he does not think anyone is there to hear them.

But agnostics do not go to those extremes. They only claim we cannot know God and must withhold our judgment about his reality. We are left uncertain, which does not mean indecisive but can mean indifferent. Perhaps God is "hidden in the shadows," and his ways are unfathomable, or maybe there isn't anything to fathom. Militant agnostics such as H. J. Blackham claim that "agnosticism does not merely mean a suspension of judgment [but] intellectual justification for a disregard of theology."

Atheism. Unlike the agnostic, the atheist does not have doubts about whether God exists; he flatly denies God's existence altogether. To the atheist, religion is a fable that we should have outgrown when we reached maturity. Instead of being born again, we should simply grow up. The absence of proof is proof of absence. If we are told a tiger is in a room and we do not find a tiger, we can conclude there is no tiger. That is, nonbelief is the default position. Agnosticism leaves the question open, but atheism purports to answer it negatively. Or, as one critic put it, everyone is an atheist when it comes to other gods, such as the deities of other religions.

The definition of atheism varies, and the meaning can matter in the evaluation of its validity. The literal translation is *a*, "without," and *theos*, "god." The general definition is "denying that there is a God," and this is the customary, positive version. A weaker form is "lacking belief in God," which is a negative or passive atheism. A third type is "rejecting belief in the existence of God." This form is usually avoided because to say that atheists do not believe in God implies there is a God whom atheists do not credit. Most atheists endorse the first, saying there isn't a God, or more technically, they affirm the nonexistence of God.

Militant atheists go further, regarding God as a dangerous idea, that society compels people to believe in this fiction or else be ostracized as heretics. Furthermore, the religious myth distracts people from solving the world's problems, telling them to trust in God, that he will provide. Marxists charge that people can be so heavenly minded that they do no earthly good. Some critics go so far as to treat the indoctrination of religion as child abuse, as when Madrasahs compel children to learn the Koran by heart. The cult of Heaven's Gate resulted in thirty-nine suicides as its followers tried to join the tail of Hale–Bopp Comet, and the People's Temple in Guyana led to the largest murder/suicide in history—about nine hundred people, including children, who drank Kool-Aid laced with arsenic. The religious wars alone testify to the harm that faith can engender, as in the present conflict with Islamic fundamentalists.

Atheism should not be regarded as a belief in the same way that theism is a belief. It is not a philosophical system asserting that certain ideas are true. Rather, it does not accept the existence of God, denying rather than affirming a faith. This distinction may be illustrated by a dispute in the Middle Ages. At the time, some theologians argued that everyone is a believer; it was only a matter of what they believed. People could believe something or they could believe nothing, but in either case they had a faith; no one was an atheist. (Ironically, in the same breath that atheism was declared impossible, it was also denounced.)

However, some philosophers pointed out that if a person believes nothing, the nothing is not the object of their belief but the absence of belief. "Nothing" was being distorted by the theologians into a "thing" word when, in fact, it was the absence of anything. In the same way, atheism is not a religion but denies that religion has any basis in fact. On this reading, atheism is no more a religion than being bald is a hair color, or not collecting postage stamps is a hobby.

Theists sometimes viewed atheism as a phase in human development, but the atheist argues the opposite: that religion is a stage in man's maturity as we move from superstition to science. We are "nature looking back at itself." Theists also charge that we need God as the foundation for moral conduct; however, there is no evidence that atheists are immoral, or that theists have a higher ethical standard. People do not stop behaving if they stop believing. It is sometimes said about the Puritans that first they fell upon their knees, then they fell upon the aborigines. Furthermore, atheists can appreciate the wonders of the earth without assuming there is a cosmic artist. As Douglas Adams remarked, "Isn't it enough to see that a garden is beautiful without having to believe there are fairies at the bottom of it too?"

The list of atheists probably begins with Lucretius, the Roman philosopher, and extends through Enlightenment thinkers, such as Baron Holbach and Denis Diderot, and such diverse figures as Voltaire, Jean-Paul Sartre, Mark Twain, and Upton Sinclair. They all maintained that the absence of God makes us free agents. As Terry Eagleton remarks, there was a time when almost everyone believed in angels and witches, and hardly anyone in atheism, but today many hold the opposite. Recently, several books rejecting God have achieved popularity: Richard Dawkins's *The God Dilemma*, Christopher Hitchens's *God Is Not Great*, and Sam Harris's *The End of Faith*. (Oddly for a liberal, Harris advocated a preemptive nuclear strike following 9/11.)

Some atheists are dogmatic and some take religion more seriously than its practitioners; they are God-intoxicated people who see the absence of God everywhere. They cannot ignore the religious impulse, and the signs of its decline are treated as a human tragedy. At best, the graying of congregations is met with mixed feelings.

Recently, religion has come in for a fair amount of criticism, from the terrorist jihads of Islam to the treatment of the Palestinians by the Israelis to the sex scandals in the Catholic Church. According to the U.S. Conference of Catholic Bishops, more than 6,100 priests have been charged with pedophilia, approximately 16,000 children molested, and $2.5 billion spent by the Church in compensation. Around 5 million babies were forcibly taken from unwed mothers by nuns in maternity homes in the late nineteenth and early twentieth centuries. Christianity has also been criticized for its tolerance of slavery, its acceptance of economic inequality, its silence during the Holocaust, and its passivity toward racism. The defense of "Don't judge the faith by its representatives," has been countered with "By their fruits ye shall know them." Europe, in fact, has become increasingly secular, even though it boasts great Gothic cathedrals and functioned as the center of Christendom for centuries. Growth in religion in general has occurred outside the European continent, principally in Africa, Asia, South America, and the Arab world.

Theism, deism, polytheism, pantheism, agnosticism, and atheism—these are the forms of belief, doubt, and rejection. How we treat religion makes a difference in our *Weltanschauung*, or worldview, so we cannot be indifferent to the question of its truth.

5

CLASSIC ARGUMENTS FOR GOD'S EXISTENCE—AND THEIR CRITIQUES

During the Middle Ages, some churchmen maintained that "philosophy is the handmaiden of theology," but a number of influential theologians thought differently. They believed that philosophy was not subservient to religion but would support it independently. This view is referred to as natural theology. Rather than fearing that thought would challenge revelation, "scholastics" such as St. Anselm and St. Thomas Aquinas used reason as an instrument to prove a spiritual reality; it was considered a gift from on high. They argued that we could find good reasons for believing that God is an existent being and not a human invention.

When theologians refuse to accept the validity of reason, they claim that faith, not the intellect, will bring us truth. But this approach affords no protection against absurdities that hide under the guise of faith. There must be some basis for differentiating between what is sensible and what is nonsensical, the reasonable and the irrational. We may want to trust our hearts, but we cannot disqualify our minds.

A PERFECT BEING MUST EXIST OR HE WOULD NOT BE PERFECT

St. Anselm, one of the notables among the rational thinkers, was an eleventh-century theologian who supported logic as an adequate means for understanding God. He thought that anyone, if he thought hard enough, could prove the reality of God to himself. Faith and reason could be reconciled, in fact, they coincided, and this could be clearly demonstrated. He declared of his major work, the *Proslogion*, "I wrote it in the role of one who seeks, by silent reasoning with himself, to learn . . . whether one argument might possibly be found, resting on no other argument for its proof, but sufficient in itself to prove that God truly exists."

Anselm found such an argument in what is labeled the *ontological proof*. Fundamentally, the proof turns on the idea of God as "a being than which none greater can be thought." Anselm argues that if we can imagine "a being than which none greater can be thought," then that being must exist, for if it were just a thought, then a greater being could exist; one that exists in reality as well as in our minds. So from the very thought of God as a perfect being, his existence must be acknowledged, since existence is part of perfection.

Differently put, God as "a being than which none greater can be conceived" must possess all positive attributes. Such a being must be wholly good, perfectly wise, almighty, and so forth, otherwise Anselm could conceive of a greater being, one that includes the things that are lacking. In addition, this perfect being would have to possess the attribute of existence, otherwise he would not be perfect. The conclusion must be that if we think of a being "than which none greater can be conceived," which is the definition of God, then we are forced to believe that this being exists.

As Anselm phrased it,

> if that than which a greater cannot be thought is in the understanding alone, then this thing than which a greater cannot be thought is that than which a greater can be thought. But obviously this is impossible. Without doubt, therefore, there exists, both in the understanding and in reality, something than which a greater cannot be thought . . . Why, then, has the fool said in his heart 'There is no God,' when it is so obvious to the rational mind that, of all beings, thou dost exist supremely?

This sounds plausible, but a contemporary of Anselm's named Gaunilo objected to this chain of reasoning and replied with his "On Behalf of the Fool." Using an analogical argument, he pointed out that a perfect island could be imagined, even though no such island exists. His argument was that just because we can conceive of something in our minds, even something perfect, that does not mean the object is real. We can think of centaurs, griffins, and unicorns, but no such creatures actually exist.

However, Anselm was not deterred. He countered that a perfect island need not have every perfection in order to be perfect as an island. We can even imagine a perfect unicorn or even a perfect lizard without attributing existence to it. But a perfect being must contain existence or he is not truly perfect. A nonexistent God would be a contradiction in terms.

But couldn't the ontological proof be criticized by saying that human beings cannot imagine perfection? As fallible creatures rooted in an imperfect world, we are unable to conceive of what perfection might be. However, for his argument, Anselm does not need us to imagine everything that must be included in perfection. For whatever else perfection contains, it has to contain existence, which is all the argument requires; an allegedly perfect being who lacked existence would not be perfect.

However, there seems to be a fatal flaw in the ontological argument, which was most forcefully presented by Immanuel Kant, an eighteenth-century German philosopher. Kant pointed out that "being is obviously not a predicate." To say something exists is not to say anything about it but indicates there is an object that corresponds to the concept. It posits the object with its attributes. As Kant stated, we do not add anything to the value of a hundred imaginary dollars by taking a real one out of our pocket.

In other words, Anselm is confusing a concept with reality. A perfect *concept* must include existence or it would not be perfect as a concept, but that does not mean there is some existent thing behind the concept. An idea is not the same as the reality referred to by the idea. A word is not a thing; a map is not a territory; and we cannot satisfy our appetite by reading a menu. In the same way, although a perfect concept must contain the notion of existence, that does not mean there is an existent thing that the concept stands for.

The seventeenth-century philosopher René Descartes offered a slightly different version of the ontological proof. Descartes maintained that "it is only what I clearly and distinctly perceive that completely convinces me." The existence of God is such a "clear and distinct idea," for the existence of God is inseparable from his perfection, just as a valley cannot be separated from a mountain.

He also presented a special argument in terms of axioms that has a reactionary, medieval smack to it: the lesser cannot produce the greater, that is, we can get less from more, but not more from less. Therefore, if we have an idea that is greater than ourselves, we could not have produced it. God is such an idea, and we as finite beings could not have conceived of the infinite; imperfect man could not have imagined a perfect deity. Descartes goes on to say that the only being capable of producing the idea of God in our minds is God himself. So from the fact that we know God, but could not have created the idea ourselves, we must admit the existence of God, who implanted the idea within us.

Unfortunately, Descartes' arguments also have serious flaws. It seems that the lesser can produce the greater, as when a snowball causes an avalanche, an acorn becomes an oak tree, or a split atom generates a nuclear explosion; the whole can be greater than the sum of its parts. Now perhaps these are not good counterexamples because the combination of causes produces the effect—the snowball plus the rocks, bushes, ice, and trees tumbling down the mountain. However, even if the lesser cannot produce the greater physically, it certainly can in the world of ideas. Here human beings seem capable of producing things greater than themselves. Through the power of imagination we can envision creatures with greater capabilities than we possess, for example, giants, dragons and even Satan. Using Descartes' argument, we could "prove" their existence.

As for "clear and distinct ideas," Descartes is often criticized for having a circular argument. That is, he believes clear and distinct ideas are guaranteed by God to be true, and we know there is a God because it is a clear and distinct idea.

The ontological proof is generally regarded as invalid, as presented either by Anselm or Descartes. Some philosophers have even criticized it on the grounds that it begs the question— presupposing what it sets out to prove. If an argument is true by definition, it is trivial. The general criticism, however, is that we cannot prove that God exists just from the thought of him. It is illegitimate to move from the idea of God to his reality without external proof. This objection applies to all *a priori* arguments, that is, those that claim to be true in advance of all experiential evidence.

The ontological argument has even generated parodies, such as that of Douglas Gasking and Raymond Smullyan, who argued that the greater the handicap of the creator, the higher his achievement. The greatest handicap would be nonexistence, so a God who did not exist would be closer to perfection than one who did. Therefore, there is no God. But this, of course, is twisted logic; an existent God is greater than a nonexistent one.

In recent years, there has been a renewal of interest in the ontological argument because of the work of Kurt Gödel, Charles Hartshorne, Norman Malcolm, Graham Oppy, and Alvin Plantinga. The discussion has centered on what is called "modal logic"—the relationship between modal propositions of the form "possible" and "necessary." In brief, Plantinga argues that if a "maximally great being" exists in a possible world, then he must exist in every possible world, including the actual one. "Maximal greatness cannot be exemplified anywhere . . . without being exemplified everywhere," otherwise it would not be maximal greatness. It follows that there is a maximally great being in the actual world, a being whom we call God. We must conclude, therefore, that God exists.

This is a complex, technical argument that can only be alluded to here, but it shows the resilience of the ontological proof. As Bertrand Russell said, "The argument does not, to a modern mind, seem very convincing, but it is easier to feel convinced that it must be fallacious than it is to find out precisely where the fallacy lies."

SOMEONE HAD TO LIGHT THE FUSE FOR THE BIG BANG

A second, traditional proof for God's existence has been labeled the *cosmological argument*, or the argument from first cause. St. Thomas Aquinas, the prominent medieval theologian, is most closely identified with this proof as presented in his *Summa Theologica* under the section "Five Ways."

The Middle Ages lasted from the beginning of the fifth century, when Rome collapsed, to the end of the fifteenth century, and Aquinas lived during the High Middle Ages (1225–1274). This was a dynamic period of history when Europe was becoming more complex and creative, the age when Gothic cathedrals were constructed, the Crusades were launched to rescue the Holy Land from the infidel, and Chaucer wrote *The Canterbury Tales* and Dante *The Divine Comedy*. Aquinas stands as the chief theologian of the Roman Catholic Church, which canonized him in 1323, and he remains one of the principal saints. He adapted a theory of the Greek philosopher Aristotle that everything tends toward some destination, connecting it to God as the being that imbued life with purpose. In *Summa Contra Gentiles* Aquinas writes, "nothing tends to something as its end, except insofar as this is good . . . that which is the supreme good is supremely the end of all . . . Therefore all things are directed to the Supreme good, namely God, as their end." Aquinas baptized Aristotle, anointing him to Christian belief.

In 1879, Pope Leo XIII declared that Thomas Aquinas was the preeminent Catholic theologian and that his works were to be studied in all Catholic seminaries and universities. If Aquinas did not write on a topic, the doctrines taught should be "reconcilable with his thinking." His demonstrations in natural theology have inspired countless followers to try to prove divine truth rather than relying upon blind faith; however, if reason diverged from faith, there was always revelation. To Aquinas, rationality could be trusted to support belief since both originated in spirit, but "Man needs divine help, that the intellect may be moved by God to its act."

Aquinas's five ways coalesce around the idea that all events in the world are subject to cause and effect. That is, everything is instigated by something that came before. Whatever happens, we can always ask what caused this, and what effect will it have. In other words, a cause-and-effect chain stretches backwards and forwards through time. However, the causal chain cannot go back indefinitely. There cannot be an "infinite regress" of earlier causes, and prior causes before that, and still more ultimate causes. A backstop must exist, a *primum mobile* or "prime mover," and that first cause can only be God. Without assuming God as the initial flick of the first domino, we cannot make sense of our consequent world.

Aquinas's first way is that of change, for anything that changes must be changed by something else, and that must be changed by something earlier. But this cannot go back and back forever in an endless series. We are "forced eventually to come to a first cause of change not itself being changed by anything, and this is what everyone understands by *God*."

With regard to the second way, Aquinas says, "a series of causes cannot go on forever," that is, we cannot have a prior cause and a still more ultimate cause, in an endless chain of causes and effects. "So we are forced to postulate some first cause, to which everyone gives the name *God*." This is his central contention.

The third way is somewhat more sophisticated, making use of the philosophic distinction between "contingency" and "necessity." A contingent event depends upon something else in order to be. For example, a tree would not exist if it were not for moisture, sunlight, and nutrients in the soil; factories would not be created unless there were bricks and mortar, land for buildings, and a demand for the product; and each of us would not have been born if our parents had not met. However, everything cannot be dependent on external factors; something must exist necessarily, carrying the reason for its being within its own nature: "So we are forced to postulate something which of itself must be, owing this to nothing outside itself, but being itself." He is the ultimate reason for everything to be.

The fourth way stretches causation to include the existence of the *ideal* that then produces lesser qualities in objects. That is, "there is something which is the truest and best and most excellent of things, and hence the most fully in being." In fact, we rate or grade objects according to this perfection, as when we judge the worth of a person's life relative to a human ideal. "Now when many things possess a property in common, the one most fully possessing it causes it in the others; fire, as Aristotle says, the hottest of all things, causes all other things to be hot." Aquinas therefore concludes, "So there is something that causes in all other things their being, their goodness, and whatever other perfections they have. And this is what we call *God*."

Aquinas's fifth way has a different character, directly tipping its hat to Aristotle. He asserts that all things appear to have a purpose in being: "Goal-directed behavior is observed in all bodies in nature, even those lacking awareness . . . But nothing lacking awareness can tend to a goal except it be directed by someone with awareness and understanding . . . and this we call *God*."

These arguments sound persuasive, but philosophers have not treated them kindly. The main criticism of the cosmological argument is that it rests on a self-contradiction. If everything has a cause, then so does God, and if God is an exception, then the world might also be an exception, in which case we have no need for God. In other words, to call God an uncaused cause contradicts the premise of the argument that all things have a cause. Why is the first cause exempt from the rule? Why must everything require an explanation but God's existence be self-explanatory?

This is not a sophisticated criticism but a child's question. If a child asks, "Where did everything come from?" the religious parent answers, "God made it." The precocious child then asks, "Who made God?" And if the child is told that no one made God, that He always was, then the truly precocious child says, "Then maybe everything always was, and God did not make the world."

Furthermore, we could ask why there can't be an infinite regress of causes, just as there can be an infinite series of effects. Recently the *Kalam* argument of Islam has been revived, according to which the universe had a beginning, and God caused that beginning. However, the argument seems based on a dogmatic assumption that there had to be a start. That is, the arrow of time could be double-ended, and go backwards and forwards, just as mathematical sequences are infinite; there is no first or last number, especially if one considers fractions and negative numbers. An analogy can be made with a sound that never ceases and may not start, but simply becomes inaudible. Perhaps there is no beginning, just as there might not be an end; both are theoretically possible. Besides, events could all be arranged in a loop, with the last effect being the first cause, like a snake swallowing its own tail. The wedding ring represents the circle of eternal love.

But if the universe is a loop, mustn't we explain the origin of the loop itself? Not necessarily. As the philosopher Paul Edwards pointed out, if we can explain every member of a series, we have explained the series. For example, suppose we are taking visitors on a tour of a college. We show them the classrooms, residences, athletic fields, laboratories, library, and so forth, but then someone asks, "Yes, but where is the college?" This question is founded on a mistake, because the college consists of all of these elements. In the same way, if we explain the parts of the world, we have explained the world; there is nothing further that requires explanation.

Another criticism is that if there must be a start to the process, why identify that beginning with God? Couldn't there be a natural explanation, such as a "big bang," a spontaneous, physical explosion of sufficient magnitude to create the universe? Do all natural events require a supernatural cause?

In 2010, the eminent physicist Stephen Hawking wrote, "Because there is such a law as gravity, the universe can and will create itself from nothing." The beginning does not have to be grounded in anything, and God is not necessary to account for creation.

In addition to these defects, if the argument were valid, it would only prove a God of deism, not the complete God of theism who designed the world and interacts with it. He would only be the first flick of the domino. The argument does not show a God of justice, wisdom, eternality, and so forth. What's more, he would not be an omnipotent or omniscient God but only one with sufficient power and wisdom to create the world. Hume even suggests that, by analogy with human creations, the argument points to polytheism more than monotheism, because complex creations require a team of designers.

Other criticisms could also be mentioned, for example, that all events have a cause but maybe the entirety does not; the whole may not resemble the parts. Also, we could question the reality of the cause-and-effect scheme altogether. Quantum physics seems able to operate without this assumption. According to some physicists, electrons pass out of existence then reappear with no causal explanation; their appearance is only statistically probable.

Some critics think that the cosmological argument commits the fallacy of "false cause." The same mistake is made by children if they believe that winter is the result of birds flying south, or that flapping flags cause the wind to blow.

Finally, the assumption of a necessary being runs counter to the philosophic view that necessity only applies to logic, not existent things. If all birds are mammals, and all crows are birds, then all crows are mammals; the conclusion follows necessarily from the premises. But there are no necessities in the world. The sun does not have to appear tomorrow, human beings need not breathe air, in fact, nothing that exists must be; everything that is, could just as well not be.

A wit once remarked, "No one ever doubted the existence of God until St. Thomas tried to prove it." There may be some truth to that. If we argue for God, perhaps we only create doubts about his reality. Trying to prove anything can be counterproductive, suggesting answers where there may not have been questions.

A modern version of the cosmological argument should be mentioned before we leave this topic. Physicists refer to "the law of entropy," or the second law of thermodynamics, which states that energy is continually being dissipated in ways that make it unavailable for use. Our oil and gas go up in smoke, the nutrients in the soil are depleted, and even the sun's heat and light are being lost to us. In short, the universe is running down like a huge clock, and its energy cannot be recovered. This may suggest that someone must have wound it up.

However, this version suffers from the same defects as the traditional argument: the clock winder would have to be wound up, the original influx of energy could be natural not supernatural, and so forth. Entropy, like a big bang, is a scientific concept that does not necessarily point to God.

To some philosophers, the existence of the world does not have an explanation. There might only be a "thatness" not a "whyness," and to ask why might be an inappropriate question.

SINCE THE WORLD SHOWS EVIDENCE OF DESIGN, AN INTELLIGENT BEING MUST HAVE DESIGNED IT

The last "way" of St. Thomas suggests another argument. As mentioned, Aquinas had adopted Aristotle's view that everything has an end or purpose toward which it tends. This is the teleological view, that nothing exists by chance, everything happens for a reason; there is a cosmic plan for everything, from the grandest to the smallest entity. As Alfred Tennyson wrote,

"That not a moth with vain desire / Is shrivell'd in a fruitless fire, . . . That not a worm is cloven in vain / Or but subserves another's gain."

The argument for God's existence that is associated with this view is called the *teleological proof*. Briefly put, the argument states that when we look out at the world we are impressed with evidence of design. Rather than randomness and chaos, we see structure and order, an inherent arrangement, and the more science reveals of life, the more impressive the arrangement appears. Now if there is a design, there must be a designer, just as a plan implies a planner, and the architecture of the universe a divine architect. If there are natural laws, then there is a lawgiver; if nature is a work of art, then the landscape shows the brush strokes of God. As Shakespeare wrote, there are "tongues in trees, books in the running brooks, sermons in stones."

In the eighteenth century, William Paley supported this argument in his *Natural Theology* with his famous Watchmaker analogy. He argued that if we found a watch on the ground in perfect working order, we would be forced to conclude "that the watch must have had a maker . . . who formed it for the purpose which we find it actually to answer." Paley writes,

> In crossing a heath, suppose I pitched my foot upon a *stone*, and were asked how the stone came to be there, I might possibly answer, that for anything I knew to the contrary it had lain there forever; nor would it perhaps, be very easy to show the absurdity of this answer. But suppose I had found a *watch* upon the ground, and it should be inquired how the watch happened to be in that place, I should hardly think of the answer which I had before given, that for any thing I knew the watch might have always been there. Yet why should not this answer serve for the watch as well as for the stone; why is it not as admissible in the second case as in the first? For this reason, and for no other, namely that when we come to inspect the watch, we perceive—what we could not discover in the stone—that its several parts are framed and put together for a purpose, i.e., that they are so framed and adjusted as to produce motion, and that motion so regulated as to point out the hour of the day; that if the different parts had been differently shaped from what they are, or placed after any other manner or in any other order than that in which they are placed, either no motion at all would have been carried on in the machine , or none which would have answered the use that is now served by it. The inference we think is inevitable, that the watch must have had a maker—that there must have existed, at some time and at some place or other, an artificer or artificers who formed it for the purpose which we find it actually to answer, who comprehended its construction and designed its use.

By analogy, when we encounter the intricate structure of the world we must infer that it too had a maker; the parts could not have fallen together by chance in just the right combination to produce a perfectly functioning mechanism. "There cannot be a design without a designer," Paley wrote, "contrivance without a contriver; order without choice; arrangement without anything capable of arranging." That is, unless we assume "the presence of intelligence and mind," the world in its orderliness is inexplicable. As George Berkeley remarked, "Everywhere we turn there are evidences of the unity of counsel and design"; even Voltaire conceded, "I cannot imagine how the clockwork of the universe exists without a clockmaker."

Another way of putting the point is that we have two classes of objects on earth: manufactured things, such as chairs, cars, and houses (D^1), and natural things, such as mountains, rivers, and people (D^2). We cannot deny that D^1 objects were designed, and neither can we deny that D^2 objects had a designer. And only God is sufficient to have produced the earth and everything that it contains.

Since the eighteenth century, the teleological argument has been reinforced by various findings, for example, that the earth is perfectly positioned in the solar system to sustain life. If it were closer to the sun we would sizzle, farther away we would freeze to death—a kind of Goldilocks phenomenon. And if the earth were too large a rock, it would collapse; too small, it would spin off into space. In addition, an envelope of moisture surrounds the earth allowing just the right amount of rainfall, just as we have the ideal combination of gases for plants and animals to exist—mostly nitrogen and oxygen. If the water on earth were too hot, it would vaporize; too cold, it would freeze and become ice. Furthermore, human beings need to eat plants and animals, and edible plants and animals are provided. The marvelous mechanism of the human body itself points to a supreme designer who organized our complex systems and organs, our balanced chemistry and physiology for ideal functioning. The intricacy of the human eye alone testifies to the genius of creation. The world is simply too complex and beautiful to have been created naturally.

Evidence of design has also been cited within the animal kingdom, where the attributes needed by different species have been perfectly distributed: the hard shell of the turtle, the ability of the chameleon to change color, and the giraffe's long neck enabling it to reach the leaves at the tops of trees. Birds have been given wings, the rhinoceros a thick hide, cheetahs speed, zebras camouflage, ducks waxed feathers, deer horns, porcupines quills, lions sharp teeth and claws, and so forth.

In his *Antidote against Atheism*, the seventeenth-century philosopher Henry More puts it this way:

> For why have we three joints in our legs and arms, as also in our fingers, but that it was much better than having but two or four? And why are our fore-teeth broad to grind but that it is more exquisite than having them all sharp or all broad . . . Again, why are the teeth so luckily placed, or rather why are there not teeth in other bones as well as in the jawbone for they might have been as capable as these? But the reason is, Nothing is done foolishly or in vain; that is, there is a divine Providence that orders all things.

This argument appeals to our common sense, and even those who rejected the reasoning paid tribute to its force. Immanuel Kant, for example, wrote, "This proof always deserves to be mentioned with respect. It is the oldest, the clearest and the most accordant with the common reason of mankind. It enlivens the study of nature . . . [and] so strengthens the belief in a supreme Author of nature that the belief acquires the force of an irresistible conviction." David Hume also wrote, "A purpose, an intention, a design strikes everywhere the most careless, the most stupid thinker, and no man can be so hardened in absurd systems as at all times to reject it . . . all the sciences almost lead us insensibly to acknowledge a first Author." Hume ultimately rejected the teleological argument, but he recognized its persuasiveness.

Even though a design and designer seems self-evident, the teleological theory may not be the last word; various criticisms can be made. The most obvious defect is that the scheme is not the kind one would expect from a wholly loving God, who is also omniscient and omnipotent. For not only is there chaos and order, but there are also conditions on earth that cause people pain, which is the problem of evil. Natural catastrophes and disease seem built into the design—from floods to earthquakes to avalanches, from cholera to malaria to leukemia, and there are savage animals and hostile environments. The habitat provided for man is not uniformly kind, filled with swamps, deserts, oceans, and jungles. Furthermore, the pain on earth would be substantially reduced if all creatures were herbivores and there were no carnivorous animals to slaughter each other for food, no predators and prey. Furthermore, the marvelous mechanism of the human body breaks down regularly, or we would not have such an enormous medical establishment.

We wonder, therefore, about the benevolence of the plan, or even whether any plan exists. The assumption that human suffering is random and not intentional may be more plausible. This is behind the remark of the writer Jules Renard: "I don't know if God exists, but it would be better for his reputation if he didn't."

Furthermore, even if the argument were sound, it would not prove a creator of the universe but only a cosmic planner who arranged his materials. Both the cosmological and the teleological arguments would have to be valid to prove a theistic God. Kant writes, "This proof can at most, therefore, demonstrate the existence of an architect of the world, whose effects are limited by the capabilities of the materials with which he works, but not of a creator of the world, to whom all things are subject." Some philosophers have even argued that, by analogy with human creations, a number of designers would have to be involved in the project, which might prove polytheism but not monotheism.

However, the main problem facing the teleological argument is an alternative theory offered by the nineteenth-century biologist Charles Darwin in a book that changed the world. In *The Origin of Species*, Darwin offered an alternative, natural explanation for the orderliness that exists. He claimed that if turtles had not possessed hard shells, chameleons the ability to change color, giraffes long necks, and so forth, they would not have survived as a species. These were the mutations called for in the life struggle, so it is not remarkable that the species now living possess the characteristics they need to survive. To think it uncanny would be like being surprised that all Olympic winners are good athletes; if they were not good athletes, they would not be Olympic winners. Or it would be like being amazed that so many major cities are located next to navigable rivers; if the rivers had not been navigable, they would not have become major cities.

Similarly, we can understand the ideal position of the earth relative to the sun, the edibleness of plants and animals, and the efficient functioning of the human body. If these elements had not been present, we would not have the world we do. All aspects of life have evolved in accordance with the *principle of natural selection*. We were once creatures with a scaly fin, then a hairy paw, and then a hand covered with skin and with an opposable thumb and forefinger.

In a famous debate, Bishop Wilberforce asked the biologist Thomas Huxley (Darwin's bulldog) whether it was from his grandmother or his grandfather that he claimed descent from monkeys. Huxley replied that he would not be ashamed of ape ancestors but only of arrogance and closed-mindedness. Evolutionists see a common ancestry for both human beings and the higher apes; the human species branched off from the tree but did not descend directly from primates.

Also, Sir John Lightfoot claimed that the universe began at exactly 9:00, October 23, 3929 b.c., but Darwin maintained there had been an evolution over millions of years. Contemporary scientists have confirmed this through decay methods of dating and other techniques, so that astronomers now estimate the start of the universe with the explosion of the big bang at about 13.7 billion years ago, the sun as forming 9 billion years later, the earth as 4.5 billion years old, and the genus *Homo* as having existed for millions of years; the oldest skeleton discovered to date, a female named Ardi, which carbon 14 dating places at 4.4 million years. *Homo sapiens* (or *homo* but not very *sapiens*) originated around 200,000 years ago. And species were not made through an act of special creation at a fixed point in time, but new species developed over millions of years as evidenced by hominid fossils; chimpanzees or bonobos are our closest relative.

Furthermore, we are not a unique planet but one of hundreds of thousands revolving around stars in the universe with the conditions necessary to produce life. In our galaxy alone there are 500 billion stars, and there are 100 billion galaxies in all. Because of the limitations of time and space, we may not ever meet other intelligent creatures, but we have vast telescopes listening for their signals.

In essence, Darwin offered a naturalistic explanation in place of a supernatural one, and that view appears preferable; if we hear hoof beats, we should think horse before we think zebra.

Although God might lie behind evolution, using it as his instrument, adding God may not be necessary. As "Occam's razor" states, we should not compound explanations beyond what is required; the simplest theory is best. Since evolution can explain the order of the world in natural, comprehensive terms, it becomes superfluous to add a God who lies behind it. When the mathematician Pierre-Simon de Laplace presented his treatise on celestial mechanics to Napoleon, the emperor remarked, "I see no mention of God here." Laplace replied, "I had no need of that hypothesis." So according to Ockham's razor, adding God is unnecessary to explain the world.

How could life have come about without God? The scientific answer is that DNA was produced by nucleotides when successful molecules replicated themselves. Water and amino acids, which are necessary for life, were contained in comets and asteroids that bombarded the earth 4 billion years ago.

Furthermore, the evolutionists argued that it is difficult to account for the extinction of dinosaurs using the biblical account of creation, but it can be explained in terms of the Darwinian model. After ruling for 160 million years, dinosaurs could not survive a catastrophic event. The impact of an asteroid threw up a cloud of dust, blocking the sun, chilling the earth, and killing most plants the dinosaurs needed for food. In fact, over time hundreds of thousands of species became extinct when they could not adapt to changing conditions, and only fossils show that they once existed. As some philosophers have pointed out, it would be odd for God to recall dinosaurs and to try mammals instead, that is, to change his mind.

In defense of the religious view theologians sometimes used questionable arguments, such as "Our ancestors might have been apes, but God adopted us," or "God planted fossils on earth to test our faith," or "He created the earth with these imprints." But the Darwinists replied that *for all we know*, God made the earth complete with fossils, just as oysters might be doing differential equations, and hibernating bears might be dreaming of the periodic table of the elements. But *as far as we know*, they are not. Similarly, it seems more reasonable to regard fossils as preserved remains of living organisms, some of which are no longer on earth. Geologists debate whether fossils are bone or stone, but no one doubts they existed well before 4000 b.c. As for marine fossils on the tops of mountains, including Mt. Everest, that does not prove the flood but the upheavals of ice ages when sea levels rose.

Furthermore, theology plays a dangerous game if it calls "God" whatever we do not know. For then the more we know, the less room there is for God. In this way, religion is edged out of the universe. This has, in fact, been a recurrent pattern. No one knew what caused lightning, locusts, earthquakes, or plagues, so these events were ascribed to the power of God, but that meant that the more science knew, the less was attributed to supernatural agency. Historically, as science advanced, religion retreated, partly because the divine was used as an explanation for what we did not know; a "God of the gaps" is vulnerable.

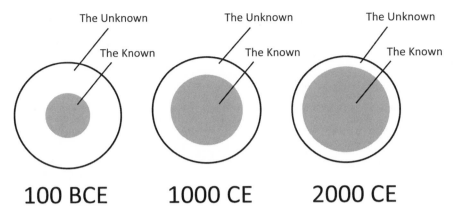

The Unknown   The Known   The Unknown   The Known   The Unknown   The Known

100 BCE   1000 CE   2000 CE

Figure 5.1.

From a logical standpoint, all we can conclude from "we do not know" is "we do not know"; we cannot say therefore we know. Negative premises do not entail a positive conclusion.

The contemporary version of the teleological argument, called *intelligent design*, has essentially the same features and suffers from the same defects; it is new wine poured into old wineskins. For example, it is argued that the "irreducible complexity" or "fine-tuning" of biological systems suggests that some intelligent force must drive the mathematics. They claim that the chances of the universe developing as it did are incredibly small. What is remarkable is not that we have survived but that we have arrived. The astronomer Fred Hoyle put it this way: to think the universe developed by chance would be like thinking a Boeing 747 was assembled by a hurricane from a scrap yard. Take the expansion rate—just one of the conditions that had to be right for the cosmos to develop. In *A Brief History of Time*, Stephen Hawking wrote, "If the rate of the universe's expansion one second after the 'big bang' had been smaller by even one part in a hundred thousand million million, the universe would have collapsed into a hot fireball." Creation was therefore a "singularity." The implication of this statement is that an intelligent mind must have created the initial conditions. (Hawking later retracted this idea, saying God is not necessary for orderliness.)

Michael Denton, a microbiologist from New Zealand, has taken a similar tack:

> It is the sheer universality of perfection, the fact that everywhere we look, to whatever depth we look, we find an elegance and ingenuity

of an absolutely transcending quality, which so militates against the
idea of chance. Is it really credible that random processes could have
constructed a reality, the smallest element of which—a functional
protein or gene—is complex beyond our own creative capacities?

However, most biologists disagree, maintaining that Darwinism is sufficient to account for the complexity and fine-tuning that exists, and that
natural selection and mutations can provide the "information" needed.
At a simple level, the mechanism of the eye was once a light-sensitive
cell; the hand a pseudopod protruding from protoplasm for locomotion
and grasping. And as Kenneth Himma remarked, "The mere fact that it
is enormously improbable that an event occurred . . . by itself gives us
no reason to think that it occurred by design."

Sir Arthur Eddington, the English astronomer, is credited with saying that chance can imitate order if the numbers are large, so that if
enough monkeys were typing on enough keyboards, they would eventually produce all the books in the British Museum. Similarly, if there
were not a single big bang but billions of them, it would be likely that
one would have the conditions necessary for life. As Carl Sagan remarked, our universe was a winner at the cosmic slot machine, even
though the odds were long. As for mathematical beauty, that need not
be purposeful; some people are naturally elegant, without even trying.

Meanwhile, the biological evidence in support of evolution continues to mount so that it has become the standard model in science,
corroborated by anthropology, geology, paleontology, archaeology, and
astronomy. Biologists may argue about the exact process—whether
there was "common descent" or "convergent evolution," "steady
change" versus "punctuated equilibria," but the overall configurations
are established. Sociobiologists claim that a chicken is a device used by
an egg for producing another egg, but not many geneticists subscribe to
this view.

Just as in photographs of a person at different ages, there is no
continuous record; there will be missing periods. Nevertheless there is
continuity. Evolutionary history operates the same way. "Missing links"
are continually being found, for example, the discovery in 2005 of three
specimens that help fill the gap between fish and land animals, and in
2006 the skull of a child was discovered, 3.3 million years old, that had
both ape and human features. Language experiments with the higher
apes—gorillas, orangutans, and chimpanzees (especially bonobos)—

have shown how close they are to human beings; chimpanzees share 96 percent of our DNA.

Evolution, in fact, is no longer a "theory" in the ordinary sense but virtually a scientific law, similar to gravity, light, and electromagnetism. It has overwhelming consensus in the scientific community worldwide. In scientific terms, a theory is the highest level of proof, far above a hypothesis or guess. As in other theories, of course, modifications are made when evidence cannot be replicated, but the essential principle of evolution remains intact.

Fairly recently, biologists have discovered that snakes, dolphins, and porpoises have limb buds in their early development, and whales have been found with atavistic hind limbs, some four feet long, complete with feet and digits; this suggests their descent from terrestrial creatures. All mammals, including humans, have gill pouches in the embryonic stage, reflecting that they were once aquatic vertebrates, and human embryos have webbed feet and hands like amphibians. Embryos first breathe liquid, and at one stage are covered with fine hair called "lanugo." The embryo also develops a tail, which usually disappear *in utero* but some children are born with tails, one to five inches long; humans also retain twice as many tail vertebrae as chimpanzees. Furthermore, people have a vertical groove in their upper lip called the "philtrum," which is a vestige of a snout. In short, the human species in its development goes through the stages of evolution.

Although evolution seems a more reasonable alternative, the teleological argument has a commonsense appeal and resonates with anyone who considers it. Even philosophers who dismiss the argument still treat it tenderly, as we saw with Hume and Kant earlier. In the end, both Hume and Kant reject the design argument, respecting its force but not its logic.

For the reasons given, especially the alternative of evolution, the teleological proof does not seem sound. St. Thomas found order in randomness, but Darwin found randomness in the order, and it is hard to argue against whales with legs, and embryos with gills, webbed feet, and a tail.

All of the classic arguments, in fact, have major flaws that make them difficult if not impossible to accept. Does that mean that God does not exist? Can we take the absence of proof as proof of absence? Some philosophers answer no, that the objections only show the *argu-*

ments for God's existence are deficient; they do not disprove the existence of God. The deficiencies only indicate that, if we are to believe in God, it must be on other grounds. However, other philosophers claim that, in the absence of rational arguments and empirical evidence, we ought not to believe in God (as atheists say). The burden of proof is always on the affirmative, and the case has not been made.

It is an open question whether we should believe until it is disproven, or disbelieve until it is proven. Which is the default position?

Still, the religious thinker maintains that Keats can compose "Ode to a Nightingale," but only God can create a nightingale.

6

THE EVIDENCE OF COMMON SENSE

We have seen that each of the major arguments for the existence of God can be questioned. They all have logical defects that render them unreliable. However, a number of other arguments have been proposed based on common sense and the reflections of religious thinkers. Some seem slight, others persuasive, and still others worthy of consideration.

AT ALL TIMES AND PLACES, PEOPLE HAVE BELIEVED IN RELIGION

In the category of less-weighty suggestions is the "common consent" argument, resting on the prevalence of religious belief. Most people in the world are believers. Not everyone believes in the same religion, of course, but the vast majority of people in United States and elsewhere affirm the existence of a God and follow institutional religion. The statistics vary between polls, but worldwide there are about 2 billion Christians, 1 billion Muslims, 850 million Hindus, 600 million Buddhists, and comparatively few atheists, about 150 million. In this country, 78 percent of the population are Christian, 1.7 percent Jewish, .07 percent Buddhist, with 14.1 percent outside organized religion altogether. Religion may be declining in Europe, Great Britain, Australia, New Zealand, Canada, and the United States, and some social scientists are predicting a "twilight of the gods," but a substantial majority of the world's people still believe in a divine being. Moreover, religion has been a part of world culture for more than 4,500 years.

The argument from common consent is that we can trust religious belief because of the extensive agreement of the world's peoples. The minority cannot be so arrogant as to believe that they are right and billions throughout the ages and across the globe are deluded. In democratic nations, in particular, we trust the majority, and the weight of history and public opinion are on the side of God. Elections are decided by popular vote, and accused criminals are judged by a jury of their peers, "twelve tried men and true." If we trust the wisdom of our fellow man in governance and law, then we can trust it in religion.

As might be expected, the main criticism of this position is that we cannot rely on majority rule in all things. The orchestra does not vote on whether to have a crescendo, the general does not wait for agreement from his troops before ordering an attack, and if we took a poll on which paintings should be in museums, the most popular works might be Elvis paintings on black velvet and dogs playing cards. In certain parts of life, the democratic model does not work. Sometimes we must defer to the authority of experts, on scientific findings and rational judgment. Hitler, after all, was elected by popular vote. Our Constitution places direct limitations on the majority in order to protect minority rights, and human rights in general. The will of the people should be respected but not if the many decide to hang the few; that would be a tyranny of the majority. In other words, democracy has its limitations, and this may be true in religion.

As for the test of time, history is littered with false ideas accepted for generations but finally abandoned. For centuries people believed that the earth is flat, women are inferior, sickness is due to evil spirits, slavery is part of the natural order, eclipses foretell disaster, and so forth. When one considers war, we cannot say that, since there has always been war, there should always be war. Some ideas honored by tradition may not be worth following.

"I could prove God statistically," George Gallup said, but that seems wrongheaded: we do not decide religious questions by taking a survey, by asking how many are for and how many are against a proposition. The majority may be wrong, the minority can be right. In the same way, two heads are not necessarily better than one; it depends upon the heads.

Another secondary argument was advanced by C. S. Lewis that is sometimes called the *argument from desire*. The thrust of it is that there are two kinds of desires: artificial and natural. Artificial desires are generated by society and vary between individuals; they include our wish for romantic relationships, for a car or a house, or for the home team to win the game. Natural desires come from within and include food, drink, shelter, sex, sleep, knowledge, friendship, and beauty. Also included is our longing for God, and just as other natural desires are satisfied, this too would not exist if it weren't capable of being fulfilled. Lewis writes,

> Creatures are not born with desires unless satisfaction for these de-
> sires exists. A baby feels hunger; well, there is such a thing as food. A
> dolphin wants to swim; well, there is such a thing as water. Men feel
> sexual desire; well, there is such a thing as sex. If I find in myself a
> desire which no experience in this world can satisfy, the most prob-
> able explanation is that I was made for another world.

This argument has a great deal of charm, but from an evolutionary standpoint it is questionable. If the natural needs of a species are not met, it becomes extinct, so it is not surprising that those species that do exist have had their needs fulfilled. But knowledge, friendship, beauty, and faith are not natural needs that must be satisfied for survival. These are psychological desires. And not everyone who longs for friendship or love actually finds it, any more than people who want meaning in their lives will inevitably discover that life is meaningful in some way. Similarly, our spiritual hungers may not be fed, and there may not be a next life where we will dwell in a heavenly kingdom and receive everything our heart desires.

A *moral argument* was also suggested by the philosopher Immanuel Kant, but it only holds force for those who accept his overall theory. Kant argues that "ought implies can": in order to say that something ought to be, we must presuppose that it can be. For example, it would make no sense to tell someone that he ought to prevent a train crash when he is unable to do so. Mistakes can be prevented, accidents cannot. Now, virtuous people ought to receive the *summum bonum*, or "highest good," which Kant believes is happiness, but there is nothing in the physical world guaranteeing that the virtuous will be happy. But since ought implies can, we must assume there is another force operative in the universe that ensures happiness will be given in accordance with virtue. That force can only be God.

Questions about this proof are immediately apparent. Granted, if we recommend that a person perform an action, we assume it can be done, but that does not mean whatever ought to occur will in fact occur, that virtuous people will be made happy because they should be. We may not live in a just universe in which virtue is rewarded and vice punished. And without that linkage, we need not postulate a God who makes sure it will occur.

IF YOU HAVE FAITH, YOU LOSE NOTHING, AND YOU MIGHT GAIN EVERYTHING

A stronger argument for the existence of God was proposed by a devout thinker of the seventeenth century named Blaise Pascal. He was something of a theologian but also a mathematician, the originator of Pascal's triangle, the mercury barometer, and the first calculating machine. Throughout his life he was torn between the spiritual and the intellectual modes of proof. Pascal wanted fervently to believe, but as a mathematician his mind insisted on logical demonstration. "It is incomprehensible that God should exist," he wrote, "and it is incomprehensible that he should not exist." Pascal seems to be a Janus figure with faces pointing in opposite directions, but he finally looked toward God. As he famously put it, *Le coeur a ses raisons que la raison ne connaît pas*, "The heart has its reasons that reason does not know."

In his *Pensées*, or *Thoughts*, notes collected after his death, he devised an argument known as "Pascal's wager" that seemed to satisfy him and to convince many others. Pascal reasoned that if we believe in God and we are right, then we go to heaven; and if we believe in God and we are wrong, we still have a happy life on earth thinking God is watching over us. On the other hand, if we reject God and we are wrong, then we go to hell; and if we reject God and we are right, we spend a miserable life on earth, deprived of divine support, justice, and love. So if we are deciding which to believe, God is certainly the better bet. As Pascal puts it,

> Belief is a wise wager. Granted that faith cannot be proved, what harm will come to you if you gamble on its truth and it's proven false? If you gain, you gain all; if you lose, you lose nothing. Wager, then, without hesitation, that He exists.

This seems a sensible argument: if we know what is good for us, we should choose to believe because, right or wrong, we are well off. Even if the worst happens and we have made a mistake in believing, theism is still a wiser bet than atheism. Above all, by opting for faith, we just might win paradise.

However, should we believe in God because it is to our advantage? Some thinkers regard this as selfish, accepting God not because we believe in him, but for our own well-being. We accept God to save our skin (or our soul), and a belief based on such cynical calculations would not be acceptable to God at all. It is founded on self-interest, not love of God, and therefore is not genuine belief at all.

Besides, on these grounds, shouldn't we also believe in the Greek and Roman deities, the gods of Egypt and those of Asia and Scandinavia just to spread our bets and be on the safe side? That is, shouldn't we accept every culture's gods because if we are right we gain everything and if we are wrong we lose nothing? Pascal meant the argument to justify belief in the Christian god, but using his reasoning, we cannot exclude any deity. On these grounds, some people contribute money to all religions, reasoning that you cannot have too many friends. But that is not faith. Furthermore, we could believe we will win a billion dollars in the lottery, that there will be peace on earth, and we will live forever because believing these things does no harm and puts us in a good mood.

Some critics have also questioned whether believing in God makes people's lives unhappy. On the face of it, that assumption does not appear factually accurate. At least theists do not seem conspicuously happier than atheists, in fact, the opposite case could be made. Believers are sometimes rigid and austere, anxious about divine wrath and retribution for wrongdoing. Rather than enjoying life, they fear a god of judgment and live by strict rules. Furthermore, they never have privacy since God is always watching them, and they feel restricted by the rules governing everyday life, especially sexual behavior, and they suffer pangs of guilt about their sins. Atheists, on the other hand, who do not answer to an all-knowing deity, can satisfy their desires without shame, and live a freer existence altogether. Without any expectation of immortality, they can make the most of their lives on earth, using the brevity of existence as a catalyst to more intense living. In other words, theism has a down side, and atheism provides some satisfactions, so it is an open question as to which people are happier. Richard Dawkins has written, "it could be said that you will lead a better, fuller life if you bet on [God] *not* existing, than if you bet on his existing and therefore squander your precious time on worshipping him, sacrificing to him, fighting and dying for him, etc."

Finally, Pascal's wager is not an argument for God's existence but for *believing* in God's existence. It does not prove his reality but argues for accepting God, if we are prudent and wise.

Even if a belief offers us great benefits, we should not believe because it would be good for us if we did so. We need good reasons for accepting a supernatural reality or we cannot maintain our self-respect. Some truths are bitter truths, some are happy ones, but an idea does not become true because it makes us happy. In fact, it is virtually impossible to trick ourselves into believing that we do know what we don't know. That is wishful thinking, and self-deception may be impossible to sustain.

Some philosophers see Pascal's wager as an example of "decision theory" or "probability theory" because the worst outcome of A is better than the best outcome of B, but that ignores the counterarguments mentioned above. It also assumes that a straightforward proof is impossible, so we must wager, but rational arguments should not be disqualified.

Pascal was conflicted about faith, and part of his uncertainty may have stemmed from his poor health. His sister wrote that he "never passed a day without pain," and he died at thirty-nine, probably of tuberculosis and cancer. His sickness probably left him isolated, lonely, and despondent, in an "infinite dependence," but he himself felt that it refined and strengthened his soul.

Pascal expressed his doubts about faith in various writings, including the following passage:

> If I saw no signs of a divinity, I would fix myself in denial. If I saw everywhere the marks of a Creator, I would repose peacefully in faith. But seeing too much to deny Him, and too little to assure me, I

am in a pitiful state, and I wish a hundred times that if a God sustains nature it would reveal him without ambiguity.

Ultimately Pascal concludes that reason supports faith, through the "wager" and other arguments, and he finds human dignity in our ability to think things through:

> Man is only a reed, the feeblest thing in nature, but he is a thinking reed. It is not necessary for the entire universe to take up arms in order to crush him: a vapor, a drop of water is sufficient to kill him. But if the universe crushed him, man would still be nobler than the thing which destroys him because he knows that he is dying; and the universe which has him at its mercy, is unaware of it.
>
> All our dignity therefore lies in thought. It is by thought that we must raise ourselves, and not by space or time, which we could never fill. Let us apply ourselves then to thinking well: that is the first principle of morality.

But then he adds poignantly, "The eternal silence of these infinite spaces terrifies me."

FAITH GIVES LIFE MEANING; AND GOD'S PRESENCE IS SEEN, HEARD, FELT

William James, the twentieth-century American philosopher, was the brother of the novelist Henry James, and a graceful stylist in his own right. A common remark is that William James wrote philosophy as if it were literature, and Henry James wrote literature as if it were philosophy. For his part, William James proposed an argument for the existence of God that carries echoes of Pascal's wager.

James, along with C. S. Peirce and John Dewey, was one of its leading lights of pragmatism, one of the few genuinely American philosophies. Pragmatism preaches that ideas should be judged according to whether their results are useful. That is, a statement is true if it "works," if it proves practical or functional for our lives. "Ideas become true just so far as they help us get into satisfactory relations with other parts of our experience," James writes, "the true is the name of whatever proves itself to be good in the way of belief." We must always ask "What concrete difference will it make in one's concrete life? . . . What, in short, is the truth's cash-value in experiential terms?"

For example, the way to judge whether we have free will is to test that belief as profitable or unprofitable in our lives. On those grounds, we ought to believe that freedom reigns because of the concrete difference it makes in our outlook. If we think that we have no choice, that an ironclad, mechanical fate rules over us, or that we are playthings of the gods, that will sap our energy and make us pessimistic. It will lead to resignation or a futile romanticism. But if we think we are in command of our existence, we can apply ourselves with proper zeal and be effective in the world. We acquire power and are willful agents of change. The choice therefore is obvious: accepting free will is the useful or beneficial option. It makes us feel at home in the world and yields a healthier result in every respect.

According to pragmatism, every philosophic question should be settled this way, that is, in terms of whether it works. We should believe in life after death, that the world is moral, and that we have a soul because that satisfies our desires.

With respect to all religious questions, belief is obviously more gratifying than unbelief, so that is the correct response. Reason cannot be used here because the intellect is inadequate to answer such questions, so we must ask which position is richer. Similarly, external verification is not needed nor is any appeal to an "absolute." We are justified in accepting the idea because it makes our lives better. The same pragmatic doctrine applies to the existence of God because truth is not objective; it is whatever proves expedient for human life. Atheism enervates our practical lives, leaving us lackadaisical and dispirited, whereas theism gives us positive energy.

In a sense, pragmatists claim we create our own reality. For example, if we are mountain climbing and are trapped on a ledge and we must leap to an adjoining ledge, we will probably make the leap successfully if we believe that we can. On the other hand, if we think we will fail, chances are that we will. Therefore, faith beforehand in the result can create the actual fact. Is life worth living? That depends upon the liver. If a person takes the right attitude, life will then be worthwhile, regardless of the circumstances.

In his essay "The Will to Believe," James first distinguishes between options: (1) living or dead, (2) forced or avoidable, and (3) momentous or trivial. An option is "genuine" if it has all three characteristics. First, a living option is a vital choice for us, such as whether to adopt atheism or theism, whereas the decision between Mahayana and Hinayana Buddhism is not real for most Americans. Second, a forced option is unavoidable. "Either love me or hate me" is not forced since we can remain indifferent, but "either accept this truth or go without it" requires a response: "there is no standing place outside the alternative." Similarly, if you are flying a plane and find you are out of fuel, you can either stay in the plane and try to glide it to safety, or you can jump out with a parachute, but you cannot decide not to decide, because that means, in effect, remaining in the plane. Third, a momentous option is significant and irreversible, such as the chance to travel to the moon as an astronaut. "He who refuses to embrace a unique opportunity loses the prize as surely as if he tried and failed," James writes.

To James, the decision whether to believe in God is a genuine option. It is a live possibility to most people, and a forced option. We cannot remain indifferent to the question, as the agnostic tries to do, because not deciding is deciding: we are behaving as if there were no God. And the decision is certainly momentous because it is important to our lives.

Since we must opt either to believe or disbelieve, which is preferable? Since reason is disqualified, the decision must be based on which option is more satisfactory. As Pascal argued, not believing leads to a dispirited, melancholy life, whereas believing leaves us hopeful. The choice is therefore clear: we should will to believe. As James puts it, we do not wish to place

> a stopper on our heart, instincts, and courage, and *wait*—acting of course meanwhile more or less as if religion were not true—till such time as our intellect and senses working together may have raked in evidence enough; . . . [to put] an extinguisher upon my nature, . . . to forfeit my sole chance in life of getting upon the winning side—that chance depending, of course, on my willingness to run the risk of acting as if my passional need of taking the world religiously might be prophetic and right.

As for the qualities of God, here too the most useful description, that which satisfies our soul is correct. God must first be considered rational so that we can react to him mentally and have a sense of comfort and security, otherwise our "religious energy" is not released. Additionally, God must be thought infinite but not omnipotent. For if he has absolute power and chose to create the world with all of its suffering, he cannot be a loving being: "No, God cannot be considered good as we understand goodness if he even tolerates our universe as it stands let alone create it deliberately and consciously. Far from satisfying God, this world must pain him beyond words." It is far better to imagine him limited in power, thwarted and grieved, and to believe that human beings can help him fight the good fight. We can cooperate with God, adding the stubborn ounces of our weight to his efforts. What we do can make a difference to the outcome, which allows us much greater control than if God were wholly in charge and the ending was already certain.

In addition, God's foreknowledge should not be thought inconsistent with free will. If an expert in chess plays a beginner, we know who will win, but we do not know the moves that will be made during the game. In the same way, God foresees the outcome of our decisions but does not know all of our choices. (This means, of course, that God is not all-knowing, but James does not acknowledge that. If God is omniscient, he knows the moves and who will win.)

James's world is attractive, and we sympathize with his no-nonsense, can-do, muscular American spirit, his impatience with theory and abstractions. But it may not be enough to call an idea correct because it works for us in our lives. An illusion can put a sparkle in our eye, a spring in our step, and roses in our cheeks. Those who are optimistic and committed can still be wrong, just as an idea does not become true because people die for it. In short, we might question the assumptions of pragmatism, which is the basis of James's argument. Truth does not depend on satisfactory answers but on how well a statement corresponds to an actual state of affairs. "The grass is green" is true when the statement matches the color of the grass, not because it is useful to think so.

As the philosopher Josiah Royce said, "We do not ask witnesses to tell the expedient, the whole expedient, and nothing but the expedient, so help them future experience." And when we say a belief is expedient, we mean it is true that it is expedient, not that it is expedient that it is expedient.

Beyond that, we wonder whether reason really is irrelevant, and whether faith is a forced option, even though it may be live and momentous. That is, there is an important difference between an agnostic and an atheist. "I do not know whether God exists," and "I do not believe in God" are different ideas, and the distinction cannot be ignored simply because the result is the same. If someone falls or is pushed off a cliff, the person may be dead, but the difference is significant, even though it comes to the same thing in the end.

MYSTICAL EXPERIENCE

Religion is one thing, theology another. Religion has to do with spiritual feelings and emotions, heart and soul, with meditation and inspiration. Theology takes those experiences and forms them into a belief system, builds a structure of ideas that explains the relation between God and humanity.

Religion usually relies on scripture, tradition, or general revelation— the evidence of God in the natural world, but when it trusts special revelation, it is based on mystical experience. The mystic claims to have a unique spiritual awareness, a different conduit to the supernatural, wholly outside of logical thought or sense perception. An "extraordinary appearance" can occur at ordinary moments when one is strolling, working, or relaxing, or under unusual conditions of sense deprivation, hallucinogenic drugs, extreme hunger or thirst, or even self-flagellation. The reports are of ecstasy and rapture, of seeing visions and hearing voices, of feeling immediately the presence of God.

Mysticism has multiple definitions: "the awareness of the divine through a special inundation of understanding," "an immediate grasping of the reality of the spiritual world," "the direct experience of divine reality," "a loving but unclear consciousness of a supernatural object that transcends the self," and "an overwhelming feeling of certainty as to the reality of God." The mystic compares the experience to falling in love or the appreciation of music, which cannot be explained but carries with it the assurance that it is genuine.

Plotinus, Jacob Boehme, Sheik Mansur, Imam Shamilin, Meister Eckhart, St. Theresa of Lisieux (the "Little Flower"), George Fox, John Ruysbroeck (the "Sparkling Stone"), Johannes Tauler, St. John of the

Cross, Al-Ghazali, Chaitanya (the "Golden"), and Emanuel Swedenborg are usually included among the celebrated mystics, and they all have given moving testimonials about their experiences. They testify to the hiddenness of God in our everyday awareness but also his abiding reality. Even the systematic theologian St. Thomas Aquinas wrote at one point, "I cannot go on . . . All that I have written seems to me like so much straw compared to what I have seen and what has been revealed to me."

But it might be more instructive to read of mystical experience as contained in various collections, for example, the accounts of Evelyn Underhill and Rufus Jones, and the following from E. D. Starbuck:

> I have on a number of occasions felt that I had enjoyed a period of intimate communion with the divine. These meetings came unasked and unexpected, and seemed to consist merely in the temporary obliteration of the conventionalities which usually surround and cover my life . . . What I felt on those occasions was a temporary loss of my own identity, accompanied by an illumination which revealed to me a deeper significance that I had been wont to attach to life. It is in this that I find my justification for saying that I have enjoyed communication with God. Of course the absence of such a being as this would be chaos. I cannot conceive of life without its presence.
>
> I remember the night, and almost the very spot on the hilltop, where my soul opened out, as it were, into the Infinite, and there was a rushing together of the two worlds, the inner and the outer. It was deep calling unto deep—the deep that my own struggle had opened up within being answered by the unfathomable deep without, reaching beyond the stars. I stood alone with Him who had made me, and all the beauty of the world, and love, and sorrow, and even temptation . . . The perfect stillness of the night was thrilled by a more solemn silence. The darkness held a presence that was all the more felt because it was not seen. I could not any more have doubted that *He* was there than that I was. Indeed, I felt myself to be, if possible, the less real of the two.

Here are a few more testimonials:

> I only remember finding myself in the midst of wonderful moments, beholding life for the first time in all its young intoxication of loveliness, in its unspeakable joy, beauty, and importance . . . My inner

vision was cleared to the truth so that I saw the actual loveliness which is always there . . . Once out of the gray days of my life I looked into the heart of reality; I witnessed the truth; I have seen life as it really is.

God is more real to me than any thought or thing or person. I feel his presence positively, and the more as I live in closer harmony with his laws as written in my body and mind. I feel him in the sunshine or rain; an awe mingled with a delicious restfulness most nearly describes my feelings. I talk to him as to a companion in prayer and praise, and our communion is delightful. He answers me again and again, often in words so clearly spoken that it seems my outer ear must have carried the tone but generally in strong mental impressions . . . That he is mine and I am his never leaves me, it is an abiding joy. Without it life would be a blank, a desert, a shoreless, trackless waste.

The earnestness of these writers cannot be doubted, and they are overwhelmingly convinced of the genuineness of their experiences and the reality of the divine. Furthermore, the accounts come from reliable sources, not just the neurotic and credulous, and they are widespread, coming from all times and places. What's more, there are similarities in the reports, even though the people were not in contact.

Jean Cocteau once said, "Artists can no more talk about art than vegetables can give a lecture on horticulture." Perhaps the same is true of mystics and their religious experience. But if the experience is incommunicable, how can the mystic describe it in two volumes?

William James, in his *Varieties of Religious Experience*, tries to describe the common denominators of the various accounts under four "marks" of the mystic state. He first lists *ineffability*, the impossibility of communicating the state to someone who has not had the experience. Those who know, can't say, and those who say, don't know. To explain the event to anyone who has not "been there" would be like trying to explain the color blue to a blind person or the key of C major to someone who is deaf. As in transcendence, the mystical experience cannot be translated into concepts much less expressed in words; it is beyond all thought and language. It might be too sacred to utter. Some truths can only be known firsthand, not learned from books, and "whereof one cannot speak, thereof one must be silent." The philosopher G. E. Moore maintains that "good" can never be taught to someone who has not experienced goodness; they will never appreciate what it is, just as the sociopath cannot comprehend remorse. The same might be said of war, depression, and racism. You have to live it to know it.

Noetic quality is listed next, which means intellectual knowledge. Mystics come away from their experience enlightened, with new insight and understanding. What they have learned may be inexpressible, but they now realize something precious. In other words, their minds were involved, not just their feelings, because meaning was transmitted and received; their path was illuminated. In fact, the experience can transform people's lives, changing them profoundly from that point forward.

Transiency is a third feature, the brief, fleeting character of the experience. It may last a few seconds or minutes, perhaps a few hours, but then it fades, leaving the mystic shaken. The feeling is so exquisite that he tries to hold onto it, but because of its evanescent, fugitive quality, that is not possible; it is like squeezing sand: the harder we grasp it, the quicker it slips through our fingers. An intense experience cannot be long-lasting, and the spiritual communion of the mystic is acute and strong.

The last characteristic is *passivity*, meaning that people do not actively seek the experience; the experience seeks them. The moment washes over them while they remain passive, absorbing impressions like a sensitized plate. Sometimes people try to induce a mystic state through extreme piety or forms of deprivation, by remaining motionless or starving themselves, but most often it comes unexpectedly. Some mystics feel that the effort itself can be self-defeating. It would be like turning on a light to see the nature of darkness, or trying to sleep, which will keep us awake. Nevertheless, our minds must be prepared to receive the experience; the ground must be fertile. The situation is similar to the arts, wherein artists must first develop their craft or they will not profit from inspiration when it strikes.

Other characteristics include a feeling of permeating love, sometimes in the form of radiant light, a spiritual "ecstasy," and a sense of the unitary character of all reality. The latter is referred to as the "oceanic feeling" in which our sensations are melted and fused, our bones become liquefied, and the drop that is oneself merges with the sea of being. This point is referred to in the Hindu religion as entering Nirvana: the self becomes one with the All. (To Freud it is the recreation of the undividedness first felt in infancy, a return to the womb.) Reportedly, it is a life-changing experience, self-authenticating, and transformative for one's worldview; we awaken the third eye.

In all of its manifestations, mysticism is a sensitive and tender outlook on human existence, and to criticize it seems almost callous. Nevertheless, mysticism is also an argument for the existence of God based on special revelation, and as such it is subject to evaluation. The main question is, "Can we trust it?"

One criticism is that the mystics differ in their interpretations of their experience. Although there are similarities in the mystic state, there is disagreement about its content, that is, the message transmitted. In the East, the believer sees the union of all being; in the West, the worshiper is overwhelmed with the distance between God's grandeur and man's littleness. Christians may claim to be in touch with Christ, Jews with Moses, and Muslims with Mohammed. Catholics may see Mary meditating, Hindus may see Shiva dancing, and Buddhists may see Gautama on a lotus blossom, rising above the sea of sorrows. What's more, the Christian and Hindu visions of the Trinity seem vastly different: Father, Son, and Holy Spirit versus Brahma, Vishnu, and Shiva. The followers will see the images they expect, and every religion seems reinforced in its dogmas by the mystical experience of its adherents. As J. B. Pratt commented, "The mystic brings his theological beliefs to the mystical experience, he does not derive them from it. . . . The visions of the mystics are determined in content by their beliefs and are due to the dream imagination working upon the mass of theological material that fills the mind."

But wouldn't God speak to each culture using their familiar forms, and wouldn't that account for the differences? Perhaps, but we are left with contradictory visions of spiritual reality and without guidance as to which we should trust. There is no consensus among the mystics that would provide direction, and certainly no common conception of God. The fact that the experience is unutterable presents a further obstacle: How do we know there is an inexpressible reality or no reality to express?

If we trust the reports of mystics who have experienced God, we should also trust those who claim to be in touch with Satan and devils. Why credit only the positive experience? Proof of angels may be proof of devils, as in Baudelaire's *Flowers of Evil*; it is a double-edged sword.

Moreover, when mystics try to bring about a mystic state, the results may be problematic. For example, if devotees hold their breath, stare at the sun, or ingest hallucinogenic mushrooms, they place themselves in an unusual state of consciousness. The images that emerge are more likely to be delusions caused by the extreme physical circumstances and not unique access to reality. As Bertrand Russell says, "From a scientific point of view we can make no distinction between the man who eats little and sees heaven and the man who drinks much and sees snakes." Both are in an extraordinary state in which hallucinations are likely to occur. We can credit normal perception, especially when it is shared by others, but the abnormal is always suspect. Initiates who whip themselves, practicing "the mortification of the flesh for the purification of the soul," are not dependable witnesses.

This leads to the main problem with mysticism, which is a psychological one. Whether in an ordinary or extraordinary state, mystical experience seems subjective, perhaps something pathological. It is heavily weighted with illusions of the senses and delusions of the mind, with auto-suggestion and forms of hysteria. Prior to seizures, people may experience an ecstasy that is due to a dysfunction of the brain. For example, Elissa Schnappell writes, "I am suddenly serene . . . rising. There is the unseen life, the illuminated world, shimmering, flooded with more light than seems possible . . . I am ecstatic. I don't want it to end. I'm about to understand something."

In short, mystics are subject to visions that are hard to differentiate from psychosis, to trances almost inseparable from catatonia, and out-of-body experiences that could be diagnosed as schizophrenia. How do we separate a mental disorder from a special revelation, a hallucination from a spiritual vision? The writer Doris Egan has remarked, "You talk to God, you're religious. God talks to you, you're psychotic." In other words when someone hears voices we do not know whether they should be canonized or institutionalized. Are they a latter-day Joan of Arc or should they be under psychiatric care? How does one validate personal experience that cannot be publicly verified?

It has been suggested that if the experience is life-altering, such as provoking exceptional acts of charity, that verifies its authenticity, but *imagining* that something has occurred could have as strong an effect as a genuine event. The paranoid mental patient who thinks he is being haunted by demons will be as frightened as someone who is awaiting execution. For this reason, doctors control for the placebo effect in medicine.

At best, mystical evidence is testimony, which cannot prove a spiritual realm much less show that a particular denomination holds the truth. The mystic has not established that God is Allah, the Buddha, or Christ, much less that he is a Catholic, Presbyterian, or a Methodist. Still, we cannot dismiss the possibility that mysticism has a special channel to the divine that is inaccessible to ordinary consciousness. The main problem comes in verifying the authenticity of the communication.

None of the arguments for the existence of God are convincing—not the ontological, cosmological, or teleological proofs, not Pascal's wager, James's will to believe, or mystical experience. One suggestion, proposed by Richard Swinburne, is that the arguments might establish a "cumulative" case for God's existence. That is, together they increase the probability that there is a God.

To discuss probability theory would take us too far afield, but philosophers counter Swinburne's claim by pointing out that if each of the arguments contain flaws, it is unlikely that collectively they constitute a proof. This could only happen if they cover each other's errors, and that does not seem to be the case.

7

IF GOD IS GOOD, WHY DO PEOPLE SUFFER?

The main stumbling block to faith comes in the form of the *problem of evil*. The problem is how to reconcile the God of theism with events on earth that bring suffering to human beings. Because these events are part of our environment and cause harm, they are referred to as *natural evils*, and they seem inconsistent with a deity who is wholly good, wise, and almighty. *Moral evil*, by contrast, refers to the awful things people do to people—war, torture, genocide, mutilation, slavery.

The problem of evil has to do mainly with the natural form. It is not a problem for atheists, who regard nature as indifferent and without intentions, but only for theists, who wonder why a loving father would allow his children to experience awful circumstances on earth. If he is omniscient, he knows people are suffering, and he is also aware of every model for constructing the universe, including those without harm. If he is omnipotent, he is not limited by given conditions or even by the devil, and he can prevent all pain if he chose to do so. Why, then, do we have the world we do?

Theodicy is the field that tries to reconcile divine goodness with earthly evil. Is A. E. Housman right in remarking, "Malt does more than Milton can to justify God's ways to man"? Should we drug ourselves to blunt the reality or find an explanation harmonious with a loving God?

Natural evils can be sorted into several categories, but they all concern the physical world we inhabit rather than man's inhumanity to man. As the Christian writer C. S. Lewis said, "It is men not God who have produced racks, whips, prisons, slavery, guns, bayonets, and bombs." The atrocities of human history can be accounted for in terms of free will, which we can use for good or ill. If we choose to abuse it, that is not God's fault (but he might have intervened when wars and genocides occurred). We are more concerned with natural evils, which are part of the earth that God created as our home. This is the world that must be explained because it involves pain from natural causes that are ultimately attributable to God.

One category of natural evils is *catastrophes and disasters*. People are afflicted by hurricanes, tornadoes, floods, earthquakes, tsunamis, avalanches, blizzards, droughts, volcanic eruptions, landslides, lightning strikes, forest fires, killing cold, burning heat, and other "acts of God." For example, 300,000 were killed in a cyclone in India in 1839; 900,000 were killed in the Yellow River Flood in 1887; 136,000 when Krakatoa erupted in 1883. More recently, a cyclone killed 500,000 in Pakistan in 1970; 655,000 were killed in the Chinese earthquake of 1978; and in 2005, approximately 200,000 were killed in the Indonesian tsunami and 23,000 in a Pakistani earthquake. In 2008, a cyclone in Burma killed 100,000. The Haiti earthquake in 2010 left 200,000 dead, and Katrina left 2,000 dead in New Orleans. These figures do not include those injured or those who have lost their homes or their livelihood. For instance, 20 million were affected by the floods in Pakistan in 2010, when a quarter of the country was underwater, and that same year floods and landslides in China affected 300 million. The toll in human misery is enormous and invites questions as to why such disasters happen.

Sickness and disease constitute another class of evils when they are not caused by people themselves, that is, by smoking, drugs, alcohol, or unhealthy foods. In this category we can place the illnesses that naturally afflict us: polio, smallpox, tuberculosis, epilepsy, cystic fibrosis, rheumatism, glaucoma, hepatitis, measles, Parkinson's disease, malaria, multiple sclerosis, influenza, cancer, cholera, typhoid fever, pneumonia, crippling arthritis. We can add the genetic disorders of blindness, deafness, deformed limbs, and brain damage, such as anencephaly. The bubonic plague (the "Black Death") killed 25 million people in 1330, one third of Europe's population; the Great Plague of Seville in 1696 killed 700,000; the Great Plague of London in 1665 killed 100,000, 20 percent of the population. About 13,000 people died of yellow fever in

1878; and up to 100 million Americans died in the 1918–1919 influenza epidemic; malaria kills 300 million people a year, and 1.5 million die of AIDS, originally contracted from the blood of monkeys. The Bible is filled with accounts of plagues and pestilences.

Watching the suffering of anyone we love can have a profound effect on our faith, and from a historical perspective, we question why outstanding people should suffer. Why should Beethoven go deaf, and Monet go blind? The most agonizing cases, of course, are those of the young, the most innocent and vulnerable members of the human race. Parents are desperate to protect their children, but even infants suffer painful injuries and genetic defects, debilitating diseases, and physical and mental handicaps. The earthly parent does everything possible to alleviate the pain and wonders why God does not do more to help—and why the affliction had to happen at all.

This thought troubled Mark Twain:

> The best minds will tell you that when a man has begotten a child he is morally bound to tenderly care for it, protect it from hurt, shield it from disease, clothe it, feed it, bear with its waywardness, lay no hand upon it save in kindness and for its own good, and never in any case inflict upon it a wanton cruelty. God's treatment of his earthly children, every day and every night, is the exact opposite of all that, yet those best minds warmly justify these crimes, condone them, excuse them, and indignantly refuse to regard them as crimes at all, when he commits them. Your country and mine is an interesting one, but there is nothing there that is half so interesting as the human mind.

Hostile environments is a third classification of evils. Here we can include topography, such as deserts, jungles, swamps (with quicksand), Arctic wastes, and barren land not fit for crops, herds, or livestock. We can get cancer from the sun and from radon in the ground; some people have allergies to plants and animals; and some plants, such as poison ivy, oak, and sumac, are toxic to people. The earth is 70 percent water, and we are land mammals who have not been given gills. What's more, 97 percent of that is salt water, with fresh water available only in lakes and rivers and unavailable to us in underground streams and ice.

There are also *wild animals* on earth that attack us if we invade their territory, threaten their young, or cross their paths when they are hungry. There are lions, cougars, tigers, and panthers; grizzly, black, and polar bears; the rhinoceros, elephant, and hippopotamus; wolves, hyenas, and wild boar; sharks, octopus, barracuda, alligators, and saltwater crocodiles; rattlesnakes, copperheads, king cobras, coral snakes, and bushmasters; scorpions, centipedes, tarantulas, the brown recluse, and the black widow. Animals will trample, claw, gore, maim, and kill us; a myriad of insects will sting and bite us, transmitting diseases such as malaria, dengue fever, and West Nile virus; and microscopic bacteria and viruses can be deadly to the human body. No place on earth is free from animals that are destructive to man, any more than there are places immune to disasters or disease. "Nature is red in tooth and claw," Tennyson writes, and says of nature's treatment of animals, "So careful of the type she seems, so careless of the single life."

Finally, we have the natural evil of *death and decay*. We wonder why human beings must be mortal, living only "four score years and ten," and why dying often involves anguish and pain, depriving us of our dignity. And we wonder why so much of our lives must be spent resting. If we sleep eight hours a night, and live for sixty years, we spend twenty years asleep. As Byron phrases it, "Death, so called, is a thing which makes men weep / And yet a third of life is passed in sleep." Furthermore, we wonder why we must undergo the metamorphosis of aging, where our body becomes disfigured and our face is a caricatures of ourselves. The fact that someone we love will be a skeleton one day makes our love both poignant and tragic.

All of these types of evils cause us to question the benevolence of God and even his existence. "God's in His Heaven— / All's right with the world," Robert Browning wrote, which means that if all's not right with the world, God may not be in his heaven.

PAIN IS PUNISHMENT FOR OUR SINS

Theologians have offered various explanations for natural evil, beginning with the idea that suffering is punishment for sin. This view takes two forms: that we have inherited original sin from Adam and Eve's disobedience, and that subsequently the human race added sins of its own. In the name of justice, both sets of sins must be punished, and this God does it through the instrument of natural evils. The world contains the precise amount of punishment that is needed for the degree of sinfulness, and in this way the scales of justice are kept in balance.

Genesis tells us God formed Adam from the dust of the earth, breathed life into his nostrils, then gave him Eve as a companion and the garden of Eden as his home. But for reasons that are obscure, God declared that they could not eat the fruit of one particular tree—a fruit that brought moral understanding. Disobedience would be on pain of death.

As we know, Eve yielded to Satan in the form of a snake, and Adam succumbed to Eve, so that they ate the forbidden fruit. In some quarters, women have had a bad name ever since, as temptresses. And by being rebellious, disobedient creatures, our ancestors lost paradise for themselves and all of their descendants, bringing suffering and death into the world.

In Greek mythology, it is Prometheus who symbolizes a rebellion against divine authority, only here we are meant to admire his spirit. He defied the edict of Zeus that human beings were not to have fire, and with the help of the goddess Athena, stole flames from the sun god Apollo as his chariot coursed across the sky. Fire, of course, represents enlightenment, civilization, and rationality, the light of understanding, so Prometheus is regarded as a symbol of righteous revolt. As the god of foresight, Prometheus knew what punishment awaited him: Zeus had him chained to the adamantine rock for 30,000 years, where an eagle consumed his liver daily, which grew back nightly. Because of his sacrifice, he is considered a humanistic hero in literature.

Of course, the exile from Eden has sometimes been judged a "fortunate fall," and the disobedience a *felix culpa*, or "happy fault." A number of theologians, from Irenaeus to John Hick, have argued this way, for not only do human beings gain dignity by knowing good and evil, but Adam's sin also paved the way for the coming of Christ, and a redeemed world is better than an innocent one.

Nevertheless, the Fall is usually taken as a catastrophic event for humankind; our ancestors should have resisted temptation—and could have done so. Adam was made "sufficient to have stood though free to fall," as Milton says, and ever since human beings have been cursed with inherent depravity. We must work for our bread, feel ashamed of our nakedness, and women have to experience pain in childbirth. "In Adam's fall / We sinned all," and Christian doctrine holds that man's sinfulness can only be redeemed through belief and by grace. "As all die in Adam, so all will be made alive in Christ," St. Paul writes.

In *Paradise Lost*, Milton retells the Genesis story, with poetic license, describing how Satan entered into the serpent and tempted Eve until "her rash hand in evil hour / Forth reaching to the Fruit, she pluck'd, she eat." Then "Earth felt the wound . . . (and) all was lost." In a poignant passage, Milton suggests that Adam chose to share Eve's punishment, loving her enough to die along with her.

From the religious perspective, some knowledge is divine and inaccessible to mortals, but like our forebears, we want to trespass beyond our proper bounds. Out of pride, we continuously test the limits, wanting to understand everything. "Faust" is a name for this *hubris*—an excessive pride that induces us to inquire into sacred realms. We should know our place and not aspire to have divine knowledge. To seek wisdom beyond our appointed realm is sacrilege. Is there forbidden knowledge, things human beings are not supposed to know?

By most accounts, the Adam and Eve story is not literally true but metaphor and myth. But assuming the story is a transcription of actual events, we wonder whether Eve was tempted by the apple or by the snake, that is, by knowledge, possessions, or sensuality, or by something phallic or rational, that serpent reason. We also wonder why a loving father would dangle the forbidden fruit before his children, tempting sin. At a deeper level, we can question why Adam and Eve should be blamed for sinning *before* they knew the difference between right and wrong, and why an omniscient God should test man when he knew the outcome of the test.

We also wonder why people should be denied knowledge of good and evil, since moral understanding seems an important part of humanness; in fact, we are scarcely human unless we know right from wrong and can choose between them. There is moral merit in resisting temptation, but only when we are aware that certain actions should be resisted. Although we find children's innocence touching, we would not want to remain innocent all our lives.

The main criticism, however, pivots round the idea of inherited sin. We might understand why Adam and Eve would be punished for disobeying God's will, but we bridle at the notion that all of their descendants should also suffer. "I the Lord thy God am a jealous God," the Decalogue states, "visiting the iniquity of the fathers upon the children unto the third and fourth generation." But it seems unjust for children to inherit the sins of their parents and to pay for their wrongdoing. We would never prosecute someone for what someone else did; that would never hold up in court. We do not hold today's Italians responsible for the Roman conquest, any more than we condemn twenty-first-century Germans for their grandparents' actions in the twentieth-century wars. In the same way, we wonder why we should be held accountable for the original sin of our forefathers.

From a psychological perspective, we might be working our way backwards, trying to find an explanation within ourselves for natural evil and mortality. That is, since we have been sentenced to death, we assume we did something awful to deserve such punishment. It must be our fault that the earth contains suffering. We tell ourselves that we sinned against God and were expelled from paradise, and that tale helps to make sense of our pain, renders it just. But the story is a little too neat and convenient.

The other form of this theory, that suffering is punishment for sin, has to do with the awful things that we have done to each other that must be atoned for. The assumption once again is that the universe has a system of justice whereby the wicked are punished and the virtuous are rewarded. People get what they deserve, and we pay for our wrongdoing by suffering from natural causes. This is the justification for the flood and for Sodom and Gomorrah. All catastrophes, illnesses, and hostile conditions on earth are retribution for our sins. When we consider the millions we have killed in war, the wounded and homeless, the starving, orphaned, and enslaved, we probably deserve an even worse world than we have. The bubonic plague in the 1330s that killed twenty-five million people was widely regarded as retribution for the unrighteousness of Europeans.

The presumption is that a scheme of cosmic retribution is in operation. In our earthly justice we often think it fair to punish people in a way that is equal to their offense. Fairness consists of retaliation in degree. In Hindu thought the "law of karma" expresses this idea, that punishment will pursue us for our crimes, as cause and effect: "God does not make one suffer for no reason, nor does He make one happy for no reason. God is very fair and gives you exactly what you deserve." Similarly, in the Hebrew religion there is the "law of talion," which lies behind "An eye for an eye," "As ye sew, so shall ye reap," and "Whoever sheds a man's blood, by man shall his blood be shed." Beginning with the early Babylonians and continuing through biblical and Roman law, it was considered just for criminals to have inflicted on them the injury they inflicted on their victims. An interesting psychological form is "talion dread," which is self-inflicted punishment. If a man feels pangs of remorse after committing adultery, he might become impotent. If a woman sees something she is not supposed to see, her vision could then be blurred; she might even become blind. This, of course, is Freud's view: hysterical symptoms come from guilt. He sees it as a highly efficient system. Instead of being punished by others, we punish ourselves, replacing our parents as instruments of justice. In cases of suicide, we are our own executioners.

In our everyday lives, we often assume that a natural system of rewards and punishments operates. If we have an accident or become sick, we ask: "Why me? What have I done to deserve this?" We then search our conscience to discover our faults, to learn why we are to blame. As children, if we catch cold after being in the snow without a winter coat or boots, we feel that poetic justice is at work. In the same way, if we overeat, become obese, and have a heart attack, that is our fault. If we do not practice safe sex and contract a sexually transmitted disease, we brought it down upon ourselves. The same can be said of the dust bowl and global warming.

The connection between wrongdoing and suffering is commonly made, and it seems reasonable to attribute this system of justice to God. The pain that people feel from natural evil can be interpreted as punishment for moral evil and therefore justified. God operates in a retributive way, and that makes natural evil consistent with a fair and good God.

The *Epic of Gilgamesh*, from around 3000 b.c., contains this theme, and it is central to the book of Job in the Old Testament. In the New Testament, it appears in Luke 13:4–5 and John 9:1–3 in connection with why the tower of Siloam fell, and why a man was born blind, respectively. This explanation is often treated in literature, especially in Fyodor Dostoyevsky's *The Brothers Karamazov*.

In the seventeenth century, G. W. Leibniz argued that the world we have has been arranged by God with complete justice, so that sinful humanity is punished exactly as it deserves. If there were more natural evil, the punishment would be excessive; if there were less, the punishment would not equal man's wickedness. Instead, we have the exact degree that justice requires, neither too much nor too little. With our limited intelligence, we may not think the scheme is fair, but *sub specie aeternitatis*, from the standpoint of God, each and every aspect is necessary. Leibniz is famous for declaring that this is "the best of all possible worlds." It was this doctrine that Voltaire targeted in *Candide*, concluding that this optimism maintains that all is well when in fact we are miserable.

The chief problem with this explanation is that no correlation exists between sinfulness and suffering. That is, we would expect sinful people to suffer and saintly people to prosper, but that is not necessarily the case. Rather, good people can undergo a series of misfortunes, and some terrible people get through life virtually unscathed. There does not appear to be any relation between what people deserve and what they get, between their character and their misery or happiness in life. Perhaps people receive their just deserts in the next life, but there is no evidence of natural justice on earth—and there is no place to lodge a complaint.

In short, the distribution is askew: the wrong people often suffer. If evils are intended as punishment, then those committing the greatest number of awful sins should experience the most terrible evils. But, in fact, that is not the case. Not only is the distribution askew but the degree of suffering is often grossly out of proportion to the guilt or innocence of the sufferer. As one commentator put it, "We would expect that the greatest scoundrels are in hospitals, that floods destroy the farms of evil men, that frost kills the crops of sinners, or that boatloads of rascals are the ones that sink into the sea." In other words, innocent people are wrongfully condemned to death. Earthquakes do not kill only terrible people, and those with cancer are not all terrible sinners; when volcanoes erupt, it is not just the wicked who are buried under the rubble, and lightning will strike the minister and the man who volunteered to repair the church steeple. In society we strive to be fair, but in the physical world, the punishment rarely fits the crime. Perhaps we are penalized by our sins, but not for them.

This answer certainly does not work for babies, who are innocence incarnate, or for animals that are incapable of sin or virtue, whose "plaint of guiltless hurt doth pierce the sky." Meat eaters cause bloodshed by their very nature. Countless animals must have drowned in the flood, but fish were exempt from destruction.

This disparity is what bothered Job, a man who was "blameless and upright, one who feared God and turned away evil," yet he lost his property through "the fire of God," his children by "a great wind," and he was afflicted with a skin disease from head to toe. At one point, Job cries, "I call aloud, but there is no justice." The answer that is offered in the Bible is not satisfactory: that the evils were the result of a contest between God and Satan, testing Job's faith. In any case, the disasters he experiences are not attributed to wrongdoing.

Archibald MacLeish, the author of the play *J. B.* (a retelling of Job), asks, "How is it possible to believe in the justice of God in a world in which the innocent perish in vast meaningless massacres." Robert Frost, in his short play *A Masque of Reason*, has God say to Job, "I've been meaning to thank you these thousands of years for teaching mankind a very valuable lesson: that people do not always get what they deserve."

Another criticism of the punishment theory is that if people deserve their suffering, evils should not be opposed; they have been visited on people for their sins. So there should not be hospitals, surgery, or medications, doctors, nurses, or medical research to prevent genetic abnormalities, cure sickness, or extend life; pain and death are just retaliation for wrongdoing. Relief efforts for tsunami or floods victims would be misplaced, and there should not be levees, lightning rods, fire breaks, irrigation projects, or early warning systems. If suffering is deserved, we should take our punishment, not try to relieve it.

Those who help in relief efforts often assume they are doing God's work, being compassionate in helping their fellow man, but if the suffering is intended by God as just deserts, it should not be alleviated. We are then helping those who are undeserving, the people whose actions have brought the disaster or disease down on their heads. If God intended suffering as punishment, humanitarian aid opposes God's will. This is why some religious people find themselves in conflict as aid workers. The dilemma is effectively illustrated by Albert Camus in *The Plague*.

As an aside, some theologians have argued against slum-clearing projects on the grounds that the poor are blessed, and that we need suffering on earth so people will long for heaven. This raises the question of whether we should leave the world better than we found it.

A final objection to this model is that it portrays God as a retributive, if not a vindictive, being. In our current theory of penology, offenders are punished in order to make them better, not to make them pay; we extend a hand rather than pointing a finger. Theoretically at least, our prisons are designed to reform, rehabilitate, and deter potential criminals and to protect society from the offender. This approach is more New Testament than Old Testament, meting out sentences according to their future effect. Instead of looking backward at the crime, it looks forward to the good the punishment will do, both for the criminal and society at large. This is in keeping with the principle that all souls are equally precious, that no one is beyond redemption, and that God hates the sin but loves the sinner. If this is our highest thinking today, presumably God would operate this way and not retaliate against evildoers. His system of justice would be based on the good for humankind, not on vengeance.

It should be mentioned that some legal authorities do not accept this objection. They argue that giving people what they deserve is the very essence of justice. The punishment must be equal to the offense, but criminals must be made to pay for their crimes. Furthermore, to pass sentence on people based on the effect it will have divorces the punishment from the crime. Innocent people could then be imprisoned if it would do them some good. It seems a better system to punish people in proportion to the severity of their offense.

The main problems, however, have to do with the human race suffering for Adam's disobedience, and the fact that no correlation exists between individual sin and individual suffering.

The Reverend Jerry Falwell recently declared that the destruction of the World Trade Center was a response to pagans, abortionists, feminists, gays, the A.C.L.U., and those prohibiting prayer in schools. But are we sure that these things are sinful, and that all those killed on 9/11 were pagans and abortionists, for example? And do we know that the people destroyed were worse than those who were spared?

SUFFERING BUILDS CHARACTER

Another proposed explanation is that suffering builds character. We must overcome adversity in order to develop into worthwhile people. All problems are challenges, setbacks are opportunities, stumbling blocks are stepping stones. Great character is always the result of challenges that have been conquered. In order to become better human beings, we need to be tempered by fire. If a person's life is wholly pleasant, with satisfaction immediately following desire, he does not grow, but if he must surmount poverty, disabilities, abandonment, and so on, then he can become a finer person. Suffering teaches us lessons; we live to learn. If the world were a paradise, there would be no incentive to progress, either personally or as a culture.

The nineteenth-century German philosopher G. W. F. Hegel took this principle as the driving force of civilization, responsible for the rise of nations. In his *Philosophy of History*, Hegel argued that the greatest civilizations of the past have emerged because of the challenges of nature. In warm climates people are inclined to relax, submit, and enjoy life, whereas in harsh conditions people are energetic and disciplined. As Machiavelli stated, "Soft climates produce soft men," but difficult conditions energize us to achieve. The nineteenth-century British sociologist Arnold Toynbee echoed this sentiment, claiming that a nation's weather, topography, temperature, and so forth must be stimulating, but not overwhelming. Relaxing in Tennyson's land of the lotus eaters will never lead to a developed society. The countries of the equator, therefore, have greater difficulties in development than those in the northern temperate zone; survival is just too easy.

History has countless examples of people who have become outstanding by overcoming their physical disabilities. Most famously, Helen Keller became a remarkable author and speaker by transcending both her blindness and deafness. "Character cannot be developed in ease and quiet," she wrote, "Only through experience of trial and suffering can the soul be strengthened, vision cleared, ambition inspired, and success achieved." Despite suffering from polio, or because of it, Franklin Roosevelt was an effective president, and Itzhak Perlman an outstanding violinist. Stephen Hawking, the brilliant theoretical physicist, is confined to a wheelchair because of Lou Gehrig's disease, and the musicians Ray Charles and Andrea Bocelli are both blind.

All athletes know that hard work is needed to achieve excellence in any sport. The dictum is "no pain, no gain." You must put in the time, pay your dues, do the work required. The same is true of achievement in art, science, literature, business, scholarship—in fact, all endeavors of life. Perspiration always precedes inspiration, and we all appreciate things more if we have to struggle for them. God, of course, realizes this, and has created a world with pain and adversity that is a catalyst to achievement.

Besides, without suffering we would never develop our potential for mercy, kindness, love, and compassion. We would not want to protect children from harm, do medical research, volunteer for charities, organize relief efforts, or generally assume responsibility for people's welfare. Disasters can bring out the best in us, uniting humanity against a common enemy. We can exercise our free will on the side of the angels, fighting the good fight for humanity. In adversity we have an opportunity to act courageously, and to empathize with the suffering of others, including Christ. In short, people develop their character to a higher level in a world of natural evils than they would otherwise, and that is sufficient justification.

John Hick, a contemporary philosopher, has written in *Evil and the God of Love*:

> The world is not intended to be a paradise, but rather the scene of a history in which the human personality may be formed toward the pattern of Christ. Men are not to be thought of on the analogy of animal pens, whose life is to be made as agreeable as possible, but rather on the analogy of human children, who are to grow to adulthood in an environment whose primary and overriding purpose is not immediate pleasure but the realizing of the most valuable potentialities of human personality.

Hick maintains that the earth is a place of "soul-making." In a similar vein, C. S. Lewis wrote in *The Problem of Pain*:

> I have seen great beauty of spirit in some who were great sufferers. I have seen men, for the most part, grow better not worse with advancing years, and I have seen the last illness produce treasures of fortitude and meekness . . . We are a Divine work of art, something that God is making, and therefore something with which he will not be satisfied until it has a certain character.

This answer to the problem of evil seems a matter of common sense, but is it true that hardship always improves people? Sometimes people are elevated, but sometimes they are also degraded. In fact, a minority may be uplifted, but the majority seem to be harmed by experiencing a disaster; some are emotionally crushed altogether. Whatever doesn't kill us can make us weaker.

When an earthquake kills a child's family, such as the 2010 earthquake in Haiti, or a parent is swept away by a flood, such as the recent flood in Pakistan, the child may be made stronger by the experience, but most likely they will be scarred, damaged, or ruined for life. If a man's wife dies of cancer, a woman he deeply loved, he may develop a finer character as a result, but he is more likely to be embittered, perhaps broken by the loss. The handicapped can sometimes overcome the odds and achieve success, like Helen Keller and Stephen Hawking, but most people will be at a disadvantage all their lives. These are the exceptions that prove the rule.

People who have been in hospitals do not usually emerge with a better character than before; the same holds true of those who survive shipwrecks or avalanches. People in poor nations who face malnutrition and starvation are not morally finer than those in wealthier nations, and outstanding people do not usually come from the slums. If it is argued that God does not give people more than they can bear, there are thousands in mental institutions who have had more than they could bear. St. Paul writes that a thorn in the flesh is stimulating, but it could also grow septic and cause death.

Undeniably, tragedy can bring people together, but at the same time it can bring out the worst in them. When a disaster strikes, such as the New Orleans flood following hurricane Katrina, the authorities call out the National Guard to stop rape and looting. Although heroic acts do occur in times of crisis, the moral level of humanity is not automatically raised. It is a good question whether people tend to exploit such opportunities or rise to the occasion, but at least they are not always unified and improved by a common threat.

Not only are people not always made better, but some outstanding figures have achieved good character with very little pain in their lives. This holds true for Aquinas, Aristotle, Bach, Chaucer, Chopin, da Vinci, Dickens, Einstein, Keats, Matisse, Newton, Picasso, Shakespeare, Shelley, Socrates, and so forth, which indicates that trials are not needed to achieve excellence.

Also, as in the retributive theory, the distribution of natural evil is askew. It does not correlate with people's need for suffering to improve their character. Those who might be deepened by pain do not necessarily encounter much of it, but those who cannot bear very much are afflicted with tsunamis and malaria, as well as locusts and droughts that ruin their crops. In brief, the number, type, and degree of evils appear unrelated to the need for disciplined character. Again, the wrong people can suffer.

But couldn't it be argued that the suffering of some can stimulate others to generous action? For example, the parents of a child with sickle-cell anemia or one who dies of leukemia might start a foundation to fight such diseases. This does happen, but then the suffering of some people is used to ennoble others, which does not seem fair. It would be a gruesome means to a worthwhile end. Good things can come from bad occurrences, but that does not justify the awfulness. Why not have a positive means to a beneficial end?

"It is better to go to the house of mourning than to the house of feasting," Solomon tells us. "Sorrow is better than laughter, for by the sadness of the countenance the heart is made better." But that implies we should seek sorrow for the sake of growth rather than trying to be happy.

Critics also point out that even if suffering were necessary for development, and the distribution were fair, we could ask why human beings were given this psychological makeup. That is, if suffering teaches us lessons we could not learn in any other way, then why were we made in such a way that suffering is necessary to learn those lessons? We might have been inspired by positive example, advancing from good to better rather than bad to good. With all models at his disposal, why would a benevolent God choose one that involves pain?

And of course, some people never recover and cannot then go on to develop fine characters. Some are killed by tumors, buried by mudslides, eaten by sharks. Trial by fire can cause fatal burns.

Perhaps this theory persists because we have a propensity to think that if something hurts, it is good for us. The bitter medicine will help the most, but the sweet-tasting one can't be very effective; the painful exercise is best, the comfortable one can't do our body much good. For this reason the boys in British public schools used to take cold baths in the morning, not warm ones. George Bernard Shaw once wrote, "The English always think they're being moral when in fact they're only un-comfortable."

People who live in the north or in rainy countries sometimes feel virtuous, assuming that if the climate changed, their character would deteriorate. Conversely, we can believe that pleasure is decadent, or at least that our relaxation must be earned by hard work. Obviously, these assumptions do not hold up; they smack of austerity and self-denial, perhaps masochism. One commentator wrote, "The stronger the winds, the deeper the roots. The deeper the roots and the longer the winds, the more beautiful the tree." But strong winds can distort the growth of trees, and a hurricane can uproot trees altogether.

WE HAVE TO EXPERIENCE THE BAD TO APPRECIATE THE GOOD

Still another explanation is that unless we have experienced the bad, we are unable to recognize the good. That is, we need sickness to appre-ciate health, rain to appreciate sunshine, hunger to appreciate food, and the prospect of death to relish living. In short, we must have grief, sorrow, and sadness to appreciate happiness. If there were no contrast, we might be happy but not realize it, and lose the whole point. God therefore allows suffering in order to make people aware of life's bless-ings.

Otherwise put, all judgments are made relative to some contrasting conditions. Unless we have a negative state, we are unable to judge another to be positive. If the weather were perfect all the time, we would not notice it; if we were continuously healthy, we would take it for granted. Therefore God permits natural evils as the bad that can enable us to appreciate the good.

This too sounds plausible. God wants what is best for us, and that entails some harm so that we can value the earth's bounty. One funda-mental question that arises, however, is whether contrasts are needed for appreciation. A baby seems to enjoy milk without having had castor oil—and not just because he is hungry; a baby bottle filled with vinegar would not be accepted. A filet mignon or lobster dinner could be enjoyable, even if we have not had ptomaine poisoning. This suggests that there are certain physical sensations that are naturally pleasurable, apart from contrasts with something distasteful. Conversely, people would not like being burned at the stake, stretched on the rack, or being hanged; it is not something one can get used to or learn to enjoy. When we feel pain, we judge it as bad, without having had a contrasting experience.

We might enjoy an experience more by contrast with something unpleasant but that does not mean we would not enjoy it at all without it. And on balance, we would rather enjoy things less and do without the suffering—especially when that suffering includes genetic deformities and childhood diseases.

That introduces another problem with this theory. Assuming that contrasts are necessary for appreciation, the amount of natural evil seems excessive for this purpose. We might appreciate a clear, balmy day relative to a rainy, cold one, but we do not need a hurricane or a temperature of 30° below zero. Having an occasional headache might help us appreciate good health, but we do not need heart disease, malignant tumors, cholera, tuberculosis, diabetes, or other ailments. In other words, there is far more evil on earth than is necessary to make us appreciate the good; as one writer put it, "the earth is soaked with tears from crust to core," which means the evil is disproportionate to the good produced.

In addition, even if contrasts are necessary, opposites are not. That is, we may need the contrast of good food to appreciate great food, but we do not need the opposite, bad food. Furthermore, the good does not become bad relative to the great; it is simply less good. In accounting, an asset is not entered as a liability even when it is small.

And as was pointed out with the previous theory, some never recover and cannot benefit from the contrast. If someone is struck by lightning, they may not be able to appreciate anything anymore.

None of these explanations seem sufficient: that natural evil is punishment for sin, that suffering builds character, or that contrasts are necessary for appreciation. The next chapter will discuss additional theories that try to resolve the dilemma. Perhaps one of these will resonate with the reader, or perhaps the problem of evil will remain a problem that must be confronted.

William Blake expressed these feelings when he wrote, "Tiger, tiger burning bright / In the forests of the night, / What immortal hand or eye / Dare frame thy fearful symmetry? . . . Did He smile His work to see? / Did He who made the lamb make thee?" Robert Frost's poem "Design" has a similar theme, wherein he reflected on a moth that had landed on a flower called a "heal-all" and was killed by a spider. The last stanza reads:

> What had that flower to do with being white,
> The wayside blue and innocent heal-all?
> What brought the kindred spider to the height,
> Then steered the white moth thither in the night?
> What but design of darkness to appall? —
> If design govern in a thing so small.

8

OTHER PROPOSED EXPLANATIONS

FOR A FREE CHOICE, THERE MUST BE ALTERNATIVES OF GOOD AND EVIL

One of the traits that makes us human as compared to animals or machines is having the ability to choose between options, that is, to exercise our free will. Machines may have artificial intelligence but not consciousness, which is a condition for free choice. Philosophers distinguish between free will, which is the ability to decide what to do, and freedom, which is the ability to do what we decide. The first is internal and central to our humanness, the second depends upon external circumstances, such as wealth and the openness of our political system. A man in prison has been deprived of his freedom and cannot affect the world as he wishes, but he can still exercise free will in choosing what he wishes. This is what Oscar Wilde meant by "Stone walls do not a prison make / Nor iron bars a cage." It is also what was meant by the Stoic slave Epictetus when he wrote, "I must die, and must I die groaning too? I must be fettered; must I be lamenting too? . . . What do you say, man? Fetter me? You will fetter my leg, but not Zeus himself can get the better of my free will."

But to be truly our own master we need both free will and the freedom to carry out our decisions, and this, it is argued, is what God provides through natural evil. He gives us a choice between the good and the bad, and by offering a genuine choice, he makes our freedom meaningful. If there were only one option, we would hardly be free. It would be like a Soviet election, with a single party and a single candidate, which is not an election at all. Evil, then, must be present for the sake of real choice, and we must endure it for the good that it allows.

In this context, being free means primarily having the power to decide between love and hate, to separate light from darkness. It means being able to choose to obey God or reject him. From a Christian standpoint, we should not seek freedom *from* God, for that is bondage to Satan, but we should express our freedom in conformity *to* the divine will. Paradoxically, if we are self-indulgent, surrendering to our desires, we become slaves to our passions, whereas yielding ourselves to God is ultimate liberation, losing ourselves to gain ourselves. God does not compel us to love him or one another, but if we do, we become truly free: "I will walk about in freedom, for I have sought out your precepts" (Ps. 119:45).

The main point of this explanation is that being free requires choices, and without the alternatives of good and evil we would lack genuine freedom and be automatons or marionettes.

However, we can ask whether evil must exist as a choice for freedom to be meaningful? We could choose between good, better, and best without the option of the bad and still have free choice. The range of possibilities would be more limited but not to the point of precluding real decisions. We could also make choices outside of a moral context—choosing a car, deciding whom to marry, electing a president. The only area that would not be open to us would be evil possibilities, which is not a bad thing.

But more importantly, natural evils seldom offer a choice. We are not faced with choosing an earthquake or solid ground, or deciding whether to be carried away by a flood. Natural evils overwhelm us without offering an alternative. Some physical problems are our fault and can be prevented, such as diabetes from being overweight, or a carcinoma from too much sun, but the evils that are part of our given environment are beyond our control. We do not elect to be swept up in the tornado, choose to have epilepsy, or decide to grow old and die. In other words, natural evils seldom offer us options and therefore cannot be justified in terms of allowing human freedom.

If tragedies did offer a chance to perform good deeds, such as blindness inspiring the invention of braille, that would be using some people's suffering as an opportunity for improving others. To cause afflictions in individuals, treating them as instruments rather than human beings, is inconsistent with a benevolent deity.

GOD'S LIGHT OPPOSES THE POWER OF DARKNESS

Another commonsense answer is that we always need balance in life, an equal measure of good and bad, blessings and misfortunes. In metaphysical terms, the universe has to be kept in equilibrium: there must be symmetry, measure, and proportion, neither an excess nor a deficiency of any one thing. And this is precisely what our world contains, both sun and rain, health and sickness, youth and old age. It is not that opposites are necessary for appreciation but that balance is needed for the universe to function at all.

This seems reasonable, however the equilibrium argument does not stand up very well. God did not need to adopt the model of balance; he could have organized the world in any number of different ways, including one in which there were only varieties of good. An all-knowing, all-powerful God is not constricted and did not have to balance good with evil. In the same way, the ocean did not need to be salty, and the ground did not need radon, any more than there had to be 117 elements rather than 3,117, or people had to breathe oxygen. An omnipotent God has logical limitations, but he could have constructed the material world in any way he imagined.

But what about the balance that is necessary with regard to the senses? If we are to be sensitive to pleasure, we must be sensitive to pain. Our senses cannot work just one way, feeling pleasure but not pain; it is a two-way street. So if we are to experience enjoyment in life, we must be responsive to suffering.

However, the question is why should there be awful events for us to experience? Our senses might have to register pain and pleasure, but that does not explain why a benevolent God would allow painful events to occur.

This leads to the suggestion that God may not be perfect, but limited—contrary to what was assumed at the outset. If God were finite in wisdom, power, or love, the problem is solved, resolved, or dissolved.

God might be limited in power. We know he cannot do what is logically impossible, so perhaps he is constricted in other ways. William

James thought that a God who depends on humanity to help him in the struggle against evil is a more satisfying kind of being to worship. For then we can ally ourselves with God in his fight against the devil, and our efforts can actually affect (and effect) the outcome. This means that God is not omnipotent but battles against "the given" or the powers of darkness, and the result is not certain but very much in doubt. On this model, evil can be attributed to Satan, but God does whatever he can to protect mankind. He is distanced from the evils of the world, and we can join with him, following the good angel on our right shoulder.

In a similar way, the Zoroastrianism, or Mazdaism, of Persia, though a monotheistic religion, describes two energy systems that are engaged in a vast, cosmic conflict: Ahura Mazda represents the creative force, truth, order, and light; Angra Mainyu stands for chaos, falsehood, disorder, and darkness. According to doctrine, good will triumph ultimately but only after a tortuous struggle against the dark power that attempts to make the world impure.

In folk religion, this scenario is also prevalent, of good and evil, right hand (*dextera*) and left hand (*sinistra*) locked in a titanic battle, which implies a dualistic system in which the Lord has incomplete power. In monotheism, an almighty God cannot escape responsibility for the pain embedded in nature; everything operates with his permission. But if Satan has comparable strength, then the terrible things can be ascribed to his agency. Sickness or injury is the work of infernal powers.

In short, in a polytheistic system the problem of evil is easily resolved: suffering is attributed to the malicious gods, pleasant experiences to the benevolent ones. The lady and the tiger are behind the same door. Evil is only a problem for religions in which God is omnipotent, where the same god is responsible for everything that happens. The good witch and the bad witch are both mother on different days.

Or perhaps God is limited in knowledge and is not aware of everything that happens. He may not know every disaster that afflicts the 7 billion people on earth; he cannot be everywhere at once. He certainly intervenes when he knows about catastrophes or disease, but he is not completely conscious of all events, including harmful ones. In designing the universe, he may not have been able to foresee how everything would unfold, that the worm was in the bud. Perhaps he is a deistic God with limited foresight, and could not predict how the potential he unleashed would be actualized. His actions had unintended consequences, and although he has perfect love for humanity, he never understood that his creation would have some terrible results. God is not to blame, his character cannot be faulted; he simply did not know any better.

Or maybe God is not perfectly good. That too would solve the problem of evil. Perhaps God does not love mankind unconditionally but according to our merits or deserts, or he loves people of one religion but not others, or he is sometimes angry, jealous, and vengeful. Perhaps his nature is mixed, not consistently benevolent. At different times he may want war or peace, retaliation or forgiveness, according to his disposition. Then we would not have to explain evil, because God could be omniscient and omnipotent but lacking in absolute goodness.

If we had to dispense with one of God's attributes we would probably begin with omnipotence, then go to omniscience, and finally absolute goodness, but most theologians would want to retain all three, plus other qualities. In other words, we do solve the problem of evil if we eliminate one of the foundations of the problem, but then we are conceiving of a different God. To most people, the price would be too high. We want a God who is perfectly wise, almighty, and wholly loving, and we want to make that being compatible with the suffering of humanity. Are we asking for an impossibility?

Could any of the attributes of God be eliminated or others added while still calling him God? For example, could we say that he is not only good but good-natured, that he has a sense of humor? Could he get bored? Is he sensual, or is that blasphemy? Could he ever surprise himself by doing something unexpected, or be amazed at people's actions? Overall, could a genuine God be less than almighty, wise, and benevolent?

WITH OUR LIMITED UNDERSTANDING, WE CANNOT JUDGE

At this point we may want to throw up our hands and declare that we are simply unable to judge. These matters are beyond our understanding, mysteries that exceed our intellect. "There are more things in heaven and earth, Horatio, than are dreamt of in your philosophy," Hamlet says, and having explored a variety of explanations, we might be inclined to agree. We may think that no answer is possible and, from a logical standpoint, that a perfect God and natural evil are simply incompatible. But this may only demonstrate the limitations of the human mind. In our skin-bound, earth-bound, finite state we cannot hope to comprehend the vision of God. In fact, it is arrogant and presumptuous to even try—perhaps that would be the same pride that prompted the Fall of man. For all we know, our black may be his white, our evil, part of his harmonious, grand design.

We are simply precluded from judging such things; they are far beyond our comprehension. We must have faith and leave the rest to God's wisdom. If we trust in him, we accept that whatever we endure is for the best. The symphony is richer for having some dissonance, and if we could hear the "music of the spheres," we could appreciate the scheme entire. Even suffering has a place in the divine plan, for everything that happens is appropriate and fitting. We will understand in the life to come, in the rapture when all is made clear. "For now we see through a glass, darkly, but then face to face" (1 Cor. 13).

Alexander Pope, in his poem *Essay on Man*, takes this approach; his intention is to "vindicate the ways of God to man":

> All Nature is but Art unknown to thee;
> All chance direction, which thou canst not see;
> All discord, harmony not understood;
> All partial evil, universal good:
> And spite of Pride, in erring Reason's spite,
> One truth is clear, *Whatever is, is right*.

This viewpoint is very appealing, asking us to surrender to hidden truths beyond reason, but can we simply place blind faith in the goodness of God, despite appearances? Wouldn't that be a type of intellectual suicide? To say, "It's a matter of faith," could mean we have run out of reasons. And we cannot adore what we cannot comprehend.

More importantly, if we cannot judge, then we cannot judge that everything is for the best or the worst; in fact, we cannot reach any conclusion. In other words, we cannot begin with "I don't know" and wind up with "Therefore I know." As we saw with the teleological argument, negative premises cannot yield positive conclusions. If we do not know, we do not know, and we cannot then call God benevolent or malevolent. In fact, things could be even worse than we imagine; we simply do not know. Once we undermine our own judgment, disqualifying ourselves, nothing can be claimed.

But what about the argument that death is necessary to make way for life; otherwise the planet would be overrun with people. Otherwise put, we can only have eternal life at our children's expense. In Hinduism, Shiva is both creator and destroyer, because all animate things need a balance of nature.

However, that is only true within a closed or isolated system. If human life could expand beyond the earth, death would not be necessary as a condition for life. If we could colonize other planets, rather than being confined to this one, death would not be necessary. We are now exploring the larger universe, and we could move outward from earth to the moon or Mars, but that option could have been made open to us from the start. And even if death were necessary, that does not justify the degeneration of old age or the pain that often accompanies dying.

Could suffering be a test of our faith? Some theologians take this view, that suffering is an ordeal or trial of our faith, so that if we trust in God, even when faced with the senseless pain of those we cherish, then we are worthy of the kingdom of heaven . But the counterargument is that a parent who tested his child's love by deliberately causing him injury or illness could hardly be called a good parent. Such a parent would not deserve a child's love. Giving a son or daughter a cold would be reprehensible, much less cholera or cancer. Therefore, a benevolent God would not function this way.

Could we accept an answer that if the earth were not so hellish, we would not yearn for heaven? But we could have been made in such a way that we would aspire to heaven, not as an escape from a world of suffering but as a finer place still. That is, we might be drawn from in front rather than pushed from behind, hoping for an even better life to come.

Could we accept pain as a warning sign of something wrong—an injury or illness? Biologists sometimes view pain this way, but that does not explain the pain that continues after we have been warned, the pain that accompanies an illness or injury.

Don't we need suffering in order to know God? We do tend to become more devout during times of stress—there are no atheists in foxholes. After disasters, the churches are full. But what kind of God is revealed in calamities and catastrophes? Certainly not a wholly loving one. If we turn to God at such times, doesn't that show human frailty and the need for supernatural support? Some critics have suggested that "though he slay me yet will I trust in him" is akin the Stockholm syndrome—a psychological paradox of relating to the oppressor. A battered wife will sometimes return to her abuser out of low self-esteem; she feels she deserves to be treated badly because she has no value. There are parallels in religion with feelings of sinfulness; we are wretches, and any pain we receive is no more than just. The psychological can vary inversely with the logical, so that we believe in God strongly when we should be most skeptical.

Sometimes the existence of evil is denied altogether. For instance, an earthquake is just a geological occurrence. It is only called evil if people choose to live along the fault line, just as a desert is only an impediment if people want to farm there. Earthquakes and deserts are not terrible in themselves but only in relation to human life. However, we can't always get out of the way of catastrophes or avoid diseases. They seem to be present everywhere on earth, including on the paths we must walk.

In the same way, it has been argued that pain may be an illusion. Christian Science is the prime example of this view. According to the founder, Mary Baker Eddy, truth and goodness are real, but evil and error are not. Just as there is no darkness but only degrees of light, and no cold but only degrees of heat, evil is simply the absence of good. Pain occurs because of fear, ignorance, and sin, and when "errors of mind" are corrected, it will disappear from our consciousness.

Appealing as this might be, it is virtually impossible to regard pain as an illusion. Few things strike us as more real. Perhaps we can reduce pain through yoga, meditation, exercise, or hypnosis, even through magnets or pyramid power, but when someone is seriously injured it is hard to attribute his suffering to an error of mind. To state the obvious, a broken leg cannot be mended by adopting the proper attitude; the mind's power over the body has its limits.

After reviewing the possible explanations, we cannot find one that we can trust. Each theory seems invalid in its own way. The problem of evil is, in fact, one of the hardest nuts to crack in religion. Perhaps we have to take Tennyson's leap of faith:

> Strong Son of God, immortal Love,
> Whom we, that have not seen thy face,
> By faith, and faith alone, embrace,

Believing where we cannot prove.

But the decision to abandon rationality is itself a rational decision, and it can lead not only to self-deception but also to the burning of heretics and beheadings of the infidel.

9

HOW CAN RELIGIOUS CLAIMS BE ESTABLISHED?

Having come this far, we may begin to wonder how much we can know about heavenly things or even if we have the right to inquire. One meaning of the Fall is that some knowledge is forbidden, that it is sacrilegious to seek wisdom beyond our appointed realm. To persist in knowing things we should not know is *hubris*, "excessive pride."

According to one strain of Christian theology, all creatures possess the degree of understanding appropriate to their station. Some knowledge is human knowledge and suitable to the needs of mortals; other knowledge belongs to immortal God, and the boundaries should not be violated. We must know our place and not presume.

From the Middle Ages on, "Faust" has been a name for intellectual pride, the yearning to transcend the limits of human knowledge. He wanted to know everything in both the profane and the sacred worlds, and he was driven to use magic and ultimately to make a devil's bargain in order to penetrate the cosmic mysteries. In the play by Christopher Marlowe, Faust dies a frightful death, which serves as an awful warning to those who want to understand things they have no right to understand. However, in Johann von Goethe's version, Faust achieves salvation precisely because of his longing to know. At the point of death, his soul is carried upwards by angels chanting, "Who e'er aspiring struggles on / For him there is salvation." He defied God but was his servant all along.

Inquiry can be dangerous, but it is far worse to be ignorant, naive, and accepting. Inevitably we will make mistakes—"Man errs as long as he doth strive" (*Es irrt der Mensch so lang er strebt*)—but "It is by error that Man can advance to the Truth." Faust was noble in his aspirations, and therefore was faithful to God. His yearning for knowledge did not condemn him to hell but allowed his election to heaven.

Goethe's *Faust* therefore celebrates the human longing to know, reflecting the spirit of the Renaissance in the modern world. We can be forgiven for our restless nature that always seeks to learn, because knowledge is essential to progress. Aristotle defines man as the creature that wants to know, meaning that we naturally seek understanding, especially of final things, and there does not seem to be any justification for keeping religious matters secret.

WHEN FAITH AND REASON COLLIDE, WHICH SHOULD BE TRUSTED?

Assuming that we accept the validity of religious inquiry, one important question that follows is the nature of religious knowledge. On what basis are we justified in accepting belief in God?

Evidentialism, as the name implies, maintains that religious claims must be based on sufficient evidence. Negatively put, we have no right to believe on inadequate evidence. Instead, we have an ethical obligation to accept only those ideas that are well founded and to doubt those that seem questionable. Knowledge can be defined as justified opinion.

In a celebrated article, "The Ethics of Belief," W. K. Clifford illustrates the evidentialist position. Suppose a shipowner knows that one of his ships is poorly built, aging, and in need of repair. Nevertheless, he allows immigrants to book passage, and in the subsequent voyage the ship goes down, drowning everyone on board. The owner collects the insurance and does not feel guilty because he could not know the ship would sink. Clifford argues, however, that even if the shipowner is sincere in thinking the ship was sound enough, "he had no right to believe on such evidence as was before him." His decision would still be wrong even if the ship made it to port safely, for a good decision is based on good reasons, not on whether it is proven right or wrong: "A bad action is always bad at the time when it is done, no matter what happens afterwards."

Clifford maintains that the shipowner represents cases where belief is unjustified, and where the consequences can be harmful. What's more, belief binds people together and strengthens their common action, so we have an obligation to accept only those ideas that are well founded. When we accept unproven, unquestioned assumptions, our mutual trust is eroded: "We want the security and power of belief to deal with life—but the pleasure is a stolen one—for the sake of a sweet fruit we've brought a plague on our neighbor."

Evidentialism, then, is the view that, logically and temporally, we must first examine the evidence, and if it proves sound, we are then justified in accepting the idea. We should not believe in the absence of evidence, and certainly not in spite of the evidence.

With regard to theism, the evidentialist claims that believers are responsible for presenting firm reasons for their faith, and that no commitment is justified without such reasons. As Antony Flew writes in "The Presumption of Atheism," the onus of proof is on the person who affirms a position, not on the one who denies it, on the proposition, not on the opposition. This makes atheism the default position. If the believer does not show evidence for his belief, then there is no foundation for faith. Flew claims that an atheist is not someone who asserts there isn't a God but "someone who is simply not a theist." The same logic applies to "atypical" and "asymmetrical." All knowledge, including religious knowledge, must be established as at least probable, because the burden of proof always lies with the person making a claim. Someone who believes there is a pot of gold at the end of the rainbow must prove there is; he cannot say, "Prove there isn't."

Finally, the person who takes the extraordinary position is required to make the case for that, otherwise the ordinary view can be maintained. For example, if a person claims that gremlins cause glitches in computers, that must be proven; if not, then we are justified in following what we know about electronics. In the same way, to believe in an invisible, eternal, supernatural being is an extraordinary idea, and therefore requires evidence before it can be accepted.

Fideism is the opposite view—that we are justified in having faith in God initially. The fideist claims that we believe by a primary act of faith, and rational arguments for God are irrelevant. Man's intellect has been "disoriented" or "clouded" by original sin, and the truths taught by scripture and revelation must be believed, even if they cannot be supported by logic. Such knowledge is immediately knowable, just as we know we are alive. We can find our left arm in the dark without a flashlight.

We have already seen examples of fideism in Pascal and William James, but fideism can be traced back to figures such as Tertullian, Immanuel Kant, Søren Kierkegaard, Ludwig Wittgenstein, and, more recently, Alvin Plantinga.

Tertullian, an ecclesiastical writer of the second century, is renowned for saying, with regard to Christ's resurrection, *credo quia absurdum* ("I believe because it is absurd."). Recent scholarship has questioned the authenticity of this quotation, but it is representative of the fideist attitude. We should be skeptical about logic because the human mind, corrupted by sin, cannot be trusted; faith alone leads us to truth. Immanuel Kant, the celebrated eighteenth-century philosopher, thought that religious belief lies outside of speculative philosophy—part of the "noumenal" not the "phenomenal" world. He wrote that he "found it necessary to deny *knowledge* in order to make room for *faith*."

Likewise, in the nineteenth-century, the Danish theologian Søren Kierkegaard disparaged reason, arguing that to demand evidence is not just unnecessary but interferes with our understanding of God. Genuine belief is a matter of will and emotion, and it cannot be separated from a personal and passionate commitment. If the "absolute paradox" of "God made flesh" is appropriated by the individual and integrated into his life, then it is true. Ludwig Wittgenstein came from a different direction, but he reached the same end point. From a linguistic perspective, each mode of language has its distinctive function. Every word is diverse, the way each tool has its special purpose, and this also holds true for religious language. It has nothing in common with any other modes of discourse, any more than tools have a general definition. Therefore, religion cannot be criticized using other "language-games" because it has different functions and rules of use.

In recent years, Alvin Plantinga has argued that belief in God is a "properly basic belief," that is, it does not depend on other beliefs for its authenticity. In this it resembles "I see a tree" and "I had breakfast this morning," which are a matter of perception and memory. In the case of religion, we have the experience of "guilt, gratitude, danger, and a sense of God's presence." These are criteria used by the Christian community, and outside evidence does not apply.

To explore the ideas of these philosophers any further would take us too far afield, but a common theme is clear. The fideists believe that faith has priority over reason, and religious belief can be affirmed in advance of any rational proof. John Calvin speaks about *sensus divinitatis*, an innate sense of the divine triggered in the face of danger when confronted by beauty, the wonders of nature, or our own sinfulness. It is an inborn faculty akin to perception, memory, and reason.

Catholicism, incidentally, opposes this view, at least since the "natural theology" of the "Schoolmen." God's existence is capable of being demonstrated by reason, Aquinas asserts, and reason can also know moral and metaphysical truths. Fideism comes mainly from Protestantism, perhaps stemming from Martin Luther, who wrote, "Reason is the greatest enemy that faith has . . . All the articles of our Christian faith, which God has revealed to us in His Word, are in the presence of reason sheerly impossible, absurd, and false."

Most philosophers are ranged on the side of evidentialism as the stronger option. If we say that religion is a matter of faith, we have no protection against mistakes, illusions, and self-deception. The Muslim terrorists who attacked the World Trade Center would be invulnerable to criticism on the grounds that faith cannot be disputed, and the Inquisition would escape censure for burning heretics at the stake. The Salem witch trials in colonial Massachusetts could not be thought of as a warning about religious hysteria overriding common sense, and the same would be true of the cult of Jim Jones in Guyana, where the followers committed suicide by lacing their Kool-Aid with arsenic. Heaven's Gate could not be criticized for assuming they would be taken up in the tail of the Hale–Bopp Comet, and neither could the Raelians, who believe that human beings were cloned from aliens. Presumably, we are required to offer sound evidence for our beliefs, drawn from the physical world or through rational argument. Augustine said, *credo ut intellegam*, "I believe in order to understand," and perhaps some things have to be believed to be comprehended, but how do we prevent ourselves from affirming only what we already believe, or want to believe? This approach could be self-authenticating. In order to acquire dependable knowledge, it seems far better to believe only on good evidence.

HOW DO WE PROVE RELIGIOUS BELIEF—OR DISPROVE IT?

In trying to establish reliable knowledge, we must pay attention to the language in which statements are contained. Some language is misleading, some is vague, some inaccurate, some confusing, some emotionally loaded. Before we can examine the truth or falsity of a statement, we must be clear about what it expresses.

In the mid-twentieth century, a group of philosophers in Britain and the United States took language as their central concern. This "linguistic turn" in philosophy tried to address problems by clarifying their linguistic meaning. Once the language was made plain, then some problems could be seen as pseudoproblems and would not need any further attention. Other problems could be seen more clearly so solutions could be found. By paying attention to meaning, we could address the issues of philosophy properly.

Logical positivism was the first school to emerge from this linguistic orientation, with A. J. Ayer as the chief spokesperson. The positivists asked, "Under what conditions can a statement be declared meaningful?" And they answered that a statement is meaningful if we can specify the observations that would confirm it as true or reject it as false. This was called the "verification principle"—that if there are tests that could count as verification and others that could count as falsification, then the statement is meaningful. Otherwise, it is meaningless, and we cannot then ask if it is true or false. It would be like asking for the truth value of "T'was brillig, and the slithy toves / Did gyre and gimble in the wabe." It is neither true nor false, but absurd.

In other words, some sentences are nonsense masquerading as good sense. Using the verification principle, the positivists gained notoriety by classifying various assertions as meaningless, including those in metaphysics, aesthetics, history, and ethics. With regard to religion, since no observations could confirm or deny the proposition "God's in his heaven," that statement and other supernatural claims are meaningless.

Most philosophers dismissed positivism because of its excessively narrow criterion. That is, only empirical verification was acceptable, otherwise a statement was considered meaningless. Ayer does not argue for empiricism but simply announces it as the basis for sensible propositions. Embarrassingly, critics also noticed that the "verification principle" itself could not satisfy the verification principle, which made it self-refuting.

A school of thought that had greater staying power was *linguistic analysis*, which took a broader perspective on meaning. To the analysts, language can have meaning on different levels, and philosophy's task is "clarificatory analysis." The philosopher must separate the modes of verification and only demand the kind of proof that each type of discourse requires. "The music of Bartok is purple" is verified differently than "Circles are round" and "The cat is on the mat."

As for religious discourse, it cannot be proven by sense evidence, yet some type of verification is needed. Something must confirm it, at least in theory, and something must disconfirm it, or it must be admitted to be nonsense.

This position is illustrated in a celebrated article by Antony Flew entitled "Theology and Falsification":

> Once upon a time two explorers came upon a clearing in the jungle. In the clearing were growing many flowers and many weeds. One explorer says, "some gardener must tend this plot." The other disagrees. "There is no gardener." So they pitch their tents and set a watch. No gardener is ever seen. "But perhaps he is an invisible gardener." So they set up a barbed-wire fence. They electrify it. They patrol with bloodhounds . . . But no shrieks ever suggest that some intruder has received a shock. No movements of the wire ever betray an invisible climber. The bloodhounds never give cry. Yet still the Believer is not convinced. "But there is a gardener, invisible, intangible, insensible to electric shocks, a gardener who has no scent and makes no sound, a gardener who comes secretly to look after the garden which he loves." At last the Skeptic despairs. "But what remains of your original assertion? Just how does what you call an invisible, intangible, eternally elusive gardener differ from an imaginary gardener or even from no gardener at all?"

Flew goes on to say that to assert something is to deny that other things are the case. So we are justified in asking what would count against the truth of an assertion: "If there is nothing that a putative assertion denies, then there is nothing which it asserts either." The parable is obviously about God, so here we can ask "what would have to happen" to constitute a disproof of his existence. As one commentator put it, "The invisible and the non-existent look very much alike."

This standard is more falsification than verification, and it does not demand empirical proof, but it does require the believer to specify *something* that would falsify the religious claim. Flew's question has hung in the air in philosophy, and it demands a judgment. Obviously our answer depends to some extent on whether we are evidentialists or fideists with regard to religious knowledge, but even the fideist can be called upon to specify "what would have to happen" to make him withdraw his belief.

IS THERE EVIDENCE FOR REVELATION, MIRACLES, AND PRAYER?

Revelation means the revealed will of God, communicated to his people through various channels. Some people who claim to be in receipt of revelations are mystics, others are prophets, saints, or disciples, and still others are ordinary people to whom divine truths are disclosed. It is a transmission from God to humans, and it carries importance because of its source and its content. The nature of the divine can be established by human reason, but the Incarnation and the Trinity are revealed doctrines established by religious experience, inspired religious leaders, holy books, and the traditions of churches.

Some revelations are *verbal*, where God speaks directly to humans; the Bible is filled with such revelations. The Pentateuch, or the first five books of Moses, are said to be dictated by God. As a prime example, the Ten Commandments were revealed to Moses on Mount Sinai in the form of two stone tablets, and "God spoke all these words." The authors of scripture heard the voice of God whispering in their ears or felt him moving their pens. For this reason some believers, such as Southern Baptists, take the Bible to be inerrant or infallible: it contains the holy word of God, which cannot be false. According to Christian theology, both the Old and the New Testaments were written under the inspiration of the Holy Spirit, and as Jesus said, it "cannot be broken" (John 10:34–36). As Timothy puts it, "All scripture is God-breathed" (3:16).

However, even if the Bible comes directly from God, that does not mean that our reading of it is infallible. Human beings do not interpret things infallibly, which opens up the possibility of error. We have various denominations of Christianity, from Catholics to Methodists to the Church of Latter Day Saints, plus the religions of Judaism and Islam. All of them rely on the Bible, and each claims an infallible reading of God's message, but they contradict each other and cannot all be accurate. True prophets are sometimes difficult to separate from false prophets.

Some theologians claim that God reveals himself through history. We cannot view God any more than we can see the wind, but we can recognize his effects. God's work can be witnessed in the beauty of the earth, the miracle of life, and the magnificence of the universe as a whole. We can see the progress of civilization, the victors in war, and the advances in ease of living—all displaying the hand of God. This was the aim of the great Russian writer Leo Tolstoy in his novels—to illustrate God's providence in the lives of families and in movements of history. In *War and Peace*, he showed the victory of the Russians over Napoleon in 1812 as according to God's will.

Academics as a whole distrust theories of history. They say we can see a pattern, in retrospect, but not a purpose to events, much less God manifest in social, political, and economic movements. Marx saw "triads" of a thesis opposed by its antithesis and culminating in a synthesis; Giambatisto Vico identified a cyclical pattern whereby history repeats itself; Darwin a melioristic model that showed progressive diversity of organisms and greater integration of functions. But to attribute any purpose to the happenings on earth, much less a supernatural one, is extraordinarily difficult to prove because of the number of variables involved. Of course, whether we believe in providence will determine whether we even look for meaning in history.

Mysticism and its opposite, *reason*, can also receive revelations, mysticism through an immediate apprehension of divine truth, reason through inspired theology. But the mystic may be in receipt of delusions, and the rationalist may not need revelation to come up with his principles. To see time as connected to space, for example, may only require the insights of physics. Thomas Paine in *The Age of Reason* also asserts that revelation might be valid for the recipient but not for others; for them it is hearsay.

Revelation, therefore, is a problematic notion. It becomes even more contentious in the form of the book of Revelation, or the Apocalypse, of John, the last book of the New Testament. Here the book of Revelation describes the final battle between the forces of heaven, earth, and hell. It predicts a time of great tribulation when natural disasters overwhelm the earth. Christ then destroys the wicked and saves his people, ushering in a time of peace. But then a second period of tribulation ensues, after which the wicked are permanently banished and a new heaven and earth are created. Those who are saved then live in a new Jerusalem, forever in the presence of God.

In the book of Revelation, Christ is the "lamb of God," Satan is the dragon or the Beast with seven heads and ten horns, whose number is 666. There are seven trumpets, seven bowls, and seven seals opened by Christ, and four horsemen of the apocalypse representing pestilence, war, famine, and death. To many commentators, this smacks of numerology—the study of the occult in terms of the spiritual significance of numbers.

This account has fired the popular imagination about doomsday, or the end time, or the second coming, and "the rapture" of the faithful. It has led to the view that the end is near, as evidenced by signs such as wars and disasters, even global warming. More symbolically, Revelation has been taken to mean that, ultimately, evil will be defeated and God will prevail; the good things will throw the last stone.

Miracles are usually defined as a suspension of natural law through supernatural forces. These miracles are usually performed by God directly, or more indirectly by Moses, Elijah, Elisha, Peter, Paul, John, and others so endowed by God. In terms of their function, they can be the seal of a divine mission, a sign and wonder, or simply a demonstration of the power of God.

According to St. Thomas Aquinas, "those things are properly called miracles which are done by divine agency beyond the order commonly observed in nature." A miracle is not just a striking coincidence or an unusual accident but a unique event caused by supernatural forces. It is a marvel or wonder produced by God in which natural law is "overruled, suspended, or modified." It is an extraordinary happening that violates the rules of physics.

In the Old Testament, miracles abound: God parted the Red Sea to allow the Israelites to escape, but the waters closed on the pursuing Egyptians; the voice of God came from a burning bush that was not consumed; the sun stood still for Joshua in the Valley of Ajalon; and ravens brought food to feed Elijah. We are also told that Balaam's donkey was given the gift of speech; water became blood; Lot's wife turned into pillar of salt; and the walls of Jericho crumbled at Joshua's trumpet blast. In addition, Daniel was saved from death in the lion's den; Jonah lived in a whale's belly; Aaron's rod became a serpent; water came out of a rock struck by Moses; and Shadrach, Meshach and Abed-nego survived inside a fiery furnace.

In the New Testament, Christ turned water into wine, and he fed a multitude of 4,000 to 5,000 people (depending on the gospel) with 5 (or 7) loaves of bread and 2 (or a few) fishes. He walked on water, calmed the storm, cast out demons into a herd of swine that then drowned, and found money in a fish's mouth—a stater, or silver coin. He performed healing miracles, such as curing a blind leper and restoring a man with a withered hand (and one with palsy), and he raised the dead, for example, Lazarus, four days after he died. Christ was himself resurrected from the dead, and was born of a virgin.

According to Catholic canon law, one documented miracle must be performed by the intercession of the deceased for he or she to be called blessed, two to be declared a saint (canonized).

In Buddhism, various miracles also surround Gautama, the Buddha. In the twin miracles, fire was produced from the upper part of his body, water from lower; then they reversed right and left. The Buddha stood up immediately after birth, took seven steps, and spoke; he created a golden bridge in the air and walked up and down on it; he levitated and passed through solid rock; he calmed a fierce elephant by touching its forehead; and he flew through the air and walked on water, and he parted waters during a flood so he could pass between them. There was an annunciation to his mother, Queen Maya, that she would be impregnated by a beautiful white elephant, which was a sign that the Buddha was about to be born.

In Islam, several prophecies are considered miraculous, such as the defeat of the Persians by the Romans, and there are "scientific miracles" in the Koran, from predicting the stages of gestation to the structure of the universe. Muhammad multiplied the waters and dates, made the root of a date palm weep, and split the moon. In modern times, reports have circulated that Allah's name has been written in clouds, swarms of bees, and in the branches of a tree, and that it appeared in a tomato, a watermelon, a flower, a squash, a hand, and a rock made of quartz.

Fairly recently, there have been reports within Christianity of a porcelain statue of the Virgin Mary that cries, of miraculous healing waters in Mexico and Germany, and of a cross of light shining from a bathroom in California. The Catholic Church has attested to the authenticity of some modern miracles that are attributed to the Holy Spirit or the intercession of saints. There are Eucharist miracles where the host bled, hovered in the air, radiated light, or became the image of Christ. Then there are celebrated cases, such as the Shroud of Turin in Italy, where Christ's face appeared on linen that is said to be his burial cloth, a holy relic that survived 2,000 years. In the Miracle of Calanda in Spain, a man's leg was restored to him two years after it was severed and buried, complete with identifying bruises and scars. In the Miracle of the Sun, 70,000 to 100,000 people in Portugal witnessed the sun dim, change color, spin, dance, and plummet to earth.

What are we to make of reports of miracles? Are they dreams, hallucinations, parables, the result of mass hysteria? Are some of them wondrous stories told of all great men to enhance their stature? Do they belong in the realm of magic, or are they fairy tales to induce a sense of a mysterious, other world? How do we decide whether a miracle really happened?

The Scottish philosopher David Hume mounted an extensive critique of miracles in *An Enquiry Concerning Human Understanding*. Hume writes:

> A miracle is a violation of the laws of nature, and as a firm and unalterable experience has established these laws, the proof against a miracle, from the very nature of the fact, is as entire as any argument from experience can possibly be imagined. Why is it more than probable, that all men must die; that lead cannot, of itself, remain suspended in the air; that fire consumes wood, and is extinguished by water; unless it be, that these events are found agreeable to the laws of nature, and there is required a violation of these laws, or in other words, a miracle to prevent them? Nothing is esteemed a miracle, if it ever happen in the common course of nature. It is no miracle that a man, seemingly in good health, should die on a sudden: because such a kind of death, though more unusual than any other, has yet been frequently observed to happen. But it is a miracle, that a dead

man should come to life; because that has never been observed in any age or country. There must, therefore, be a uniform experience against every miraculous event, otherwise the event would not merit that appellation.

In other words the preponderance of evidence shows the uniformity of nature, so every testimony in favor of a miracle is outweighed by that evidence. Hume goes on to say that no testimony can establish a miracle unless its falsehood would be more miraculous still.

Furthermore, to make belief in miracles credible there would have to be (1) a sufficient number of witnesses, (2) of good sense and education, (3) with sound reputation and integrity, (4) and a public performance of the incident. There has never been such an instance. Also, Hume says, we have to combat the human tendency to believe in the strange: "The gazing populace receive greedily, without examination, whatever soothes superstition and promotes wonder."

Finally, reports of miracles are questionable because they occur mainly in "underdeveloped" countries: "It forms a strong presumption against all supernatural and miraculous relations, that they are observed chiefly to abound among ignorant and barbarous nations . . . in proportion as we advance toward the enlightened ages, we soon learn that, there is nothing mysterious or supernatural in the case." In brief, miracles happen much less today than in biblical times, if they happen at all.

This essay, "On Miracles," has been criticized on several fronts. The main objection is that Hume's argument is taken as true *a priori*—an idea that is accepted in advance of sense evidence. That is, the laws of nature are believed to be true because they are without exception and a miracle is an exception therefore it can be ruled out by definition. However, the laws of nature may not contain everything possible; as the philosopher John Locke remarked, there could be "laws of supernature." Hume only describes what is physically possible or perhaps only what is common, but that might be narrow-minded.

A related criticism is that the uniformity of nature is based on historical precedent, but it is possible that something new could appear that is unprecedented. What has been need not always be. Uniqueness and singularity can appear in the world, and that is what a miracle is claimed to be. What was assumed to be a law of nature may cease to be so.

Antony Flew gives a milder interpretation of Hume's position, saying that he did not mean miracles were an impossibility but that there should be "an everlasting check" on belief in miracles. Miracles could happen but, in point of fact, they do not occur. Other philosophers downplay the importance of miracles to faith. Dostoyevsky wrote that people need miracles even more than they need God, however miracles may not be essential to belief. There is no word for miracle in the Old or the New Testament. If miracles are genuine, that tends to support belief in God, but if not, that does not undermine the belief system.

From a philosophic standpoint, we cannot say that miracles are impossible, but we should maintain a healthy skepticism about their authenticity for some of the reasons that Hume cites.

Prayer takes multiple forms, but the common factor is communication with God, usually to ask him to grant a request. As Diane Robinson remarked, "Prayer is when you talk to God; meditation is when you listen to God." Petitionary prayers are made for oneself, and intercessory prayers for others. Some prayers are made for guidance, some as expressions of worship, or the confession of sins, or in deep contemplation. There are prayers for the sick and dying, and for the success of loved ones. People will utter prayers of thanksgiving, ask for victory in war, plead for the repose of souls, want mercy, grace, and peace, or express their thoughts or emotions in conversation with their Lord.

There does not seem to be a proper way to offer prayer, certainly not a uniform one. People will ring a bell, burn incense, light a candle, offer sacrifices, anoint others with oil, make the sign of the cross, bow their heads, say the rosary, close their eyes, raise their arms, knit their fingers, face Mecca, or fly multicolored flags printed with prayers that are blown to heaven. They will wear a hat, uncover their heads, play an instrument, be silent, speak in tongues, paint their faces, recite scripture, assume a lotus position, sing, whirl, chant, sway, kneel, dance, genuflect, or prostrate themselves. There is private and corporate worship, usually requiring a quorum, with the sexes separate or together, prayers to God, to a saint, to Mary, or a person of the Trinity. And people will ask for benefits, protection, or healing for themselves, their enemies, or their loved families, in a house of worship or in the forest, wherever God is thought to reside. Often in the West we utter the Lord's Prayer, "Our Father who art in heaven . . . ," ending with "Amen," or "so be it."

Prayer can be an utterance or incantation, a hymn, the spinning of a wheel, a reading from the *Book of Common Prayer*. There are morning and evening prayers, bedtime prayers ("Now I lay me down to sleep . . . "), and grace before meals ("For what we are about to receive, may the lord make us truly thankful, and may we always be mindful of the needs of others."). Prayers are said three times a day in Judaism, and five times a day in Islam, when the muezzin utters a call to worship from the prayer tower. In Buddhism, prayer accompanies meditation when a mantra is recited, a sacred formula expressing respect to a guru or invoking a deity.

The key question, of course, is does prayer work, especially petitionary or intercessory prayers? Sometimes people pray and they get what they want, but sometimes they do not. The first tends to confirm people's faith, but the second is often explained away by saying God knows best. One theologian claims that God answers all prayers, but sometimes the answer is no. But that is disingenuous. By "answering" is meant reacting positively, and the real question is whether there is a God who hears, judges, and responds to people's prayers.

We do know that the most common prayers, of petition, thanksgiving, and worship, do work for the health of the devotee. Such prayers lower blood pressure and heart rate, and decrease anxiety, stress, and depression. However, that seems to prove the effect of *believing* in prayer and its efficacy, rather than the supernatural power of prayer.

Studies in social science do not show that prayer makes any difference to the outcome of events. Recent studies at the Mayo Clinic, Duke University, and a study published in the *American Heart Journal* found that intercessory prayer had no effect on recovery. This held true if the patients did not know that prayers had been offered; if the patient did know, then a positive effect was observed. These findings suggest the power of the mind over the body; they do not show that prayer itself is effective. The same results have been noted for yoga, meditation, a positive attitude, and placebos.

One study in Great Britain, done with tongue in cheek, examined the longevity of the royal family. Since a great many people prayed "God save the Queen," the queen should live longer than average if prayer worked. In fact, the queens of England had the usual life span.

From a philosophic standpoint, we question the extent to which "selective memory" plays a role in belief in prayer. People tend to remember successes and to forget failures, which makes prayer self-reinforcing. It's the carrot of positive reinforcement. Some theologians have argued that prayer gives people peace of mind, but that is only true if people believe in it. We also wonder whether the successes are greater than chance; only then could it be considered a causal factor. But that does not seem to be the case.

In addition, there are certain similarities with gambling. Logically, the steady gambler is the steady loser because the odds are always with the house. But the gambler does win occasionally, and this "intermittent reinforcement" has enough psychological force to keep the person gambling. Does this type of reinforcement also operate in prayer, so people believe in it, despite the evidence? And people in a life threatening situation whose prayers for safety have been answered will, of course, always outnumber those whose prayers have not.

The Greek philosopher Epicurus wrote that the gods would not be perfect if our pleas could affect them in any way. The same point is made in Western religion when we say that if God is all-knowing, he does not need to be reminded of his responsibilities; what's more, an all-knowing God does not change his mind. He should be aware of all of our needs, and there are no unknown facts that we can point out. However, the fact that people pray could be the condition for granting the request. This raises the question, of course, of why a benevolent God would not do what he should do without people's prayers. Why wait for cries of help?

It should also be noted in passing that although our society pays lip service to the power of prayer, it is not given credence in our daily affairs. We do not depend on prayer to improve the economy, to affect international relations, or to correct social injustice. Business decisions are not based on prayer, any more than the courts accept "the devil made me do it" as a defense. For all intents and purposes, we behave as if prayer is irrelevant, and although it surfaces at times of crisis or in ceremonies, we do not rely on it for everyday matters.

10

FAMOUS CHALLENGES TO FAITH

Religion has faced opposition from a number of quarters, and various theorists have attempted to explain away the religious phenomenon. Attacks have come mainly from psychology, politics, and philosophy. What they have in common is confidence that the physical world known by the scientific method is the only world and a basic skepticism about any supernatural realm. They generally hold that our senses disclose reality, corroborated by the experience of other people, whereas religion springs from psychological need, political manipulation, and philosophic mistakes. These challenges to religion deserve to be heard and evaluated.

RELIGION IS AN INFANTILE NEUROSIS: FREUD

Some psychologists have cast doubt on whether religion is based on reality or whether it is a symptom of an underlying emotional problem. When there are psychological criticisms, they focus on our emotions of anxiety, longing, and hope, sometimes the fear of abandonment.

As we discussed concerning early beliefs, when primitive peoples were confronted with the terrifying forces of nature, they looked for reasons why they were suffering; if there were only physical causes, the environment would be intolerable. There had to be some explanation behind the animal attack, the bout of malaria, the drought that ruined their crops and brought them to starvation. Natural forces were unsatisfying as an explanation, so they attributed these events to unseen spirits, agents with intentions like themselves. Even death was thought the violent act of an evil will, not a random event. This provided some degree of security because people could appeal to these spirits, to their understanding and compassion. Through prayer and sacrifice, the anger of these beings could be placated. If people knew what prompted the gods to act, they could be appeased, bribed, influenced, and begged to be merciful. Then human beings could feel they had some control over the threatening aspects of nature. This may be what Homer meant in saying, "All men have need of the gods."

But, the critics charge, these gods were a human invention to foster the illusion of control and to provide a defense against fear. The same impulse operates today, but we have more sophisticated theologies. When events occur that are beyond our power, we feel vulnerable and seek protection. To imagine a god who acts according to a hidden plan gives us safety and the reassurance we require. "Religion is an attempt to gain control over the sensory world, in which we are placed, by means of the wish-world," Freud writes. Not only does belief provide power over nature, but it also allays our anxiety that everything might be absurd and pointless, that chance rules our lives and the void awaits us. Our psychological makeup demands that events have meaning; we need to identify a pattern in history. We especially need to believe in life after death, for ourselves and those we cherish, and this is reinforced by the culture. Our society maintains a mass delusion for the sake of security and stability.

Religion, then, is considered cowardice. We create an imaginary being that will save us from being extinguished and give our existence some purpose. If we could face life with greater courage, religion would be unnecessary and become outmoded.

This is the general indictment, but does it undermine religious belief? Today we have far greater control over the natural world than we did in a primitive state, yet religion persists. If life has become safer and pleasanter, shouldn't religion decline and be replaced by technological power? In other words, if religion is based on fear, and if there is less to fear, religion should be gradually disappearing. Some religious leaders did maintain that as life became more comfortable, people would turn less to religion; they opposed social improvements, such as wage hikes and higher levels of health. But even though the standard of living has risen, people continue to attend church.

And can we make the generalization that believers are cowards and atheists are brave? It seems a distorted view of human nature to say that people are so weak and vulnerable that they need divine support in order to function. On the contrary, the human race has shown remarkable resiliency in migrating across continents and in combating animals, natural disasters, and extreme weather conditions. Those who fight wars in the name of God may be mistaken, but they are not weak, neither the crusaders nor the jihadists.

But the skeptical psychologist replies that the world is still a frightening place, and the inevitability of death persists. We not only fear the destructive forces of nature that continue to threaten us, but we also fear violence from our fellow humans, both on the street and on the battlefield. We are also afraid of our own passions that can lead to homicide or suicide. Faith reassures us that we are part of a larger cosmic plan and "the end is not the tomb."

In addition, sociologists have pointed out that, in fact, religion is declining in the West, at least in terms of institutional worship; the only increase has been in developing nations, principally in Africa and in South America. There is a shortage of applicants for the priesthood, and when people have problems, they do not turn to clerics for answers; they are more likely to consult a friend or a therapist. Even the weather can be predicted more accurately, so we do not generally pray for sunshine or rain.

As for believers being courageous, the counterargument is that they initially turn to faith to quiet their fears, and then behave bravely when supported by faith. In Freudian terms, they are more afraid of their own fear than they are of the enemy.

If religion is based on a generalized anxiety, did people invent God to reassure themselves, or did God make us fearful so we would turn to him for support?

Sigmund Freud, the founder of psychoanalysis in the nineteenth and twentieth century, is probably the most influential critic of religion. Although his stock is not high in the field of psychology, which now allies itself more with experimental science than evidence from psychoanalysis, he has support in literary criticism, especially biography, and in the therapeutic community. His insights resonate strongly with those who have read *The Interpretation of Dreams*, his pivotal work, *Civilization and Its Discontents*, and *Three Essays on the Theory of Sexuality*. His book *Totem and Taboo* contains his account of the origins of religion, and *The Future of an Illusion* is a more general attack on the validity of religion.

In general, Freud dismisses religion as "an infantile neurosis." God is a projection of our earthly father as a divine protective power—a myth that must be abandoned if we are ever to become mature, healthy adults: "The face that smiled down on us in the cradle, now smiles down on us from heaven."

According to Freud, we idolize our father when we are children as the epitome of all virtue. We are wholly reliant on him for food, shelter, and protection, for all the necessities of life. However, as we grow older, we detect flaws and limitations in this supposedly ideal being. He is not perfectly intelligent or strong or kind; he disappoints us, and is not always reliable.

At this critical point, the unhealthy personality cannot accept the truth and let go of an ideal image. He becomes arrested in his development and invents a cosmic father who embodies the perfections that daddy lacks. The separation anxiety cannot be endured, so he must create a substitute parent in a spiritual realm. This heavenly father is entirely loving and will never hurt or disappoint us. Through his power, he offers protection from all dangers. He knows our inner thoughts and can give us what we desire and guide us through life by his infinite wisdom. Above all, he can grant us eternal life, provided we worship him, abandon our pride, and acknowledge we are wholly reliant on his blessings—"except as ye become as little children." We must believe in him without reservation and obey his rules, even when they surpass our understanding. If we humble ourselves in worship, confess our wrong-doings, and ask for his mercy, he will then forgive our sins and grant us a place in heaven.

The healthy personality, on the other hand, accepts the shortcomings and inadequacies of her earthly father and moves forward toward maturity. Here the individual realizes that his father is similar to other people, with virtues and vices, but he is generally decent and tries insofar as he can. In other words, if a person is strong enough, he does not need to invent a father in heaven but can take an honest, clear-eyed view of life. This acceptance of reality enables a healthy development and an adult personality.

Religion is therefore a developmental abnormality, with belief in God as a symptom of the disorder. Mature individuals resolve their disillusionment with their father; they face life as it is and assume responsibility for themselves. Unhealthy people have a childish need to cling to God as an idealized father and remain dependent children, living a life of fantasy.

This is Freud's main account of religion, but he offers another version based on what he assumes happened in prehistory. Originally, Freud speculates, humanity was arranged in clans called "the primal horde." The father was the dominant (alpha) male who had sexual access to the mother and all the females. However, his declining powers and the sons' ascending ones eventually led to his being overthrown and slaughtered by them; afterwards they consumed his body in order to absorb his qualities.

But this atavistic crime of patricide set up tensions within the psyche, which led to moral prohibitions, especially a taboo against incest. The primitive horde experiences collective guilt over the murder of its patriarchal leader, and this guilt also produces a belief in the father's ghost hovering over the clan. The sons feel a sense of fear, reverence, and obedience to this spirit, whom they project as God.

This theory is part of a larger system of Freudian thought, centering round his notion of the "Oedipus complex." In the play by Sophocles, Oedipus is the ill-fated king of Thebes who inadvertently kills his father and marries his mother. When he realizes this, Oedipus tears out his eyes because some truths are too painful to see.

To Freud, this scenario is universal—at least in our desires and imagination. All boys want to marry their mothers and feel a primitive rivalry with their fathers. The tension and guilt over these desires induces a "castration anxiety" because the son fears retaliation from the father, aimed at the offending organ. The boy eventually represses these impulses and only expresses them later by marrying a girl who resembles his mother. In this way he fulfills his wishes vicariously, in a socially approved way. The guilt persists, however, because he is having sexual relations with a female proxy, a mother substitute. Boys supplant their fathers and become the dominant male, but the sense of shame and sin make them venerate their fathers and turn them into idealized beings or God. Sex is therefore freighted with inhibitions because we are committing incest and the father-God is watching.

To Freud, religion is not wrong, the way a mathematical equation can be wrong but a delusion because it is "derived from human wishes."

A contemporary of Freud's named Carl Gustav Jung, an influential therapist in his own right, maintained the opposite. He held that religion is not a consequence of arrested development or a "neurotic relic." Jung was part of Freud's inner circle, but he came to believe that rather than religion being a neurosis, the *absence* of religion would produce neurosis. Jung thought that faith is based on emotional needs, but needs so basic to human nature that they cannot be denied without causing mental disorder. Science, as astronomy, physics, or chemistry, cannot replace the "fictional and emotional processes" served by religion. If we are believers, the impersonal becomes warm and events are endowed with significance. This satisfies our deepest yearning for a larger meaning to our lives.

Worldwide, most people are believers, so Freud's theory would imply that the bulk of mankind is neurotic. Jung treats people as essentially sane—partly due to their having faith. Freud writes, "The whole thing is so patently infantile, that it is painful to think that the great majority of mortals will never be able to rise above this view of life." Jung, on the other hand, thought that the road to adulthood went through religion, that faith derives its strength from the fact that it satisfies our universal desires.

As for the primal horde, this story was extrapolated from the anthropology of the time and has not been corroborated. It was a hypothesis that explained belief in God, moral taboos, and "drive renunciation," but it borders on mythology. Some critics see the primal horde and the Oedipus complex as fantasy elements within a rational scheme.

Freudianism itself may be a substitute religion, a resurgence of religion within Freud's own psyche. Many of the elements have a religious smack—our original sin of rebellion against the father, the need for confession to resolve our problems (on the therapist's couch), the unconscious, which is more fundamental than reason, our basic desires for sexual gratification, and guilt as equivalent to sin.

One open question remains: Can religion be judged a fiction because of our motivation in accepting it? Even if religion were proven to originate in our need for a perfect father, does that mean there is no reality corresponding to that need? Some scholars refer to this as "the fallacy of origins," dismissing an idea because of its source. On the other hand, if religion arose from our wishes rather than reason or revelation, wouldn't that make it a human construct?

In any case, Freud's views on religion are provocative but may not be convincing. The Oedipus complex may be more of a myth than the religion he dismisses. Feminists have certainly criticized him for analyzing only father-religion and for claiming that women are wounded men and have "penis envy." He also extrapolated from patients, who were wealthy, repressed, nineteenth-century Viennese women to the female sex in general. Women apparently baffled Freud, for he famously asked, "What do women want?" And once his patients learned his system, they began dreaming in Freudian symbols, which contaminated the evidence altogether.

One general criticism of Freud is that he thinks all reasoning is rationalization, that is, finding an excuse for what we want to believe anyway. But if that is true, then Freudian theory is one elaborate rationalization and cannot be taken as true. What's sauce for the goose is sauce for the gander.

RELIGION IS THE OPIATE OF THE MASSES: MARX

Karl Marx, the nineteenth-century founder of communism, was just one in a series of thinkers who attributed religion to political schemers. In the sixteenth century, Niccolò Machiavelli also held this view, but to him that was not a criticism. In his *Prince* and *Discourses*, he recommended that shrewd leaders use religion to keep their subjects obedient. He wrote that it is

> the duty of princes and heads of republics to uphold the foundations of the religions of their countries, for then it is easy to keep their people religious, and consequently well conducted and united. And therefore everything that tends to favor religion (*even though it were believed to be false* [my italics]) should be received and availed of to strengthen it.

Machiavelli offered rulers a handbook of governance that included the use of cruelty, violence, and deception, for it was better to be feared than loved. In his *realpolitik*, religion was simply a useful instrument for maintaining power.

And the seventeenth-century English philosopher Thomas Hobbes recommended religion to monarchs for the same reason: that it would keep subjects passive. In his *Leviathan*, Hobbes wrote that rulers should be careful to fulfill three ends: (1) to impress upon the people that the decrees do not proceed from the monarch's fancy but are the will of God, (2) to promote the idea that whatever is prohibited by law is also prohibited by God, and (3) to promote religious ceremonies, sacrifice, and festivals so people think that disasters such as famines or lost wars are due to God's wrath. That way blame is kept from the monarch.

Marx described religion the same way, but he judged it an oppressive force that opposed social, political, and economic liberation. Marx did not want to maintain the status quo but to foment a revolution that would free the workers from the harsh conditions of their labor. He called himself "a philosopher with a hammer," and said that philosophers have tried to understand the world, but the point is to change it.

In *Capital* and *The Communist Manifesto* (with Engels), Marx presented an account of the European society of his time as split between the *proletariat*, or workers, and the *bourgeoisie*, or the owners of industry. In order to survive, the proletariat must labor in factories where they are routinely exploited by the bourgeoisie. Men, women, and children are compelled to work, and they are given low wages, long hours, and unhealthy and unsafe working conditions. "If you don't come in on Sunday, then don't come in on Monday," a sign in one mill read. Meanwhile, the bourgeoisie live in luxury off the backs of the poor, and have all the trappings of wealth: fine houses, carriages, furnishings, and clothing, but the workers live in squalor, close to poverty. The proletariat labor far more than is necessary to sustain themselves, and the excess labor goes to making the bourgeoisie rich.

Religion pacifies the industrial workers so that they accept their condition, which is virtual slavery. By creating fantasies of a better life to come, it makes them content so they can face their economic reality. As one critic put it, "Religion helps them to forget why they are suffering and causes them to look forward to an imaginary future when the pain will cease instead of working to change the circumstances." That is, it distracts them from their temporal, earthly misery. Or as one sympathetic canon put it, "We have used the Bible as if it were a mere constable's handbook, an opium dose for keeping beasts of burden patient while they were being overloaded, a mere book to keep the poor in order."

To Marx the economic conditions needed to be changed; then there would be no need for religion. At the moment, "Religion is the sigh of the oppressed creature," Marx writes, "the heart of a heartless world, and the soul of soulless conditions. It is the opiate of the people." Religion drugs people into believing they can achieve salvation in a distant heaven, which is a clever device to prevent them from revolting on earth. It distracts the proletariat when it should enrage them to fight against their hardship and deprivation.

Religion to Marx is "parson-power" and the church, the "barking dog of capitalism"; it is a way of stifling people's desire to improve their economic and social circumstances. Christianity and Judaism collaborate with government and industry to keep workers passive; it tells the faithful to trust in God for help. It preaches acceptance of one's lot in life and champions the virtues of patience, humility, and self-denial. If we are struck on one cheek, we should turn the other and not return injury for injury. It preaches that the meek shall inherit the earth and that the last shall be first; that the poor are blessed and a rich man can no more enter heaven than a camel pass through the eye of a needle. It tells people not to lay up treasures on earth for moth and dust to corrupt but to look toward the spiritual treasures in paradise.

This gospel is ideal for the wealthy and powerful who exploit these sentiments; then the workers will not revolt against the inequality or strive to acquire power. Marx maintains, in fact, that religion is the product of those who control production, and it serves the interests of the ruling class. "Religion is what keeps the poor from murdering the rich," he writes, and those responsible for the suffering are the very administrators of the opiate we call religion. Or as Napoleon succinctly phrased it, "Religion is excellent stuff for keeping common people quiet." The wealthy supported slavery in the ancient world, serfdom in the Middle Ages, and they exploit the workers in the industrial age—all with the blessings of religion: "The parson has ever gone hand in hand with the landlord." The church has allied itself with the upper class and the rich, who use the police and the military to maintain control. Those who enforce the law have the power to take people's freedom or to end their lives.

Marx cites the Sermon on the Mount, which urges people not to fill their barns with the earth's goods, but he asks, "For whom were these remarks intended?" Not the church, because it has some of the best filled barns in Europe and didn't show any sign of emptying them. Not the financiers, because they continued in positions of power. It had to be intended for the workers, who didn't possess barns to begin with. It removed them from the economic struggle by making poverty the symbol of religiosity.

To Marx, God is an imaginary figure because the only reality is the material world, and that means our financial circumstances. What's more, God is a harmful illusion, created by people who enslave themselves by accepting the dream of a heaven to come. He would agree with the revolutionary Mikhail Bakunin, who wrote, "I reverse the phrase of Voltaire, and say that if God really existed, it would be necessary to abolish him."

But faith cannot be eliminated until the social, political, and economic dimensions of society are transformed. The working people must be put in charge, not the wealthy class, who are in league with the state and the church. Religion will only disappear when the workers are freed from their misery, for then there will be no need to escape through religious superstition.

Marx may be right in part, but to claim that religion is the invention of political schemers does not explain the religious impulse. At times, government leaders may manipulate religion for political purposes, but the original desire for God seems to come from within human beings. It seems implausible to say that it was created by the rich in order to control the poor.

"Religion is the opiate of the people" is one of the most quoted phrases in history, and, undeniably, religion does make us more tranquil and accepting of our lot in life, but that may not be the reason for religion. It may only be a consequence of belief.

The criticisms of Marx's views of religion are always part of a larger critique of his political philosophy. The Marxist system advocates the leveling of wealth and a classless society, but that requires a government that is authoritarian, if not totalitarian. (Besides, wealth does not always indicate class.) In addition, that doctrine eliminates the freedom to acquire wealth because of the inequality that follows, but curtailing economic freedom reduces the incentive to work; it is partly responsible for the collapse of several Marxist economies. His system also calls for a revolution and for the workers to be the new rulers, but whatever class the rulers are drawn from, once they are rulers, they are part of the ruling class. We have seen examples of this in the Soviet Union, and Marx himself declared that all people will act in their self-interest. In addition, freedom of speech, press, assembly, religion, travel, and other rights must be eliminated by the state so people do not revert to the bad old ways, but it seems extreme to deny fundamental human rights for the sake of an imagined utopia. Furthermore, Marx advocates a violent revolution to dislodge the capitalist leaders because no one will ever relinquish power voluntarily. But he also claims that following the revolution, and after a period of dictatorship by the proletariat, the leaders will voluntarily step down.

What's more, Marx predicted the inevitable collapse of capitalism, that capitalists are their own gravediggers, but the trend of world history is toward more capitalist economies; he predicted the revolution would occur in industrial nations, but agricultural nations have been more receptive to Marxism; and he predicted class warfare, but that proved to be a self-negating prophecy. The owners of industry improved the conditions of workers, thus preempting revolt. More importantly, the logic of the Marxist system has produced brutality on a massive scale. In Stalin's Soviet Union, it led to the death of 20 million people; in China, Mao Zedong killed 40 million; in Cambodia 1.7 million died at the hands of the Khmer Rouge, 21 percent of the population. As one commentator, Karl Popper, remarked, whenever too great a disparity exists between means and ends, the system is morally bankrupt.

GOD IS DEAD: NIETZSCHE

The nineteenth-century philosopher Friedrich Nietzsche is usually identified as a founding figure of *existentialism*, a movement that flourished in Europe between the two world wars. His major books include *Thus Spoke Zarathustra*, *The Gay Science*, *Beyond Good and Evil*, and *The Genealogy of Morals*. As for his religious views, they are spread throughout his works, but appear especially in *The Anti-Christ*.

As the name implies, the existentialist wants to focus on human existence and how it can be lived fully. One of the originators, Søren Kierkegaard, believed we only escape despair and live fully if we accept God as a vital presence in our lives. Nietzsche took the opposite tack, arguing that belief turns us into slaves, unable to gain mastery over our existence. Other existentialists range along that spectrum, and include the philosophers Martin Heidegger, Jean-Paul Sartre, Karl Jaspers, and Gabriel Marcel, and literary figures such as Franz Kafka, Fyodor Dostoyevsky, and Albert Camus.

The existential movement takes as its starting point the actual conditions of human beings in the world. That is, the existentialists begin at the level of our actual and concrete lives, and then ask what it means to be a human being, especially in our contemporary age. Further, they ask what is required to maximize our existence when faced with the truth of the human condition. We want to live authentically, not with comforting illusions but in the light of reality, to consciously pursue a rich and deep existence. The answer as to how that should be done separates the various existentialists, but they are united in believing that existence is the most insistent question.

If we begin at the level of human beings in the world, we find that we are prey to anxiety, dread, forlornness, alienation, anguish, and boredom, all of which must be transcended to lead satisfying lives. Anxiety, for example, is a fundamental state that has philosophic significance, and it differs from simple fear. In fear we are afraid of some specific object—of heights, an epidemic, being alone, nuclear weapons. In anxiety, however, we cannot specify the source of our uneasiness; in fact, we will often say it is nothing. But that in itself is revealing. We are not anxious about something but about nothing, about nothingness, the void, the cessation of existence. We live our lives in perpetual dread of being snuffed out, and we deny our eventual death. François de La Rochefoucauld says we can no more look at death directly than at the sun. We defend ourselves by objectifying the fact of man's mortality, refusing to apply that truth to ourselves. But to live fully, our temporary, ephemeral state must be accepted. As Camus wrote, "There is no sun without shadows, and it is essential to know the night." We should face our condition and use it as a catalyst to more intense living.

As human beings we have the power to transcend such facts; we are free in our choices and actions. In fact, reflection on our situation enables us to choose our own existence. Animals or objects are unaware of their mortality and the brevity of their lives, but we understand that we will die one day and can decide the type of life we want to live in the meantime.

For this reason, the existentialist says that in the case of human beings, *existence precedes essence*, but for animals the reverse is true. In other words, we are first thrown into life and then develop our essential selves through the decisions we make. In the case of a chair or a frog, they contain their essence when they come into existence, and they cannot develop further. With people, however, we choose ourselves through our actions, defining the kind of person we want to be, and we are always free to choose otherwise and become a different person.

One of the significant decisions we make concerns religion, and our choice can either enhance our existence or lessen its authenticity. To some, faith produces the only genuine existence; to others, religion detracts from life, and to accept God is an act of "bad faith." Sartre, for example, claims that if there were a God, then essence would precede existence; we would have been fashioned by a creator and lack the freedom to form ourselves. Nietzsche belongs to the atheistic camp, and he maintains both that God does not exist and that believing in him is dishonest. "Faith," he declares, is "not wanting to know what is true," and it is "an eternal song over the waves in which reason has drowned."

In a well-known passage in *The Gay Science*, Nietzsche writes:

> Have you not heard of that madman who lit a lantern in the bright morning hours, ran to the market place, and cried incessantly, "I seek God! I seek God!" As many of those who do not believe in God were standing around just then, he provoked much laughter. Why, did he get lost? said one. Did he lose his way like a child? said another. Or is he hiding? Is he afraid of us? Has he gone on a voyage? or emigrated? Thus they yelled and laughed. The madman jumped into their midst and pierced them with his glances.
>
> "Whither is God," he cried. "I shall tell you. We have *killed him*— you and I. All of us are his murderers. But how have we done this? How were we able to drink up the sea? Who gave us the sponge to wipe away the entire horizon? What did we do when we unchained this earth from its sun? Whither is it moving now? Whither are we moving now? Away from all suns? Are we not plunging continually? Backward, sideward, forward, in all directions? Is there any up or

down left? Are we not straying as through an infinite nothing? Do we
not feel the breath of empty space? Has it not become colder? Is not
night and more night coming on all the while? Must not lanterns be
lit in the morning? Do we not hear anything yet of the noise of the
grave-diggers who are burying God? Do we not smell anything yet of
God's decomposition? Gods too decompose. God is dead. God remains dead. And we have killed him. How shall we, the murderers of
all murderers, comfort ourselves? What was holiest and most powerful of all that the world has yet owned has bled to death under our
knives. Who will wipe the blood off us? What water is there for us to
cleanse ourselves? What festivals of atonement, what sacred games
will we have to invent? Is not the greatness of this deed too great for
us? Must not we ourselves become gods simply to seem worthy of it?
There has never been a greater deed; and whoever will be born after
us—for the sake of this deed he will be part of a higher history than
all history hitherto."

The madman must mean that God is dead in that the traditional
Lord of the earth is no longer believable; he is dead to us. But Nietzsche does not rejoice at man's liberation. Rather, he feels an acute sense
of bewilderment, loss, and abandonment, expressed in various ways.
The wheel lurches, the compass spins, and we are cast adrift. "Things
fall apart," as W. B. Yeats puts it, "the center cannot hold; Mere anarchy
is loosed upon the world." We wander in a trackless waste, howling to
the moon for the lost pack leader. Or as Matthew Arnold wrote, "The
Sea of Faith / Was once . . . at the full, and round earth's shore / Lay like
the folds of a bright girdle furled / But now I only hear / Its melancholy,
long, withdrawing roar."

Nietzsche's madman says, "Must not we ourselves become gods,"
that is, fill the vacuum and create new values for the future of mankind?
The madman, of course, corresponds to Shakespeare's fool, who is wiser than those around him, perhaps wiser than he knows, but Nietzsche
calls churches the tombs and sepulchers of God. He takes a humanist's
position, saying we do not need to resurrect God but replace him as an
outmoded concept. We should now trust in man himself.

Nietzsche proposes heroic virtues to replace the outmoded values of
religion—the virtues of bravery, strength, decisiveness, and daring,
rather than humility, peace, kindness, and compassion. Mankind must
adopt an aristocratic morality, of excellence and a "will to power." The

individual must predominate over the collective, assertiveness over meekness, freedom over equality, and originality over conformity.

Democracy and socialism declare that everyone is the same, that no one is better than anybody else, but the truth is that some people are superior, others inferior, both by their natural qualities and their achievements. Democratic movements, therefore, are an impediment to the advancement of mankind. Christianity too blocks man's progress by endorsing deference to authority and acceptance of the human condition. Weakness is valued, making a virtue of necessity. "In truth," Nietzsche wrote, "there was only one Christian, and he died on the cross." Religious people could be outstanding, but they practice the most conventional behavior. The church has stifled innovative thinkers, opposing greatness with routine worship. Because of its values. Nietzsche says, "I call Christianity the One great Curse, the one great inward corruption . . . the one immortal mark of shame of the human race."

Nietzsche proposed a dual system of ethics: there is master morality and slave morality, the values of the shepherd and those of the sheep. The bulk of society accepts the prevailing mores, following a herd mentality in their style of dress, food, sports, and in their politics and religion. They want to blend in, not stand out, to follow and be safe, but that only leads to lethargy and stagnation. The weak always resent the powerful people, and thus trust that they will inherit the earth because they lack the courage to take the earth.

Master morality is radically different, and open to anyone with the strength to embrace it. The "higher man," the *Übermensch*, or "superman," is a self-affirming individual, original, dominating, and beyond good and evil. He is a superior human being with great abilities and power, a lord or demigod who imposes his own values on the society:

> *I teach you the overman*. Man is something that shall be overcome. What have you done to overcome him? All beings so far have created something beyond themselves; and do not want to be the ebb of this great flood and even go back to the beasts rather than overcome man. What is the ape to man? A laughingstock or a painful embarrassment? And man shall be just that for the overman: a laughingstock or a painful embarrassment.
>
> Behold, I teach you the overman. The overman is the meaning of the earth. Let your will say: the overman *shall be* the meaning of the earth! I beseech you, my brothers, *remain faithful to the earth*, and

do not believe those who speak to you of otherworldly hopes! Poison-
mixers are they, whether they know it or not.

    Once the sin against God was the greatest sin: but God died, and
these sinners died with him. To sin against the earth is now the most
dreadful thing.

Nietzsche's philosophy is provocative and romantic, but also dangerous. He advises us to let superior people rule and lead us to a higher
future, and he divides humans into masters and slaves. He tells us to
"live dangerously," "make war," to live under the volcano, and destroy
magnificently, like Napoleon; that God is dead and we must become
supermen to replace him. But much of that smacks of fascism, and Nazi
Germany thought of him as their philosopher. The Nazis did distort his
views, for example, identifying his "blonde beast" with "Aryans" from
the north, when Nietzsche only meant lions, but some of his ideas do
lend themselves to a fascist interpretation.

    Moreover, Nietzsche's distinction between superior and inferior
people makes him highly undemocratic, and he rejects religion mainly
because of its egalitarian effect. In an age when we strive for equality,
this seems wrongheaded. Furthermore, he believes that religion supports deference and slavishness, but as in the case of Marx, he underes-
timates the militancy of religion. Religious wars, for example, have occurred repeatedly, including the Crusades between the eleventh and
thirteenth centuries to wrest the Holy Land from the Muslims, the
French wars in the sixteenth century between Catholics and Protestants, and the Thirty Years' War in the seventeenth century in what is
now Germany. In Islamic warfare today, we have ample evidence of
religion driving violence. Finally, Nietzsche makes the sweeping statement that the churches and institutions have misrepresented Christianity, and that we should not value love, pity, or charity, or be altruistic
toward mankind. This strikes us as callous and inhumane.

    Nietzsche, along with Marx and Freud, has shaped our contempo-
rary awareness—his thoughts may be brilliant, but his conclusions are
probably wrong. As the American philosopher George Santayana said,
Nietzsche is "the belated prophet of romanticism," who preferred "the
bracing atmosphere of falsehood, passion, and subjective perspectives"
to truth.

    Throughout his life, Nietzsche remained an uncompromising critic
of religion, and he warns us that, even if religion died, we must be on

guard against its aftereffects: "After Buddha was dead, his shadow was still shown for centuries in a cave—a tremendous, gruesome shadow. God is dead; but given the way of men, there may still be caves for thousands of years in which his shadow will be shown.—And we—we still have to vanquish his shadow, too."

11

THE STORMY RELATIONS BETWEEN SCIENCE AND RELIGION

AS SCIENCE HAS ADVANCED, RELIGION HAS RETREATED

Religion's conflict with science began effectively in the Middle Ages when religious authorities clashed with the emerging disciplines of science. According to orthodox theology, God is responsible for all natural phenomena; only he can understand and control events in the universe as a whole. Science can never know why things happen, only how. Furthermore, scientists are allied with the devil: the laboratory experiment could be a magic spell, the foaming beaker a witch's brew producing enchantment. Besides, chemists often sought "the philosopher's stone" that would turn base metals into gold, which meant that they prized earthly rewards over the treasures of heaven.

This antagonism played out in various fields of science, and it continues today in opposing views on artificial contraception, stem-cell research, surrogate motherhood, cloning, evolution, intelligent design, and other topics. Fairy or crop rings are sometimes attributed to the hand of God, but scientists have identified a subterranean fungus that grows in circles.

In the Middle Ages, various astronomical events were given spiritual significance, including comets, meteors, eclipses, and rainbows, the movement of the moon and stars, day and night, the waxing and waning of the sun in summer and winter. Churchmen saw these phenomena as signs, wonders, omens, and warnings, but scientists sought explanations in physical laws.

For example, *comets* were seen by religious leaders as divine signs, often foretelling the birth of a great man. A radiant sky surrounded the birth of Moses, the Chinese sage Lao-tze, and Gautama the Buddha, and a heavenly light led the Magi to the manger of Christ. Earlier, comets were viewed as fireballs or thunderbolts thrown by an angry god, such as Zeus. The myth of dragons might have originated in fiery, long-tailed comets.

Comets also functioned as warning signs, which is how most School-men interpreted them. "Comets portend revolutions of kingdoms, pestilence, war, winds, or heat," Origen wrote, and this view was endorsed by St. Thomas Aquinas. A comet was believed to foretell the Norman Conquest, literally woven into history in the Bayeux tapestry. In fact, comets as portents became an article of faith throughout Europe.

Queen Elizabeth I referred to comets, eclipses, and falls of snow as warnings against sin. She prescribed an "order of prayer to avert [his] wrath . . . to be used in all parish churches." Martin Luther in Germany sermonized, "The heathen write that the comet may arise from natural causes, but God does not create one that does not foretoken a sure calamity."

Sometimes comets were called "harlot stars," doing the work of the devil. The theologian Andreas Celichius went so far as to identify comets as signs of human depravity, visible to mortals. The vapor is "the thick smoke of human sins, rising every day, every hour, every moment, full of stench and horror, before the face of God, and becoming gradually so thick as to form a comet." By contrast, some people today think "shooting stars" mean good luck.

The most notable example of comet superstition occurred during the Crusades. When European armies were about to conquer Constantinople, a comet appeared, which alarmed Pope Calixtus III, who therefore decreed "several days of prayer . . . that whatever calamity impended might be turned from the Christians and against the Turks." Unfortunately, the prayers were not answered. Even though Calixtus excommunicated the comet, the Moslems took Constantinople, which today is Istanbul. Halley's Comet, as it came to be known, appears every seventy-six years.

From a scientific standpoint, comets are "celestial bodies composed of a solid mass at the center and a luminous tail of dust and gas. They have a cylindrical shape, a nucleus of 16 x 8 x 8 kilometers, and a tail of 20 million kilometers. Solar wind and interstellar dust blast their ions, dust and fragments, and their brilliant light is produced by the interaction of matter and antimatter."

We understand today that comets are composed of common elements of hydrogen, carbon, nitrogen, and oxygen, and that they circle the sun in an erratic, elliptical orbit. They are gigantic, dirty snowballs, for when the tail crosses in front of the sun, the crystals that compose them are illuminated. The Latin name, *stella cometa*, means literally "hairy star."

In the Middle Ages, *meteors*, or falling stars, were terrifying and meant impending chaos, perhaps the end of the world. Alternatively, meteors appeared each time a baby was born, and a candle lit in the sky, or a falling star, could indicate that a life has been extinguished.

Meteors that struck the earth were generally thought to come from heaven. This includes the black rock in the Kaaba at Mecca, worshipped as a holy object by Muslims. The legend is that it was once white but turned black because of human sin. Furthermore, in Islam, good angels are believed to throw showers of meteors at bad angels, driving them from the heavens.

From the perspective of astronomy, meteors are fallout from comets, and their collision with earth is predictable. We have 150 craters caused by meteors, including Meteor Crater in Arizona and the Tunguska explosion in Siberia, and the impact of a meteor caused the extinction of dinosaurs when a cloud of dust covered the sun.

Like comets, *eclipses* were always taken as emblematic of the gods' displeasure, foretelling imminent calamity. Darkness falling upon the earth during daylight hours was naturally taken as sign of disaster—a warning that God could withhold the light from the world forever. This was the fear that preceded the winter solstice, when each day is shorter and darker than the one before. Eclipses occurred at the deaths of Prometheus, Hercules, Alexander the Great, Romulus, and Julius Caesar, which reinforced the view that they betoken evil. Charlemagne's son, Emperor Louis, may have died of fright at an eclipse, and as a result Europe was later divided into Germany, France, and Italy.

Eclipses were simply bad omens, a sign of catastrophe: if it was dark at midday, then the natural order was askew. The word "eclipse" in Greek means "abandonment," and people feared the light and warmth would desert them and not return. The sun gave life, and for it to be blotted out was a terrifying event. In Chinese mythology, it was a great dragon that devoured the sun, and the people would pound on drums to frighten it away. In India, the people immersed themselves in water to fight the sun-eating dragon.

Besides the darkness, eclipses had another fearful dimension. To the medieval mind, they resembled the iris of the eye and could be viewed as God seeing every sin. A disk of blackness, with a white line around its edge is the eye of God, glaring down from heaven in anger. The same interpretation was made of a lunar eclipse, especially since the moon appears blood red as the shadow of the earth moves across it.

Numerous biblical passages refer to eclipses: "And on that day I will make the Sun go down at noon, and darken the earth in broad daylight" (Amos 8:9); "The sun shall be turned into darkness and the moon into blood" (Acts 2:20); and "The sun will be darkened and the moon will not give its light" (Matt. 24:29). A solar eclipse allegedly occurred at the time of Christ's crucifixion: "There was darkness all over the land" (Matt. 27:45).

As we know, Columbus did not follow this religious view any more than he accepted a square world or a flat earth. When he landed in what is now Jamaica, the local people would not provide him with food and supplies. He knew from astrological charts that a lunar eclipse was due, so he threatened to make the moon disappear. When the moon began to fade, the terrified natives gave him everything he wanted. Once Columbus had his provisions, he made the moon return. This trick was also used by Mark Twain in *A Connecticut Yankee in King Arthur's Court.*

The scientific explanation, of course, is much simpler. Today we understand a solar eclipse as the obscuring of the sun's light by the intervention of the moon.

Contrary to eclipses, *rainbows* were usually taken as signs of divine blessing and favor, a "charmed phenomenon." They were viewed as a tangible bridge of light leading to the divine. In Genesis, God displays a rainbow to seal a pact with humankind that he will not destroy the world again with a flood: "I do set my bow in the cloud, and it shall be for a token of a covenant." Partly as a religious exercise, schoolchildren in England were taught the rainbow's colors of red, orange, yellow, green, blue, indigo, and violet, using the mnemonic "Richard Of York Gave Battle In Vain."

Thanks to Isaac Newton, we now understand that a spectrum of light appears when the sun shines through rain; the drops refract the light into variegated colors.

In the Middle Ages, religion also opposed the practice of *medicine* for a variety of reasons, but mainly because it contradicted the traditional beliefs about disease and the human body. Within Christianity the body is considered the seat of the passions and of carnal sin—our animal desires for food and drink, shelter, sensuality, and all our "baser needs." This is the devil's hook. He invades human beings by tempting the flesh. As the temple of the soul, the body should be kept inviolate through celibacy, penance, fasting, and the mortification of the flesh. In cases of physical illness, the body becomes sick, but it is the soul that should be treated for impurity.

It follows that cures for diseases should be sought not from physicians but from churchmen; corporeal illness is a manifestation of a sick soul. Cures were only possible through prayer and grace, for God could intervene in accordance with his judgment and mercy. The sick person himself was to blame; he brought it upon himself. By his sinfulness, he had let the devil in and was suffering from demonic possession. The bubonic plague in the 1330s that killed 25 million people was widely regarded as retribution for the unrighteousness of the people.

Medicine, therefore, was generally resisted, for the body would only recover if the soul were cured; treating the body would never redeem the soul. By extension, holy relics might cure people—the bones of saints, a hair of a martyr, charms, amulets, and exorcisms, but physicians' remedies would not. Besides, we were meant to suffer on earth as penance for original sin, so doctors were interfering with God's will.

Nevertheless, medicine was permitted to some extent, especially if accompanied by the prayers of a priest. But in treating patients, physicians had to follow the classic Greek texts, which pivoted around the four "humors." These bodily fluids determined a person's health: blood, phlegm, black bile, and yellow bile. Each was associated with basic elements of earth, air, fire, and water, the four ages of infancy, adolescence, adulthood, and old age, the four Gospels, the signs of the zodiac, and even the directions of the compass. Good health consists in keeping our bodily fluids in harmony, and one's personality reflects whether there is an imbalance among the humors. The predominance of blood meant a cheerful, optimistic, confident disposition (sanguine); phlegm was associated with a calm, apathetic, unemotional personality (phlegmatic); black bile meant melancholy, gloom, despondency; yellow bile signaled irritability, anger, a choleric attitude toward life (bilious).

To restore a patient's equilibrium, the physician had to control the person's diet. Different foods—cold, hot, wet, or dry—regulated a person's bodily humors. Warm pasta cleans stomach lining; barley soup was good for humid intestines; roses, which are cold and dry, will reduce inflammation of the brain. Contact with sacred waters is also restorative, be they fountains, rivers, fonts, or spas. Also essential is the use of signatures—cures for diseases marked in nature by God. For example, the red juices of bloodroot are good for the blood; the yellow fluid of celandine cures jaundice; eyebright with its oval spot cures eye diseases; and the sinuous shape of bugloss can be used to treat snakebites.

Bloodletting (phlebotomy) was a related cure that for centuries was thought effective. By choosing the proper vein, releasing or restricting blood flow, physicians controlled the humors. In actuality, bloodletting often resulted in an infection, a severed nerve or artery, and uncontrollable bleeding. Usually patients just grew weaker, or they simply died. Bloodletting, in fact, was one of the most harmful practices in the history of medicine. Today, doctors have adopted the reverse procedure of blood transfusions.

Although medicine was practiced under the careful supervision of the Church, doctors were generally identified with infernal sorcerers, practicing the magic of satanic cults. A popular proverb said, "Where there are three physicians, there are two atheists."

Medicine and surgery were carefully distinguished: physicians dealt with internal problems, surgeons treated wounds, fractures, skin diseases. Because of a religious injunction against "shedding blood" (with the exception of bloodletting), surgeons were severely limited. They were only allowed to amputate limbs on the battlefield, but the anesthetic potions that were used—hemlock juice, opium, and henbane—often proved fatal.

The dissection of cadavers was considered especially sinful, because it showed disrespect for the dead. Bodies had to be smuggled into basement laboratories, and there were severe penalties for grave robbing. Dissection was also prohibited because it revealed one of the divine mysteries: how the body functioned. That was for God alone to know. It was even feared that both sexes would be found to have an equal number of ribs; since the creation of Eve, men should have one less. Andreas Vesalius created a controversy in 1543 when he suggested that men and women had the same number of ribs.

Today the conflict between medicine and religion has reached a truce. We dissect cadavers in medical schools, conduct autopsies, harvest organs, use artificial body parts, and routinely perform transplants. The fact that hospitals are named St. Francis or St. Mary's shows the hostility has ceased, both toward medicine and surgery. A minor conflict does still exist between faith-healing and medical science, but it surfaces mainly when parents allow a child to die, praying for their recovery rather than seeking medical help.

Mental illness (madness) was treated by medieval theologians as a satanic influence; people were "fiend-sick," and spiritual measures had to be taken to restore their souls. Sometimes these measures were humane: holy water, sacred relics, the breath of priests, visiting holy sites, drinking potions from church bells. The first step was to attack Satan's pride, which was his dominant characteristic. Obscene curses and vile insults should be hurled at him so he would leave the body of the madman. Books of exorcisms contained hundreds of imprecations calling Satan a mangy beast, filthy sow, loathsome cobbler, envious crocodile, malodorous drudge, swollen toad, perfidious boar, greedy wolf, entangled spider, bestial drunkard, lustful and stupid one. Thunder-words might also frighten away Satan, for example, "Schemhamphora," "Athanatos," "Tetragrammaton," and "Eheye."

Gradually, however, inhumane measures were used. The Church accepted the notion that the indwelling demon had to be punished, which meant torture of the "lunatic." The point was to exorcize the devil, and the devil's power was such that gentle treatment would not be enough. This conviction opened the door to the cruelest acts of the Middle Ages and some of the saddest chapters of religion. Satan was being punished, but it was the lunatic's body that was tortured. Flogging, hanging, ducking, pressing, the thumbscrew, the rack, the garrote, the wheel, the iron maiden—all were used on the insane person. According to one report, the Jesuits in Vienna exorcized 12,652 devils in the year 1583. The specific justification cited was that Christ cast out demons and drove them into a herd of swine.

Incidentally, the same methods were used against heretics. Anyone accused of heresy was tortured until they confessed, and everyone eventually confessed. Because blood should not be spilled (aside from phlebotomy), people's joints and bones were cracked instead. This practice went on for hundreds of years

Belief in demons flourished throughout the Middle Ages, which can be seen in Gothic cathedrals where there are representations of Satan and his hideous fiends, scourging people, poking them with tridents, dragging them to hell in chains. Carved gargoyles were placed at the cathedral corners and as downspouts of gutters. They are beneficial grotesques, designed to frighten off evil spirits. They were described as "sermons in stone," teaching the illiterate that the devil is never far away. Stained-glass windows also depicted demons and monsters; one window in Chartres cathedral shows the exorcism of an insane man, a horned and hoofed hobgoblin spewing from his mouth. Demonic possession is still part of Catholic doctrine, and exorcism is prescribed in cases of profuse blasphemy, speaking in tongues, supernatural abilities, knowledge of hidden things, and an aversion to anything holy.

So much pain and misery could have been avoided during the Middle Ages if doctors had been allowed to apply scientific knowledge. Because of dogmatic beliefs, thousands of people have suffered terribly from curable diseases or were needlessly tortured as a consequence of superstition. Gradually, medical treatment has come to be judged consistent with God's will, and health a divine blessing.

Science also clashed with religion over *cosmology*, or the structure of the universe. Medieval theologians accepted the theory of a monk named Cosmas, who, in *Christian Topography*, declared that the earth is a flat rectangle, perhaps a disk, surrounded by four seas. Its dimensions are four hundred days' journey long, two hundred wide, and the four corners of the earth symbolize the four seasons and the twelve months of the year. Gigantic walls enclose the land and seas and rise to support "the pillars of heaven." Two levels make up this oblong box, divided by the solid vault of the heavens: the lower one stretches from the earth to the stars and contains human life; the upper one is the home of divine beings, including angels, who carry out God's work: "We say therefore with Isaiah that the heaven embracing the earth is a vault, with Job that it is joined to the earth, and with Moses that the length of the earth is greater than its breadth."

Further iterations concerned the next world. A hell exists below the earth where sinners descend and live for all eternity; good souls are resurrected, rising to heaven above. The tower of Babel was an impious attempt to build a tower "whose top may reach heaven."

A few theologians and a majority of scientists rejected the flat-earth notion, preferring the spherical theory of Protagoras. As previously cited, Columbus was convinced the earth was round and bravely sailed across the Atlantic. His crew was uncertain and believed they could be attacked by sea serpents waiting to devour ships, or that the horizon had an end and they would fall off the edge into perdition. The common belief was that the sun was red in the evening because it looked down on hell.

Our cosmic picture is quite different: the earth an elliptical planet orbiting the sun, which is one of 400 billion stars in the Milky Way galaxy, which is one among 100 billion galaxies. We no longer fear the thunderbolt, treat comets as omens, cower at eclipses, or hesitate to use medicine for physical or mental illness. We have harnessed atmospheric electricity, and church steeples have lightning rods. We don't hesitate to orbit the world in space capsules, and the planets of our solar system may soon be pockmarked with human footprints. One cynic remarked that science flies people to the moon, but religion flies terrorists into buildings.

Poets sometimes deplore the way that science has removed the romance of nature, analyzing the physics of falling stars and rainbows. The worry is that science murders to dissect. William Blake calls a star the "bright torch of love" and the "fair-haired angel of the evening," but physicists describe the star as emitting electromagnetic radiation as a result of nuclear reactions. Goethe refers to the moon's "sweet soothing eye . . . watching like a gentle friend," and Shelley asks of the moon, "Art thou pale for weariness, / Of climbing heaven and gazing on the earth . . . ?" But astronomers speak of lunar volcanoes and impact craters, a structure formed from the crystallization of a magma ocean. Today we do not wonder how many angels can stand on the head of a pin but how much information we can store on a microchip.

Science may diminish beauty by parting the veil of mystery, but it can also enhance our appreciation. Snow-capped mountains may be less romantic when geologists tell us about the temperature and pressure that formed them, but we are also able to admire them at another level. In the same way, when astronomers inform us that the sun is 93 million miles away from earth and its light takes 8 minutes to reach us, traveling at 193,281 miles per second, that can increase our sense of awe and wonder; we certainly do not stop appreciating the sunrise or sunset. And we still like the taste of apple pie even when we know how apples grow and how pies are baked.

Of course, science also gives us power and makes us feel less vulnerable. We need not fear natural phenomena quite so much once we understand their mechanisms and feel some measure of control over them.

WHY DID THEOLOGIANS REFUSE TO LOOK THROUGH GALILEO'S TELESCOPE?

The most celebrated attack by religion on science was made by the Catholic Church on Galileo Galilei (1564–1642), the Italian astronomer, physicist, and mathematician. Galileo rejected the second-century, Ptolemaic notion that the sun circles the earth, and accepted the Copernican theory that the earth revolves around the sun. This was a heliocentric rather than a geocentric view of the cosmos, contrary to Church teaching, and it provoked a direct confrontation with ecclesiastical authorities. At a trial by the Inquisition, Galileo was prohibited from believing the evidence of his own eyes, thus setting up a conflict between religious authority and scientific evidence.

Einstein called Galileo "the father of modern physics—indeed of science altogether," partly because he used the experimental method and stated his findings in mathematical terms. "Philosophy is written in this grand book the universe," Galileo wrote "but the book cannot be understood unless one first learns to comprehend the language and to read the alphabet in which it is composed. It is written in the language of mathematics." Galileo believed that science did not oppose religion but revealed the grandeur of the divine order, expressed in mathematical symbols.

We know that Galileo discovered a mathematical law that governed acceleration, observing that the swing of a pendulum always takes the same amount of time; this enabled him to design the pendulum clock. He also found that objects remain in motion unless an external force, such as friction, acts upon them. This became Newton's first law of motion, that objects moving at a steady speed in a straight line will continue doing so indefinitely, and an object at rest will remain at rest. Galileo also invented a thermometer, an advanced microscope, and a more accurate method for calculating the gunpowder needed for cannons. He left drawings of candles and mirrors for increasing light indoors; a schematic for an automatic tomato picker; and a design for the first ballpoint pen. His most famous experiment was to drop balls of different weights from the leaning tower of Pisa, and when they reached the ground at the same time, that proved velocity is independent of mass.

However, Galileo is best remembered for his work in astronomy: the patches of light and shadow on the moon are mountains and craters, much like earth; there are sunspots or solar flares; the Milky Way is not a nebulous cloud but a vast array of stars; and Jupiter has moons.

His astronomical studies convinced him that the earth was not the center of the universe, with other heavenly bodies orbiting around it, but a remote planet wheeling around the sun in a concentric circle, along with other planets.

Churchmen saw his findings as a threat to the orthodox, geocentric theory. It implied that humankind was not at the heart of creation, which reduced man's centrality, significance, and dignity. It was, in fact, an intellectual revolution, challenging the biblical account of creation. The authorities concluded that Galileo had to be suppressed, especially since he supported this theory with science; that in itself was suspect. His views contradicted Aristotle, Plato, and the approved interpretation of the Church. According to scripture, the sun "runneth about from one end of the heavens to the other," and "God fixed the Earth upon its foundation, not to be moved forever." (A competing theory of Tycho de Brahe claimed the planets revolved around the sun, but the sun revolved around the earth.) What's more, Galileo claimed that the moon shines by the sun's reflected light, when according to Genesis, the moon is itself "a great light." One cardinal stated, "To assert that the earth revolves around the sun is as erroneous as to claim that Jesus was not born of a virgin."

Galileo argued that biblical interpretation should always be subject to new understanding, and that scientific theories, such as Ptolemy's, should not be considered dogmas of faith. All knowledge is conditional and open-ended. He once wrote, "I do not feel obliged to believe that the same God who has endowed us with sense, reason, and intellect has intended us to forgo their use." But in 1624, he was summoned before the Inquisition under "grave suspicion of heresy."

The hearing took place when Galileo was sixty-nine years old. He was threatened with torture, imprisonment, and death if he did "abjure, curse, and detest" his work. Galileo acquiesced to every demand, and pleaded for mercy, citing his "regrettable state of physical unwellness." But although he recanted, he was convicted of heresy and sentenced to life imprisonment. The punishment was later commuted to house arrest, but it was never rescinded, even though he went blind. His books were ordered to be burned, and Church officials attempted to destroy everything he had written. The "Papal Condemnation of Galileo" reads, in part:

> The proposition that the Sun is the center of the world and does not move from its place is absurd and false philosophically and formally heretical because it is expressly contrary to Holy Scripture. The proposition that the Earth is not the center of the world and immovable but that it moves, and also with a diurnal motion, is equally absurd and false philosophically and theologically considered at least erroneous in faith.

Galileo was compelled to kneel before the Inquisition, to renounce his belief in the earth's movement, but according to the popular account, as he rose he said, *E pur se move*, "and yet it does move."

The dispute between Galileo and the Catholic Church concerned which mode of knowledge is more trustworthy: the findings of science or the holy word of scripture. Religious officials relied on the canonical Bible and the theological commentary built up over the centuries; these sources revealed God's timeless truths. Changes were made but only according to divine revelation. Alterations in doctrine had to be approved by Church councils after deliberation and prayers for guidance.

Galileo regarded himself as a devout Catholic, but he trusted empirical science more; he assumed that systematic experiments, supported by mathematical proof, yielded the most reliable knowledge. To truly

know, we had to examine the physical evidence, formulate an explanation, and verify that hypothesis by successful prediction and replication.
Science was more a matter of method than subject matter. Astronomy
and astrology both deal with the stars, and chemistry and alchemy both
concern physical substances, but they are not all sciences. Galileo found
it particularly frustrating that churchmen would not look through his
telescope. From their perspective, they did not want to be fooled by
fallible senses about matters that they knew from the Bible were false.

That was the crux of the dispute. As one philosopher put it:

> The individual, alone in a laboratory, with evidence acquired through
> careful research, might reach conclusions contrary to the teachings
> of the church. The evidence could, in fact, be overwhelming, and
> anyone was free to examine the proof. Once open inquiry was per-
> mitted the Bible might then be called into question, and the entire
> edifice collapse like a house of cards. Strict control over knowledge
> was needed and, if necessary, the Inquisition could be summoned to
> enforce the articles of faith.

In 1992, 359 years after Galileo's trial, a papal commission under John
Paul II admitted the Church's error and offered an apology. The condemnation was reversed, and a statement issued by the Vatican stated
that the creator worked through Galileo's spirit.

Some questions that have come down to us are whether science and
religion can be reconciled, how much latitude should science be allowed, and does science have to be censored when it conflicts with
religion? Which mode of knowing is more reliable, and which parts of
scripture should be taken literally and which symbolically? Should the
Bible be issued in loose-leaf form or firmly bound as timeless truths, as
God's last will and testament? One lesson we have learned is that real-
ities do not disappear by being suppressed.

WORLDVIEWS OF RELIGION AND SCIENCE: CONTRADICTORY OR COMPATIBLE?

When religion and science reach different conclusions, three responses
have been identified by scholars such as Ian Barbour:

1. One possibility is to see a deeper *compatibility* between them. For example, we could claim that God was the spark for the big bang, and that he favored humankind and provided the ideal conditions for life on earth. If other intelligent creatures are discovered elsewhere in the universe, that would show God's creation is even grander than we imagined. Similarly, the conflict between creationism and evolutionism may be only apparent. Perhaps God used evolution as the instrument of his creation. For instance, it has been suggested that the process of natural selection was infused into nature by God, as was survival of the fittest. This instrumental view is the basis on which the Catholic Church now accepts evolution. Pope Pius XII in *Humani Generis* declared that evolution explains "the origins of the human body," and in 1996 Pope John Paul II called it "more than a theory."

This assumes, of course, that the Bible is largely symbol, myth, allegory, and metaphor, not literal truth; it must not be taken at face value. Scripture, it is argued, is for transformation rather than information, and the stories of the Bible offer us insight into reality. If we look for meaning not fact, then the mysteries of God can be brought within our grasp.

There are numerous examples of such reconciliation. The billions of years of evolution in human time correspond to the six days of creation in Genesis, a day in the life of God being that much longer. The parting of the Red Sea could mean that if we have faith, our way will be made safe. (Or perhaps the Israelites crossed at low tide, and God sent a rising tide to drown the Egyptian army.) The Bible does endorse having slaves, but that only means a servant, a division of labor between the overseers and the workers. As for the story of loaves and fishes, people's hearts were so filled with Christ's love that they shared their food with each other.

The story of Jonah being swallowed by the whale was meant to show God's caring and forgiveness, because after three days and nights, Jonah was spewed out onto the land; what's more, the large fish could have been a ship, with wooden ribs. When Moses smote the rock and water flowed forth, the rock represents God, the water, his truth and knowledge. The voice in the burning bush could be the wisdom imparted through nature, and the angel that appeared as a pillar of fire simply illustrated the grandeur of the firmament. In the gospel of Mark, when Christ restored sight to the blind men, they were made to "see the light." When Christ changed water into wine, people drank a liquid that seemed transformed because of their newfound understanding. And Lazarus's resurrection does not mean a dead man came to life, but that we are all able to be reborn, to make a new start with fresh hope. As one writer put it, whatever the last trumpet will be, it will not be the sound of a trumpet.

This approach can certainly reconcile differences between religion and science, especially the accounts in the Bible and scientific evidence. However, the main question is how far can we take symbolic interpretation? As far as we know, seas cannot part, water cannot become wine, people cannot survive inside a whale, and dead men cannot be brought back to life. Is it too convenient to plead metaphor when conflicts occur with scientific facts? If metaphor is invoked only in tight corners, it could be the clang of the escape hatch. And are the fundamental ideas of Christianity also metaphor, such as the Fall and redemption, Christ's resurrection, and the reality of the Trinity? We do not want to go too far down that path, and we are not sure how to differentiate between a literal truth and purely figurative meaning.

A related, reconciliation approach is to add the religious explanation to the scientific one. In that way, the two are harmonized. However, as discussed under the teleological argument for God's existence, to try to graft God onto science has not been very successful. The main obstacle is Occam's razor, or the law of parsimony: explanations should not be compounded beyond what is required. Since science explains the arrangement of the world, it's superfluous to add a God who lies behind it. Or as the philosopher David Hume phrased it, we should not multiply causes without necessity.

In other words, if a simple, natural explanation is sufficient, we do not need a complex, supernatural one. If evolution accounts for life, there is no need not to postulate a God who used evolution as his instrument of creation. If the big bang explains the universe, it is superfluous to add God as the force behind the primal explosion. Besides, we would be back to an "infinite regress" in which we could ask, "What, then, started God?"

2. Another approach is to say that religion and science operate in *separate and distinct realms*, and therefore cannot be in opposition. They are talking about different things. The paleontologist and science writer

Stephen J. Gould takes this approach. Religion and science are two distinct fields or "non-overlapping magisteria" and their authority does not clash. Science covers "the empirical realm: what the universe is made of (fact) and why it works the way it does (theory). The magisterium of religion extends over questions of ultimate meaning and moral values." If the one asks, "How does it all operate?" and the other asks, "What does it all mean?" they have no quarrel. Science and religion are different but equal, and this, Gould believes, is "a simple and entirely conventional resolution to . . . the supposed conflict."

Einstein expressed this idea when he wrote "science without religion is lame, religion without science is blind." The two address different aspects of our experience, but they need each other for a complete picture of the whole.

Unfortunately, the areas do overlap and conflicts do arise. Religion assigns spiritual causes to events, but science uses physical explanations. When a hurricane passes them by, the pious believe their prayers have been answered, but the meteorologist, checking his Doppler radar, identifies a high-pressure system that diverted the tropical depression. If a patient recovers after being given up for lost, the minister thanks God for a miracle cure, but the doctor regards it as a misdiagnosis. An earthquake that kills thousands can be attributed to the people's sinfulness, but the geologist explains it in terms of shifting tectonic plates as a result of increased temperature and pressure along a fault line.

Can we say God is ultimately responsible for the hurricane missing the town, for the low-magnitude earthquake, and so forth, or are we adding explanations unnecessarily, as Occam's razor claims? If the physical explanation is sufficient, do we need to include a metaphysical one also?

Miracles, in particular, run afoul of Gould's separate-but-equal thesis. Miracles are a suspension of natural law, so we can look for an explanation in divine intervention or in the laws of physics, chemistry, and biology.

3. A third response is to acknowledge a *genuine contradiction* between the truth-claims of religion and that of science. This is pointed up especially in scripture, which fundamentalists believe to be inerrant. But even if the Bible is infallible, that does not mean we interpret it infal-

libly. Errors can creep in, especially since much of it was transmitted orally.

The Bible today is a source of inspiration but not scientific knowledge, because its account of the world seems mistaken on a number of facts. These discrepancies set up a direct conflict with the findings of science.

The earth is not flat (Dan. 4:10–11; Matt. 4:8); nor is it stationary (1 Chron. 16:30; Ps. 93:1; Ps. 96:10). It is not a disk sitting on pillars with a rotating dome, carrying the sun, moon, and stars, and water does not leak through as rain from the windows of heaven. The sky is not a solid crystalline structure, the moon does not give off its own light, the earth began 4.7 billion years ago, not 6,000 years ago, and the universe is 15 billion years old. The world was not created before light and stars, any more than birds and whales existed before reptiles. To amass enough water for a flood to cover the earth appears impossible, and Noah's boat would have been swamped in any case, overloaded with tens of thousands of animals; Noah would also need to go to Antarctica for penguins, and Australia for kangaroos.

Insects have six legs not four; the camel does not have an undivided hoof; the hare does not chew its cud; a bat is not a bird; and snails do not melt. It also seems doubtful that Jacob made his flocks conceive by showing them striped rods; that languages arose from one source (the tower of Babel); that if you have faith you can handle poisonous snakes and never be bitten (snake-handlers are bitten regularly); or that "it raineth not on the earth for three and a half years." There also seems to be some exaggeration: Adam is reported to have lived 930 years, his son Kenan, 910, his third son, Seth, 912, his son Enoch, 805, and Methuselah, 969 years. Even allowing for metaphor, the life spans seem excessive.

Theologians tell us when Christ was born and died, but scientists say we do not know the year when these events happened, much less the day. Christmas was set during the pagan celebrations of the winter solstice—a time of rejoicing and revelry. Easter likewise replaced the pagan carnival at the return of spring, following the spring equinox.

In brief, religion and science do seem to contradict each other. We would like a neat reconciliation, but at bottom, the two appear to have different worldviews. Either God designed heaven and earth, placed people in the world for a purpose, or billions of years ago a primal atom exploded, resulting in stars, planets, and the chance evolution of the human species. These seem to be *alternative* models—which accounts for the centuries-old warfare between religion and science.

In many ways, science militates against our deepest desires, presenting a stark picture of the human condition. Psychologically, we want to believe that we exist for a reason, that our lives have a narrative, and that we are moral beings living out a cosmic drama of sin and redemption. We want to believe in life after death, with heavenly rewards for being good. We want a universe that contains pity, forgiveness, brotherhood, and justice rather than one that is cold, empty, and dark. We need purpose and value, security and comfort, the power of prayer and the hope of miracles, in short, the consolation of faith.

Galileo took away our centrality, placing us at the edge of the universe. Darwin took away our spirituality, treating us as mere clever animals inhabiting that remote planet. And Freud later removed our rationality, treating us as motivated by emotional, unconscious drives. In the light of these attacks, we want to dismiss science altogether. It does not nourish our spirit as the Bible does. However, the challenge that science offers to religion cannot be ignored; it must be confronted.

Does science slay beautiful theories with ugly facts? Is it a choice between "heartless science" and "mindless religion"? These are two windows on the same world, but the view is vastly different.

Sometimes science itself is considered a faith that strains credibility as much as religion, especially the findings of modern physics. Einstein, for example, claims that time does not flow evenly but is relative to space. Hence the poem:

> There was a young lady named bright
> Who traveled much faster than light.
> She left home one day in a relative way,
> And came back the previous night.

12

HOW RELIGION RELATES TO SOCIETY

IS ETHICS BASED ON RELIGION?

When religious people are asked why an action is right, they will reply that is the will of God. We should not kill, steal, or lie, and we should love both our neighbor and our enemy because that is written in the Bible. In other words, God is the authority behind all values. We can trust that certain actions are right and others are wrong because we have the word of God behind them, and there cannot be any greater validation.

In the Old Testament, the Ten Commandments express the moral code that has governed much of Western civilization:

1. I am the Lord your God.
2. You shall not make yourself an idol . . . for the Lord your God is a jealous God.
3. You shall not make wrongful use of the name of the Lord your God, for the Lord will not acquit anyone who misuses his name.
4. Remember the Sabbath day and keep it holy.
5. Honor your father and your mother, so that your days may be long in the land.
6. You shall not murder.
7. You shall not commit adultery.
8. You shall not steal.
9. You shall not bear false witness.

10. You shall not covet your neighbor's house; you shall not covet your neighbor's wife.

These divine commands have been widely accepted, but questions have also been raised about some of them. For example, jealousy is not a virtue and should not be imputed to God. To never forgive someone who misuses his name seems a harsh judgment, and to honor your father and mother so that you will have a long life seems a selfish reason.

More significantly, some of the edicts contained in the Old Testament appear to be rooted in more primitive times rather than in universal values; some, in fact, seem immoral. For example, the last commandment goes on to say that you should not covet your neighbor's male or female slave, which could be a tacit acceptance of slavery. More explicit approval appears elsewhere in Exodus:

> When you buy a male Hebrew slave, he shall serve six years, but in the seventh he shall go out a free person, without debt . . . If his master gives him a wife and she bears him sons or daughters, the wife and her children shall be her master's . . . When a man sells his daughter as a slave, she shall not go out as male slaves do. If she does not please her master, who designated her for himself, then he shall let her be redeemed.

Similarly, questionable are the requirements to sacrifice animals (Jer. 7:30–31; 21–22): "You should present a burnt offering to the Lord of livestock, turtledoves or pigeons,—a male without blemish, and it will have a pleasing aroma to the Lord." There are even references to killing innocents. Jephtha promised God that if he were given the power to slay the Ammonites, he would kill the first person to come out of his house; he kept his promise, even though it turned out to be his daughter (Judg. 11:29–40). Abraham is also prepared to sacrifice his son Isaac in response to God's command, but the angel of the Lord intervened at the last moment. A voice called from heaven saying, "Do not lay your hand on the boy or do anything to him; for now I know that you fear God, since you have not withheld your son, your only son, from me" (Gen. 22:1–2).

Today we sentence people to death for only the most heinous crimes, principally murder, but the Bible prescribes the death penalty for a variety of offenses: for not being a virgin at the time of marriage, not obeying your parents, not observing the Sabbath, using God's name in vain, worshiping other gods, committing adultery, being homosexual, being a witch, and for cursing. This strikes the modern mind as excessive. Furthermore, the Bible apparently accepts polygamy, since Abraham married Sarah, Hagar, and Keturah; Esau married Judith and Bashemath; and Solomon had 700 wives, plus 300 concubines (Judg. 8:30). It also advocates child-beating; "If you beat them with a rod, they will not die" (Prov. 23:13). Some critics have claimed that incest is accepted, since Adam and Eve's children and Noah's grandchildren must have intermarried; there were no other people on earth. Feminists also point out that women are treated as inferior throughout scripture and told to submit to their husbands: "The husband shall be head of his wife, as Christ is the head of the church" (Eph. 5:22–26). Women are also described as unclean and temptresses.

The lesson seems to be that not all parts of the Bible can be taken as absolute truth. We have to judge which parts are worth accepting and which parts merely reflect the values of that historical period. Perhaps we need to select the principles that are valuable, and reject such things as slavery, animal sacrifice, and the subordination of women.

"Exegesis" seems necessary—the critical examination and evaluation of biblical texts. This implies that moral values are not derived from the Bible, because we judge the worth of scriptural passages according to an independent standard of value. Not everything we read in the Bible can be called divine truth; some parts might be distorted, human judgments.

The New Testament contains moral values also, especially the section referred to as the "Sermon on the Mount." Here we have the heart of the Christian message:

> When Jesus saw the crowds, he went up the mountain, and after he sat down, his disciples came to him. Then he began to speak, and taught them, saying: "Blessed are the poor in spirit, for theirs is the kingdom of heaven. Blessed are those who mourn, for they will be comforted. Blessed are the meek, for they will inherit the earth. Blessed are those who hunger and thirst for righteousness, for they will be filled. Blessed are the merciful, for they will receive mercy. Blessed are the pure in heart, for they will see God. Blessed are the peacemakers, for they will be called children of God. Blessed are

those who are persecuted for righteousness' sake, for theirs is the
kingdom of heaven . . . You have heard that it was said, 'An eye for an
eye and a tooth for a tooth.' But I say to you: Do not resist an
evildoer. But if anyone strikes you on the right cheek, turn the other
also; and if anyone wants to sue you and take your coat, give him your
cloak as well; and if anyone forces you to go one mile, go also the
second mile. Give to everyone who begs from you, and do not refuse
anyone who wants to borrow from you. You have heard that it was
said, 'You shall love your neighbor and hate your enemy.' But I say to
you, love your enemies and pray for those who persecute you, so that
you may be children of your Father in heaven; for he makes his sun
rise on the evil and on the good, and sends rain on the righteous and
the unrighteous. For if you love [only] those who love you, what
reward do you have?"

This is a clear departure from Old Testament thinking. In Christian
terms, it is an affirmation of selfless, unconditional love. The Greek
term used is *agape*, which contrasts sharply with erotic love, *eros*.

In *eros* there is a desire to possess the person or object loved. We
want the other person to belong to us and to claim ownership—often-
times in a romantic relationship, exclusive ownership. It is essentially a
self-centered form of love because we are concerned with satisfying our
desire for the other person rather than satisfying the other person's
need for us. In some way, we wish to be personally enriched by absorbing their traits or by appropriating the person altogether. By making
another our own, incorporating them within ourselves, we feel an en-
largement of our being, even though it may mean the other's diminu-
tion. We do not exist for the other person but rather he or she exists for
us, and we maintain the relationship just so long as we continue to
benefit from it. Sacrificing our own good for the sake of the other
person is contrary to *eros* love, for we do not desire what is best for the
other, but only what is best for ourselves.

In *agape*, by contrast, our feelings for someone else are so strong
that we desire his or her good even above our own. Our love impels us
to dedicate ourselves to the other person's welfare. If we accept an
agape ideal, which means acting selflessly instead of selfishly, then we
remain in a relationship as long as we believe that we are good for the
other person. If that point is passed, and we are not helping the person

we love, then regardless of whether it is beneficial for us, we will sever the connection.

To the Christian, *agape* is the only genuine love. It is not a business transaction in which each party seeks an advantage, but a commitment to the other person's well-being, above our own. And the *agape* we give does not have to be earned by the other person because it is not based on merit or deserts; in the same way, it will not be withdrawn if the person disappoints us. For it is not what the person does but what he or she is that matters. People are lovable because of who they are not by virtue of their accomplishments, and we forgive them their faults while maintaining love for the person.

The Christian moralist who affirms *agape* rather than *eros* wants this mode of functioning to apply not just to romantic attachments but to our attitude and conduct toward all humankind. Charity, as St. Thomas Aquinas said, is "the mother and root of all the virtues" (*caritas est mater omnium virtutum, et radix*). And to be charitable means loving humanity, our brothers and sisters, without reservation, as God the Father intended and Christ exemplified. People may not be of equal worth, but we can carry the same love for them in our hearts. *Agape* should typify all personal relations and replace envy, malice, spite, greed, lust, hate, and selfishness.

For the Christian, the supreme prototype of *agape* is, of course, God's love for humankind, which lay behind his sacrifice of his only son. That love was not awarded because of any merit on man's part, that is, because the human race deserved it, but because pure love is of an unqualified character, an unreserved giving. God loves humanity for its own sake, and human beings should love God in the same way, not for the good he can provide by granting our prayers or guaranteeing us heaven, but solely because he is God. And our caring attitude toward our fellow human beings should be prompted by our common relationship to God in *agape*: "This is my commandment, that you love one another as I have loved you" (John 1: 12), and "Let no man seek his own but each his neighbor's good" (1 Cor.10: 24).

In Christian ethics, this leads to a fundamental paradox that must be embraced: as we give, so do we receive; as we lose ourselves, we gain ourselves. When we subordinate our egos in *agape*, deferring to our Lord and our fellow human beings, we become infinitely richer.

The *agape* ideal also leads to a special conception of *justice*, which also distinguishes Old and New Testament thinking. Unlike the ancient Hebrews, who believed in giving people what they deserve, the Christian wants to give them what they need. The Hebrews thought of justice as balancing the scales in accordance with the *law of talion:* that whatever offense people commit, something equivalent should be done to them. The Hindu notion of karma is based on the same principle. As applied to law, a person should be punished in proportion to the severity of the crime, neither more nor less. If the punishment is commensurate with the offense, then justice has been done.

In contrast, Christian ethics tries to meet a person's needs, regardless of what the conduct might deserve. Instead of rewarding or punishing people in proportion to their merits, the New Testament stresses helping people to improve; their sins are used as a gauge of their need for love, not an index of how much they should be punished. No thought is given to paying for the crimes or getting even, but only to meeting the fundamental need that motivated the crime. We do not want to make people pay, but to make them better; not to point a finger but extend a hand. Divine justice, as the New Testament theory is called, concentrates on needs rather than deserts, redemption of the person rather than retribution for the crime.

Without question, unconditional love is an ideal worthy of respect. It characterizes the best relationships and the highest ideals of punishment. In the Christian system, it describes God's interaction with man as pure love. However, Christian ethics has encountered opposition on several fronts, including charges of its impracticality.

This criticism pivots round the reality of human relationships. Certainly, if both parties are saintly, they will each give to the other unselfishly, but people are not always evenly matched in generosity. In ordinary life, people can and do take advantage of unselfishness, and if one person gives and the other takes, the giving person will become a mark, a victim, or casualty. For example, if a man is unfaithful to a woman, she may forgive him out of love and understanding. Operating in terms of *agape*, she might reason that, regardless of what he deserves, what he needs is support. But suppose his response is to exploit her generosity and to betray her again, expecting that she will continue to be understanding. Then her sacrifice would be pointless, in fact, she may have encouraged his cheating by default, that is, by not asserting herself and opposing it. His character is not improved, and she has only succeeded in making herself miserable. Suppose further that the woman is a battered wife, and her caring only feeds his abusiveness, that turning the other cheek only gives him another target. How far can the woman be expected to go before her passivity becomes self-destructive and feeds his violence?

Also, the person who operates a business according to *agape* principles is doomed to fail. A banker, for example, cannot follow the maxim "Do not refuse anyone who wants to borrow from you." He would soon declare bankruptcy. In the capitalist system as a whole, people will not succeed if they do what is best for their competitors. Similarly, in international relations, Christians who act for the well-being of their country's enemies will soon endanger their own nation. A brutal dictator, for instance, would like nothing better than nonresistance to his aggression. If everyone adopted the *agape* ideal, then the Christian approach would work, but in a world where only some operate selflessly and the rest selfishly, altruistic people become irrelevant. Little good is achieved, and a great deal of suffering can result.

Christian theologians recognize the practical difficulties involved in applying *agape*, and they make various concessions to business and *realpolitik*. These compromises are more or less successful but they stray very far from the pure ethics of Christianity. The Protestant theologian Reinhold Niebuhr, for example, concludes that we must abandon the law of love and engage in evil actions if we are to improve the world politically. Individuals may behave in just and loving ways toward one another, but "all human groups tend to be more predatory than the individuals which compose them . . .they take for themselves whatever their power can command." Therefore, we cannot expect to make moral progress through withdrawal or pacifism but only through employing the evil tactics of the opposing group. We must get our hands dirty, and "if we repent, Christ will forgive and receive us." Niebuhr may be correct in his assessment, but his theory does point up the impracticality of using Christian ethics in contexts where power is dominant.

In addition to the criticism of impracticality, Christians face a dilemma over the principles of morality versus the spirit of love. For example, one of the biblical rules is "Thou shalt not kill," but under certain circumstances it seems allowable—in the name of love. Religion has often supported killing in war if the cause is just and innocent lives are being protected. Killing could also be justified in defending one's family from attack, not using excessive force but the force necessary. What's more, abortion might be permissible when a mother's life is threatened by a pregnancy. If a choice must be made, we may decide in favor of the mother and accept the death of the child as a "foreseen but unwilled side effect." Moreover, some religious leaders claim that a doctor may withhold treatment from a dying patient as long as the person consents, is suffering from a painful, incurable disease, and death is imminent.

The point is that *agape* can conflict with moral rules, and then a difficult choice must be made. For instance, the pacifist takes the Bible literally and believes in noninjury, but church leaders, out of love for humanity, will bless warships and tanks. In the same way, we know we should be honest, but we hide a disturbing truth from someone with a bad heart, just as we tell white lies to protect someone's feelings. In *Les Misérables*, we sympathize with Jean Valjean for stealing a loaf of bread for his sister's family, just as we might forgive Robin Hood for stealing from the rich to give to the poor. Within the Christian system, we are not sure whether love or rules are paramount, especially since love can be used to rationalize violence.

Aside from specific problems with Jewish or Christian ethics, philosophers have an overall criticism about trying to derive moral values from religion.

This criticism can be traced back to ancient Greece, specifically the writings of Plato. In his dialogue the *Euthyphro*, a discussion takes place over the relationship between ethics and religion. Socrates, who is the chief spokesman in most of Plato's dialogues, meets a young man named Euthyphro in the anteroom of a court. Socrates is there to defend himself against a variety of charges, mainly that he is impious and has corrupted the youth. Euthyphro, on the other hand, is there to bring charges against his own father for being impious—which implies strong knowledge of the nature of piety. Socrates therefore questions him, ostensibly to gather ammunition for his own defense.

At first Euthyphro defines piety as that which the gods love and impiety as whatever they hate. But Socrates points out that the gods do not always agree. What is pleasing to Zeus may be disagreeable to Cronus or Uranus, and what Hephaestus likes, Hera may dislike. But after this initial sparring, Socrates then poses the key question: Is the pious or holy "beloved of the gods because it is holy, or holy because it is beloved of the gods?"

Socrates: [Is it] because it is pious or holy, or for some other reason?

Euthyphro: No, that is the reason.

Socrates: It is loved because it is holy, not holy because it is loved?

Euthyphro: Yes . . .

Socrates: Thus you appear to me, Euthyphro, when I ask you what is the essence of holiness, to offer an attribute only, and not the essence—the attribute of being loved by all the gods. But you still refuse to explain to me the nature of holiness.

In other words, the gods must love piety for some reason. There must be something in the nature of piety that makes it worthy of being loved; it is not worthwhile because the gods love it.

To update the example, an action is willed by God because it is right, rather than being right because it is willed by God. We should love our neighbor because that is the correct thing to do, and therefore it was commanded by God. He does not act arbitrarily, inventing moral rules, but he recognizes what is right in itself. In other words, even God cannot make the right wrong or the wrong right, pulling morality inside out, like a glove. He must acknowledge the independent value of certain actions and command them on those grounds.

For this reason we cannot claim that morality is derived from religion or rely on the authority of God in the Bible. Dostoyevsky wrote, "If God is dead, everything is permissible," but ethics does not depend on religion, so even if religion declined, we could still have ethical principles. As the philosopher P. Nowell-Smith remarked, "We must judge for ourselves whether the Bible is the inspired word of a just and benevolent God or a curious amalgam of profound wisdom and gross superstition. To judge this is to make a moral decision, so that in the end, so far from morality being based on religion, religion is based on morality." Even Mother Theresa expressed doubts about her faith, but she led a life of dedication to humanity, perhaps as a secular saint.

One principle most of the world supports is the Golden Rule, which is found in every religion and which can be endorsed on its own merits. Judaism has a negative version, sometimes called the "silver rule," Christianity a positive one. The Hebrew Talmud states, "What is harmful to you, do not to your fellow men," and Matthew says, "Therefore all things whatsoever ye would that men should do to you, do ye even so to them" (Matt. 7:12). This sentiment is voiced by a number of religions. In Islam, "No one of you is a believer until he desires for his brother that which he desires for himself." In Hinduism, "This is the turn of duty; do naught unto others which could cause you pain if done to you." In Buddhism, "Hurt not others in ways you yourself would find hurtful."

The cynical view, of course, is that we should not do unto others as we would have them do unto us because they may not have the same tastes; a masochist, for example, who enjoys receiving pain, should refrain from following the Golden Rule. Similarly, a shopkeeper should not give his goods away because he would appreciate that as a customer, and a jailer should not let a prisoner escape because he would want that himself if the situation were reversed. Nevertheless, human beings are reasonably consistent in what they find good.

Although ethics may not be derived from religion, it can certainly be motivated by religious impulses; in fact, there may not be any greater incentive. This can be beneficial or harmful, depending on the ethical code. Some writers identify religion as spiritually charged ethics. As Matthew Arnold wrote, "Religion is ethics heightened, enkindled, lit up by feeling." Nevertheless, ethics seems autonomous and distinct from religion, and its principles must be independently grounded.

CHRISTIANITY AND CAPITALISM: UNEASY BEDFELLOWS

Christianity has always had an awkward relationship with wealth. The gospel of Matthew says, "Do not store up for yourselves treasures on earth, where moth and rust consume and where thieves break in and steal; but store up for yourselves treasures in heaven, where neither moth nor rust consumes and where thieves do not break in and steal. For where your treasure is, there will your heart be also" (Matt. 6:19). Or again in Matthew, "No one can serve two masters, for a slave will either hate the one and love the other, or be devoted to the one and despise the other. You cannot serve God and wealth" (Matt. 6:34). And St. Thomas Aquinas thought we should not amass wealth but aim at subsistence only. Charging interest on loans was particularly odious; any interest is usury, "a sin against charity." We should not take advantage of someone's misfortune.

Is being wealthy a disqualification for being a Christian? The Bible does say that a rich man can no more get into heaven than a camel pass through the eye of a needle. Capitalism, which aims at maximizing profits, fostering a consumer culture, and the acquisition of material goods, has wrestled with this issue, especially the inequalities in the distribution of wealth. It is an open question whether capitalism is consistent with Christianity or antagonistic to it.

Communists, of course, charge that Christianity and capitalism are incompatible. Within capitalism, the poor are not blessed and the rich are generally admired; they have the highest social status. Marxists claim that distributing wealth equitably is more consistent with Christ's teachings than the inequalities we see today. In 2005, for example, 1 percent of the population held 21.2 percent of the national income, and the earnings of corporate executives was 55 times greater than the industrial worker; 85 people in the world had more wealth than 450 billion people. For some to have a vast fortune and others to be malnourished and die of starvation does not show a loving attitude toward humanity. To the communist, a government that honors Christian values should level wealth, flatten the pyramid, so that no one has any more than anyone else. Should we limit economic freedom for the sake of social equality?

Two twentieth-century social scientists have contributed most significantly to this discussion: the German Max Weber, whose classic work is *The Protestant Ethic and the Spirit of Capitalism*, and the Englishman R. H. Tawney, who is known for *Religion and the Rise of Capitalism*. In their analyses they reach similar conclusions, but they differ in their judgment as to whether Christianity has been beneficial or harmful to society.

Weber coined the phrase "the Protestant work ethic," which encapsulates his perspective. He claimed that Christianity, in general, and Calvinism, in particular, advanced capitalism by making worldly success a sign of religiosity. "To wish to be poor was the same as wishing to be unhealthy," he said. People who are hard-working and prosperous are exhibiting holy virtues. We should all be disciplined, thrifty, efficient, and rational. In some religions, such as Hinduism and Confucianism, the faithful are innerworldly, striving to escape life through asceticism and mystical experience. But except for monasticism, Christianity is a worldly religion. Its adherents demonstrate their faith by pursuing profit in the marketplace through industry and moneymaking. Consumption is a sin of pride, as is indulgence in pleasure, but business enterprise is a blessed activity, "the performance of a duty in a calling." Therefore, the rich man can get into heaven as long as he isn't a materialist.

The Calvinists, specifically, held a doctrine known as "double predestination" whereby God decides in advance who will be saved and who will be damned. They maintained this belief because it awarded maximum power to God. People could not earn salvation by their own efforts but only through divine grace, otherwise God would be superfluous and the system mechanical. But, Weber claimed, even though the issue was already decided, people became wealthy as a sign that they had been favored by God and were among the elect. This was the reason for success in business, and it became the motivation behind America's financial growth.

Religion and capitalism went hand in hand, reinforcing each other to build both the churches and the economy. To Marx, the material conditions produce the social forms, that is, capitalism created the version of Christianity that it needed. To Weber, religion is a powerful, independent force that shaped the capitalist institutions.

Tawney is critical of the effects of Christianity while admitting its power, paying it a left-handed compliment. To Tawney, religion reflected the structure of social privilege, and the Church of England was "a class institution making respectful salaams to property and gentility." He though the Protestant Reformation created an unhealthy division between business and morality, nurturing "an idolatry of money and success" instead of working toward a just society. In the Middle Ages, making a profit was something shameful, but in Protestant teachings, creating wealth and owning property were equated with the will of God. Accumulating capital was considered honorable, if not sanctified. Profit, in fact, was evidence of a pious character, and it should be reinvested in the capitalist system. In Calvinism, of course, riches showed God's blessings and displayed proof of a successful existence.

Tawney thought that socialism expressed the true spirit of Christianity, free from acquisitiveness. Capitalism corrupted people, encouraging a selfish individualism rather than an egalitarian brotherhood. It deprived work of its intrinsic value, rendering it a means for material gain. We needed to promote a different attitude toward labor, restoring the pride of the worker in his product. Above all, we needed to renew the connection among religion, morality, and the economy by instituting a Christian socialism. To Tawney, the alliance between Christianity and capitalism is a devil's bargain. No compromise is possible between "the Church of Christ and the idolatry of wealth, which is the practical religion of capitalist societies."

Where does the truth lie? In *The Wealth of Nations* the chief theorist of capitalism, Adam Smith, wrote there is "an invisible hand" that guides the marketplace: As each person pursues his own welfare, the whole will be enriched. Today we question this wisdom. Companies pollute because it is cheaper than protecting the environment; people buy SUVs even though they contribute to global warming; greed in the financial markets is largely to blame for the Great Depression and the Great Recession. That is, everyone is not necessarily better off if each person seeks his own advantage.

But that consideration aside, is the pursuit of financial gain and the acquisition of wealth compatible with Christianity? One of the paradoxes of our nation is that we preach self-sacrifice in our family relationships and self-interest in the business world. We have never resolved the tension between altruism and egoism. Can religion and economic gain be harmonized in a capitalist system, or is selfishness the best motivator? Do we have to pay the devil his due?

Ironically, Republicans, who have co-opted religion as part of their platform, are most in favor of the free market, which operates without the influence of religion. They want a laissez-faire economic system, despite the resulting inequality in wealth, favor development over environmental protection, and support a large military budget rather than returning good for evil. Is Christianity irrelevant in our practical affairs, a sentimental piety reserved for Sunday worship?

SEPARATING CHURCH AND STATE, RELIGION AND POLITICS

Separating church and state is embedded in our American tradition and enshrined in the Constitution. This principle is usually ascribed to the seventeenth-century English philosopher John Locke, who maintained that religion falls within the purview of private conscience, and such privacy must be protected from governmental authority.

But the person most closely associated with the doctrine is Thomas Jefferson, who articulated it in a letter to a Baptist congregation. Jefferson referred to a "wall of separation" between religion and the government because "religion is a matter which lies solely between Man and his God." He cited Martin Luther's notion that the two kingdoms are fundamentally different. James Madison, the principal author of the Bill of Rights, also wrote in favor of a "total separation of the church from the state," that "a practical distinction between Religion and Civil Government is essential to the purity of both; it is guaranteed by the Constitution of the United States." He is referring to the First Amendment: "Congress shall make no law respecting an establishment of religion, or prohibiting the free exercise thereof." It is usually called "the establishment clause," and it guarantees freedom of religion, just as the Constitution asserts freedom of speech, of assembly, and of the press. Citizens should be free to practice their individual religion or not to practice any religion. (Interestingly enough, the Constitution is silent on God.) The U.S. Supreme Court has referenced the separation doctrine more than twenty-five times but has not defended it unanimously.

In establishing the separation of church and state, the founders may have been reacting to the European power struggles that surrounded this issue, especially the battle between Henry VIII and the pope over the power of the nation-state vis-á-vis ecclesiastical authority. The pope was God's vicar on earth but the counterdoctrine was "the divine right of kings."

Despite America's principle of the separation of the two institutions, religion does appear in parts of our government. "So help me God" is included in the presidential oath of office, and "In God we trust" is stamped on our coins. Congress has salaried chaplains and offers prayers at the opening sessions—as one wit put it, an ecclesiastical garnish on a secular salad. In court we swear to tell the truth "so help me God," and the phrase "under God" was added to the Pledge of Allegiance in 1954. Various religious symbols, such as the Ten Commandments, have appeared on public buildings, and Christmas trees are regularly erected in civic centers. The wall between church and state seems to be porous, perhaps because we have not separated religion and politics.

The issue surfaces, for example, in debates over prayer in public schools. Liberals argue that, by law and tradition, prayer belongs in church or at home but not in a public institution. Furthermore, since the state mandates school attendance, school prayer puts pressure on atheists to worship God. Conservatives, on the other hand, see the rejection of school prayer as denying them the right to exercise their religious freedom. They also regard it as an erosion of fundamental American values because religion has been part of our nation since its founding.

So far the legal decisions have been against school prayer. The dominant argument has been that we should not use a public institution for religious purposes; we cannot trespass the boundaries. Also, the right to practice one's religion is not being denied, since that right can be exercised at home and elsewhere.

Should those who want prayer in schools use political action to influence the Supreme Court?

Another recent issue concerning politics and religion is gay marriage, which has been approved in some states, explicitly prohibited in many others. As part of the "culture wars," religious conservatives insist that marriage is between a man and a woman, but religious liberals and the nonreligious want to extend marriage to same-sex couples. In the United States, a majority of the population are in favor of gay marriage, thirty-six states. Across the world, some nations are supportive of gay rights, others impose harsh penalties for homosexual acts. For example, gay marriage is legal in Canada, Spain, Holland, Belgium, Portugal, but illegal in Saudi Arabia, Korea, Egypt, India, and Argentina; in some countries, committing a homosexual act is a capital crime.

Homosexuality is clearly condemned in the Bible, and there is no mention of gay marriage. Leviticus says, "Thou shalt not lie with mankind as with womankind; it is an abomination" (Lev. 18:22), and there shall not be "man lying with a man as one lies with a woman" (Lev. 20:13). Romans refers to "men committing shameless acts with men," and Sodom and Gomorrah were destroyed because the people "gave themselves up to sexual immorality and perversion"; this is taken to mean homosexuality. But as we have seen, we do not accept everything in the Bible as divine truth. Rather, we select sound principles from scripture using our moral judgment, and that should be our reference point in evaluating homosexuality.

Should we conduct a political campaign for or against gay marriage based on our religious views?

Still another area of disagreement concerns euthanasia, which can be defined as inducing an easy death in cases of terminal illness involving extreme suffering when death is imminent. Religious conservatives view euthanasia as a type of suicide, perhaps assisted suicide, and that is prohibited to human beings. The Catholic Church (and the American Medical Association) is opposed to active euthanasia on the grounds that we should not decide when life ends. The liberal view is that we continually interfere with the gates of life and death. In medicine we preserve life where there would be death, in war we bring about death where there would be life. This is simply another case of interfering in nature for the sake of human welfare. This was the basis on which Oregon passed a "death with dignity" act, which was upheld by the Supreme Court in 2006.

A related question is whether we should eat meat. Vegetarians sometimes argue, "Heart attacks are God's revenge for eating his furry creatures," but the carnivores counter, "If God didn't want us to eat animals, he wouldn't have made them of meat." (Of course, the latter position is akin to saying, "If we were not meant to cut down trees, they would not have been made of lumber.")

Should issues of euthanasia or vegetarianism be decided on religious grounds?

Interestingly, institutional religion has largely supported our nation's wars, despite the doctrine of the brotherhood of man and returning good for evil. Prayer and sacrifice have mainly been directed toward military victory for our troops. Globally, of course, religious differences have been the cause of numerous wars, from the Muslim conquests to the Crusades, from the wars between Catholics and Protestants to the jihads of radical Muslims. "Religion has caused more misery to all of mankind in every stage of human history than any other single idea," Madalyn Murray O'Hair writes. Of course, wars were also fought by atheists, including communists and fascists, which shows that war has other causes, not that religion is not one of them.

Should our religious position be translated into political activism? Should we, perhaps, run for public office to make euthanasia illegal or to codify a right to death corresponding to a right to life?

One overall point of contention between liberals and conservatives is whether clerics should express their political views—whether a Catholic priest should condemn abortion from the pulpit, or whether a Baptist minister should preach in favor of capital punishment, like an imam calling for holy war. Likewise, we question whether government officials are at liberty to express their religious ideas. Although we demand that our political leaders be pious, we are not sure whether they should voice their faith as governmental officials.

If people have strong religious convictions that inform their views on social issues, don't they have the right, even the obligation, to express them? In fact, wouldn't it be odd if a person's religious beliefs were not a part of their public discourse?

In the United States, we have settled on a "doctrine of restraint," whereby we exclude the use of religious reasons to support public policy. The philosopher John Rawls has articulated this position: religious beliefs can motivate support of political positions but only when the basic reasons are public ones. Citizens are not justified in advancing a political agenda on the basis of private religious convictions. If the policy is demonstrated as good for the state and its citizens, then religion can be used as further support. In a religiously pluralistic society, we must respect the beliefs of our fellow citizens, and that means not using a particular religion as the basis for legislation. The philosopher Richard Rorty goes so far as to completely privatize religion, but the consensus today separates church and state and allows religion into politics, provided there is secular justification for public action.

This holds true for issues of environmental protection, nuclear weapons, new reproductive technologies, global warming, abortion, and so forth. In American political life, the doctrine of restraint should extend even to faith-based initiatives of the religious right. Both liberals and conservatives are required to present rational arguments for political positions. We want to avoid a theocracy where power is derived from religious authority rather than underlying moral principles.

13

IMMORTALITY: A DIVERSITY OF BELIEFS

THE CYCLE OF NATURE, AND AN ETERNITY OF INFLUENCE

In today's mental climate, when people consider immortality, they may think in terms of science and technology, breakthroughs in the laboratory. Since the biological sciences have dramatically increased our life span, why not expand it infinitely? If we could switch off the mechanisms of aging and death, and cure all diseases, then life would never have to come to an end. Of course, there would remain the threat of accidents, violent attacks, starvation, war, and suicide, but at least we could control the effects of sickness, disease, and physical degeneration. Aging is already managed to some extent through such procedures as transplants, pacemakers, and stem cells to replace damaged tissue in the heart, blood vessels, and other organs. And strictly speaking, no one ever dies of old age but of a specific cause, such as organ or system failure, and such causes are theoretically curable by medical treatment, pharmaceuticals, or surgery. Why couldn't human beings live forever?

People sometimes argue that we were not meant to be eternal. "Man is mortal" and has a fixed life span, perhaps "three score years and ten" (Ps. 90:10) or "a hundred and twenty years" (Gen. 6:3). There is an inevitability about death, it is assumed, one of the few constants. However, are there any necessities in nature? In logic, if all fish have gills, and tuna are fish, then necessarily tuna have gills. But in the physical world, can we even say the sun must appear tomorrow? There may not be anything unalterable about what has been a part of nature.

Some organisms are immortal in their natural state. For example, one species of jellyfish (*turnitopsis nutricula*) replenishes its cells continually, alternating between old and young forms, and water bears (also called tardigrades) appear to continue indefinitely. Hydras do not undergo aging, and bacteria are immortal as a colony. Perhaps we could incorporate their strategies and attain an equivalent immortal state.

Various books have appeared recently that purport to identify ways of living longer. We are advised to exercise daily, adding strength exercises, to eat a healthy diet with different colored vegetables and a minimum of meat, to cut down on calories and reduce food intake altogether; we should certainly avoid obesity and not smoke or drink too much. In addition, we should be optimistic, have a sense of purpose, and be surrounded by people who want us.

But extending life is not the same as living forever. One field of science that touches on the possibility of physical immortality is *cryobiology*—the study of how subfreezing temperatures affect biological systems. This research lies at the intersection of physics and biology. The cryobiologist investigates the way in which cells, tissues, organs, and whole organisms can survive in a frozen state and when reanimation is possible. We know the negative effects of extreme cold in hypothermia and frostbite, but subzero temperatures could also have positive value. The most intriguing question, of course, is whether mammals such as human beings can be frozen when they contract some lethal illness, then have the cadavers thawed when a cure is discovered.

Nature contains various examples of the freezing and thawing of biological organisms. A freezable frog can live for six weeks at temperatures down to 6°F below zero. Some insects can survive at 79°F below zero. Polar fish produce their own antifreeze proteins and maintain themselves at one degree below their freezing point. Some tree branches can survive at 30°F to 40°F below zero, undergoing a "vitrification" process, that is, turning into glass. Nematoid worms have been frozen and were reported to live in suspended animation for four years. Some mammals, such as bats and the Alaskan squirrel, are able to "supercool" their bodies below freezing and then restore their vital functions later. There is similar evidence regarding turtles, clams, and oysters in northern climates.

For some years now, science has duplicated the feats of nature, for we can now freeze and restore human skin, semen, eggs, and embryos, and this cryonic suspension is now a multimillion-dollar business. We are also able to freeze heart valves, blood vessels, and components of knees for transplant. The heart and kidneys have been frozen for a short period of time, as have dog intestines, spleen, and lungs. The negative effect of freezing can also have medical applications, as in cryosurgery, where it is used to eliminate unwanted cells, such as tumors.

These reports are promising, but they must be carefully screened and sifted for exaggerated claims. In some cases, the organisms are truly frozen, in others simply cooled; and sometimes there is only partial recovery with some residual injury.

But what about the prospects for freezing people at the point of death, then thawing their bodies so that they become animate once again? And could that process be repeated endlessly, creating in effect a biological immortality?

In terms of the present state of our technology, that seems highly unlikely. Some companies promise clients that they can be frozen and reanimated at a future point when cures are found for the illnesses that killed them, but there is little evidence that this could be done. Such companies have been accused of practicing pseudoscience, and some have been sued for fraud. According to cryobiologists, the process of freezing destroys tissues and causes disintegration, so restoring a large mammal to life may be impossible. Cadaver freezing and thawing does not seem scientifically feasible for reanimation, and for the present, at least, brain death appears irreversible.

Cloning is the other field of biology that deals with immortality—of a kind. Cloning involves removing the nucleus from an embryonic stem cell and substituting the nucleus of a donor cell, resulting in the development of a duplicate organism. Growth is stimulated by electricity and chemical baths, and after three to eleven days the inner cells are harvested for therapeutic cloning, or implanted in a woman's uterus for reproductive cloning. Technically, the process is called "somatic cell nuclear transfer."

Therapeutic cloning is the less controversial application, and it shows promise in treating cardiovascular disease, AIDS, cancer, Alzheimer's, spinal-cord injuries, and Lou Gehrig's disease, among others. It could also repair or grow body parts, such as ears, teeth, hair, skin, or even a new liver, heart, or limb. But reproductive cloning is more applicable to the issue of immortality; here an exact replica of a whole organism is produced. Thus far, clones have been created of fish, rabbits, pigs, cattle, mules, horses, deer, cats, dogs, monkeys, and, of course, Dolly the sheep, who was the first clone. Procreation occurs not through the union of sperm and egg but through the manipulation of body cells.

Success with cloning animals naturally raises the possibility of cloning people—creating a new human being with the same genetic identity as an existing one. Fire ants and honeybees clone themselves naturally, and twins are natural clones, so why not create an identical copy of ourselves through artificial means? Clones are, in fact, identical twins born at different times.

Cloning animals has extensive commercial possibilities. Prize cattle or sheep can be bred much faster, and champion dogs or racehorses could be reproduced with the same genetic makeup. Species threatened with extinction could be saved, such as the African elephant, giant panda, white rhinoceros, and the mountain gorilla. If a child's puppy or kitten dies, the pet could be restored to them, identical to the original. More significantly, a couple that loses a child could have an exact copy made.

At present, human cloning is prohibited worldwide; the risks of genetic abnormalities or a reduced life span are simply too great (Dolly died young). The main objections, however, are religious ones. The Vatican calls cloning "a crime against humanity" because it is asexual reproduction, divorced from lovemaking; a cloned baby may not even have a soul. For the same reason, the Catholic Church condemns in vitro fertilization and the implantation of embryos. Reproductive cloning is also criticized as reducing the sanctity and dignity of human life and making it difficult to establish separate human identities; it might only reflect the narcissism of the parents, who want to duplicate themselves. On the other hand, infertile couples, who cannot have a baby by any other method, could use cloning as an alternative method of reproduction, and single people and same-sex couples could do the same. Feminists see the issue as ensuring the reproductive rights of individuals. If the technology becomes safe, why shouldn't people be allowed to have children any way they choose, including cloning?

In terms of immortality, cloning is not a perpetuation of the person. Although the same biological material is formed, the individual is not the same. People are more than their bodies, in fact, our identity seems a matter of our character, memory, personality, disposition, outlook, and, in short, the immaterial factors. Personhood begins where DNA leaves off. A frog may be duplicated, but a person is more complex, and it is the difference that makes the difference. Robert Frost once defined poetry as "what gets lost in translation"; in the same way, people cannot live on through a series of clones who are essentially other people.

Related to cloning is the creation of *cyborgs*, short for "cybernetic organisms," a mixture of the human and the mechanical. In collaboration with bioengineers, medical researchers have introduced a variety of artificial parts into our bodies, mainly to improve our health and physical functioning. The resultant cyborg is part natural and part synthetic, both organic and inorganic. Bones are combined with steel, flesh, and blood with wires and circuits, so that the person is partially transformed into a machine.

We already accept the notion of cyborgs when we introduce pacemakers or hearing aids, use teeth implants or contact lenses, insert plastic joints in our fingers, elbows, or knees, have disks inserted in our spinal columns, and attach prosthetic devices, such as artificial arms or legs. In a larger sense, clothing makes us cyborgs, protecting us against the weather with artificial skin, and we have a technological outer layer of cars, trains, and submarines, planes, and rockets to give us speed and mobility.

Basically, cyborg engineers insert artificial parts into our bodies to repair something that has malfunctioned or to make it function better than the natural part; the aim is the improvement of human life. But could it be a way to live forever? When an essential organ becomes defective and death could occur, why not substitute an artificial component?

That prospect generates anxiety, and hope. As we exchange more and more of our physical body for synthetic materials, the fear is that the human being could disappear altogether. This may not be a way of achieving immortality but a replacement of our humanness. And if our brain were replaced by a miniaturized computer, that might mean the person himself would be different. It might not even be the same individual.

One type of natural immortality that is open to us is a *cyclical* one in which our body dies, is buried, fertilizes the soil, which then grows various types of vegetation. The plants feed animals, and humans then consume both plants and animals, and breathe the oxygen plants produce. We recycle ourselves. There is also the immortality described by physics. According to the law of conservation, energy is neither created nor destroyed, so at death our energy is transmuted to another form but is never lost. It is like light or sound that never disappears but only becomes impossible to perceive. From such perspectives, we are eternally a part of nature.

However, this type of eternal life is not very reassuring. It is nowhere near as satisfying as living forever as ourselves, as conscious, continuous beings. In fact, none of the forms of physical immortality seem reassuring. Cryobiology is not promising for eternal life, and cloning does not reproduce the same person, only a genetic copy. By becoming cyborgs we may surrender our human and personal identity altogether, and being part of the life cycle does not offer much comfort.

Another naturalistic version is an *immortality of influence* where we live forever through the people we affect. Not everyone grows old, just as not everyone dies; some will vanish without a trace, others live on through those they inspire. The essential character of the person can survive, reverberating into the future. Their lives stop but do not end. For this kind of immortality we do not have to change the world, but if we leave our mark and are remembered, then our lives continue after death. Physical existence is certainly fleeting, but we can perpetuate ourselves by our impact on other people. "If something comes to life in others because of you," Norman Cousins writes, "then you have made an approach to immortality."

Teachers sometimes take comfort in this thought. They stay in place and their students move on, but they hope they have made a difference. Sometimes artists will create their work not so much to express themselves as to communicate their vision to those around them and to those still unborn. The spatial arts of painting, sculpture, and architecture can create lasting monuments, and the temporal arts of music, dance, and drama are more ephemeral but still leave an impression. Statesmen hope to affect the course of history and hope their legacy will be an improvement in the human condition. Mothers and fathers try to raise their children so they will thrive, and the parents then live on vicariously, shaping the next generation and extending themselves into the future. They are like stones thrown in a pond; the ripples spread outwards and never end, even though they may no longer be visible.

The "butterfly effect" in chaos theory expresses this idea—the view that the flutter of a butterfly's wing in China can ultimately cause a hurricane in the Caribbean. Everything is connected through the web of space and time. This includes our effect on the lives of others. The poet John Donne expressed our interconnectedness in these famous lines:

> No man is an island, entire of itself; every man is a piece of the continent, a part of the main; if a clod be washed away by the sea, Europe is the less, as well as if a promontory were, as well as if a manor of thy friends or of thine own were; any man's death diminishes me, because I am involved in mankind; and therefore never send to know for whom the bell tolls; it tolls for thee.

Such reflections do provide consolation, but for most people their influence will not extend very far, and being remembered is a poor substitute for self-remembering. We want to remain ourselves and be aware of ourselves for all eternity.

Another form of immortality is termed *timeless instants*, where events appear to be frozen and time seems to stands still. Mathematicians report such moments when they understand objective relations between numbers, a universal and eternal mathematics. In the aesthetic experience of listening to music, reading literature, or viewing a painting, we can feel transported beyond our temporal lives. The experience of love can have the same effect, as can religious ecstasy. Tolstoy reports that living in God is eternity; it is not a reward for virtuous living.

But again, most people want more than an immortality of influence or timeless instants of existence. They want life after death in a conscious state, to live on as sentient, whole beings.

The prospect of our own death is unimaginable. As the philosopher C. D. Broad wrote, "It is easy enough to think of someone else as having really ceased to exist, but it is almost impossible to give more than a cold intellectual assent to the same proposition about oneself."

WESTERN HEAVEN AND EASTERN REINCARNATION

Religion sees immortality in spiritual not physical terms. Each of the various world religions has a different concept of life after death, but in nearly all of them it is a central article of faith.

"Everyone would, if he could, live forever," Miguel de Unamuno said, "the desire for immortality is inseparable from the desire for God." And Plutarch writes, "The hope of eternity and the yearning for life is the oldest, as it is the greatest, of human desires." Dostoyevsky agreed, writing that in religion we long for eternal life even more than we seek God.

According to the *Hindu* religion our souls undergo a series of reincarnations, inhabiting new bodies at the moment of death. Everyone is born into a caste or fixed social class, and the level at which we are reborn is determined by the moral quality of our previous lives. This mechanical, principled system is called the "law of karma." In Hinduism, those who have had the best thoughts, words, and deeds "enter a pleasant womb," that of a Brahmin priest or a Kshatriya nobleman; those with mediocre to poor past lives become shopkeepers or craftsmen, called Vaisyas, or laborers, called Sudras; but those whose conduct was despicable "enter the womb of a dog, or the womb of a swine, or the womb of an outcast"; they are the ones with bad karma.

This series of lives, in different castes and forms, is not viewed by the Hindus as something hopeful; rather, they feel themselves chained to the wheel of rebirth (*samsara*) and seek ways to escape from it. They want deliverance from this vale of tears, from illusion and endless repetition, the perpetual becoming that never resolves itself into being. If they could be reborn as a Brahmin, they would be in a position to merge with the All at death, to lose their separateness and identity and become one with everything. They would enter *Nirvana*, a condition of ecstasy in which they are aware of being absorbed into *Brahma*, the world soul. The spark would then join the universal fire, the drop dissolve in the ocean of being. The self, which is an illusion, is extinguished.

Buddhists, on the other hand, while retaining the idea of reincarnation and the hope of freedom from rebirth, reject the idea of caste. They believe that anyone can achieve salvation provided they are willing to seek enlightenment as monks, to follow the Four Noble Truths and the Eightfold Path.

The first noble truth is that of Suffering: "Birth is suffering, decay is suffering, illness is suffering, death is suffering . . . clinging to existence is suffering." This means that sorrow, or *dukkha*, pervades all of life—hunger and disease, the collapse of the body as it ages, and the pain that accompanies death. Even if one is not tormented by these inherent evils, the times will bring upheavals, turmoil, and destruction.

Second, is the noble truth of the Cause of Suffering: "Thirst that leads to rebirth . . . thirst for pleasure, thirst for existence, thirst for prosperity." That is, the sorrow we experience springs from our desires. We yearn for material comfort, goods, and property, the satisfaction of our physical appetites, and for intellectual, aesthetic, and spiritual satisfactions. Each of these proves disappointing, so we exist in a state of disappointment, not having what we want and not wanting what we have. Even when we achieve satisfaction our pleasure is short-lived, for our experience is always transitory (*anicca*). Life is characterized as a ceaseless process of change, an endless mutability with no rest in actual being. Time itself is an evil, and our richest enjoyments are tainted by the realization that this too shall pass away. The skull always grins in at the banquet, ruining the feast.

Third, is the noble truth of the Cessation of Suffering: "the complete cessation of this thirst—a cessation which consists in the absence of every passion . . . with the destruction of desire." In other words, sorrow can cease if we eliminate our cravings (*tanha*) and no longer seek to satisfy our wants. This requires a deep knowledge of ourselves so that we can control and then extinguish the yearnings that lie within.

The fourth noble truth is the holy Eightfold Path of right behavior that leads to the end of suffering: "Right Belief, Right Aspiration, Right Speech, Right Conduct, Right Means of Livelihood, Right Endeavor, Right Mindfulness, Right Meditation."

For example, right belief pertains to a genuine understanding of the world and ourselves, especially as elucidated in the Four Noble Truths. Right aspiration means we should strive to conduct ourselves properly, to avoid sensuality and refrain from harming any living thing, and right speech refers to clear thinking and expression, not harboring ill-will or saying hurtful things to people. If our belief, aspiration, and speech are correct, then right conduct automatically follows.

Finally, if we follow each of these steps on the path, right rapture is achieved in which we are delivered from earthly sorrow. We slip into a trance close to that of a saint (*arahat*), and attain the ecstasy of Nirvana. All greed, hatred, and ignorance are erased, and we are enlightened as was Gautama, the Buddha. The process of striving ceases at enlightenment (*bodhi*), at which point we become deathless (*amata*).

One important qualification, however, is that we must become monks to attain salvation. In an informal way, that is what anyone becomes who approaches enlightenment. However, the monks as a group must commit themselves to an ascetic life. They have to wear a simple saffron robe and have no family or personal property. They must be celibate and beg for their food each day, leaving none for tomorrow. In short, they have to renounce all earthly desires, in return for which they earn salvation.

The Buddha did not believe that the soul inhabited a succession of bodies; in fact, he denies the reality of the soul altogether (the doctrine of *anatman*, or "no soul"). Rather he maintained that our character is reincarnated, continually producing fresh individualities until such time as we no longer seek existence. Between one life and another is a "going," or *gati*. To take some Buddhist analogies, it is not like the passing of a bird from nest to nest but rather like a poem going from a master to a student, or one candle being lit by another.

Judaism also rejects the concept of an everlasting soul initially, mainly because it does not appear anywhere in the Bible. Also, the Jewish religion does not contain an incarnate savior who has appeared on earth promising immortality. The soul is merely a breath connected to the life blood. When God withdraws his spirit, which unites body and soul, "it goes down to Sheol or Hades where it leads a shadowy existence, without life or real consciousness." Only God (*Yahweh*), the ruler of heaven and earth, was thought to have eternal life. On this view, the spark of the soul does not live on after the body perishes. Human beings are simply enjoined to lead a worthwhile life, without hope of a heavenly reward or fear of eternal damnation.

However, later developments in Judaism accepted a belief in the resurrection of the righteous dead with the coming of the Messiah. Those "in the bosom of Abraham" would be granted immortality, but the wicked dead would not be resurrected; they would remain in torment forever.

For *Christians*, the soul is vital, and resurrection is mentioned in the letters of St. Paul, but there are no references to immortality in the Gospels:

> Behold, I shew you a mystery; We shall not sleep, but we shall all be changed, in a moment, in the twinkling of an eye, at the last trump: for the trumpet shall sound, and the dead shall be raised incorruptible, and we shall be changed . . . O death, where is thy sting? O grave, where is thy victory? (1 Cor. 15: 51–52; 55)

At the Second Coming of Christ, every person will be judged "according to his deeds," and all those born again will live eternally in his presence, but sinners will be deprived of his glory forever. In Catholic teachings, there is also a realm called "purgatory," where souls in an incomplete state of grace are purified before going to heaven; "limbo" used to be where unbaptized infants reside (but this teaching came into question in 2007).

Life after death is thought to consist of either heaven or hell, paradise or perdition. Heaven is described as a spiritual realm where those who have accepted Jesus as the Christ will have fellowship with God: "He will wipe every tear from their eyes. There will be no more death or mourning or crying or pain . . . There will be no more night . . . for the Lord God will give them light" (Rev. 21:4; 22:5).

But unlike Islam, the Christian heaven is not sensuous; there is no suggestion of wine or sex, and all vestiges of hunger and thirst are absent. It is described as a spiritual place of eternal worship, praise, and adoration, and a wholly fulfilling relationship with God. There is peace, blessings, honor, and glory, and the saved will contemplate the face of the Lord for all eternity.

Hell is described more graphically, especially in Matthew. In most Christian versions, hell contains intense heat, sulfur, and serpents, demons with pitchforks; it is a cavern filled with fire yet strangely dark. The biblical passages read: "I am tormented by flame" (Luke 16:24); "But the fearful and unbelieving . . . shall have their part in the lake that burneth with fire and brimstone" (Rev. 21:18); "And [God] shall cast them into a furnace of fire" (Matt. 13:42); "And the smoke of their torment ascendeth up forever and ever: and they have no rest day or night" (Rev. 14:11). There are torments of the body and of the soul, burning floors, outer darkness, bondage, thirst, worms, and whips. A more liberal interpretation sees hell as a never-ending consciousness of one's sinfulness and, above all, eternal separation from God.

Dante's epic poem, *The Divine Comedy*, written in the fourteenth century, strongly influenced Christian conceptions of the afterlife for hundreds of years. Divided into three canticles of *Inferno* (Hell), *Purgatorio* (Purgatory), and *Paradiso* (Heaven), Dante describes the exact fate awaiting every type of earthly existence.

In *Inferno*, the first circle is reserved for the unbaptized, who are denied God's presence for eternity; the second, for those overcome with lust, who are now unable to touch anyone again; the fourth, for the greedy, forced to push giant rocks forever; and the sixth for the gluttonous, who are facedown in the mud, gnawed by Cerberus. *Inferno* is the best-known section of Dante's book, containing the inscription above the portal: *Lasciate ogni speranza, voi ch'entrate*, "Abandon all hope, ye who enter here."

In *Purgatorio* there are seven terraces for the seven deadly sins: the envious have their eyes sewn shut, the slothful run continuously, and the prideful carry heavy weights so they cannot stand. *Paradiso* has spheres for the contemplative, those who fought for Christianity, those who performed acts of goodness out of love, and so forth. Although Dante intended his poem as an allegory, his circles were taken as divine truth.

Islam has a similar notion of the end of time, when Allah will reveal himself fully and pronounce doom or blessings on everyone who has ever lived. In that day of reckoning, "When the sun shall be folded up, and the stars shall fall, and when the mountains shall be set in motion . . . and the seas shall boil . . . then shall every soul know what it hath done . . . Every man's actions have we hung round his neck, and on the last day shall be laid before him a wide-open Book" (Koran 81; 17:13).

Allah will reward the believers and the righteous but mete out foul punishment to the infidel and those who question the veracity of the Koran (34:3–5). After death, everyone will be resurrected, some going to hell (*Johannam*) for a period of purification before going on to paradise (*Jannat*); some will remain in perdition forever.

In Islam, the afterlife is depicted in vivid, physical terms: heaven has deep, cool rivers of crystal waters, succulent fruits, fertile fields, "rivers of wine," and beautiful mansions with seventy-two attending virgins of "perpetual freshness." Those in heaven will wear costly robes, bracelets, and perfumes, and eat from priceless vessels at exquisite banquets surrounded by gold and precious stones. "They will sit with bashful, dark-eyed virgins, as chaste as the sheltered eggs of ostriches" (Koran 37:40–48). "They shall recline on jeweled couches face to face, and there shall wait on them immortal youths with bowls and a cup of purest wine" (56:7–40). Hell, on the other hand, is a place of bubbling, molten metal, sulfurous liquids, and an all-consuming conflagration. "Garments of fire have been prepared for the unbelievers. Scalding water shall be poured upon their heads, melting their skins and that which is in their bodies. They shall be lashed with rods of iron" (22:19–22, 23). "The unbelievers shall endure forever the torments of hell. The punishment will never be lightened, and they shall be in speechless despair [forever]" (43:74).

Paradise for women is less clear, except that they will be reunited with their husbands and children. Hell is much the same, but populated by more women than men!

Both Hinduism and Buddhism have been criticized on a number of points of doctrine. For one thing, suffering may not characterize human life. To the Eastern mind, life is a trial filled with change, loss, and death, and to view it as enjoyable is an illusion (*maya*). Existence is basically an evil state, so in each new lifetime suffering is simply repeated. But in the West, continual suffering does not seem to characterize human existence, and we do not feel the need to escape through renunciation and austerities. Disease, aging, and death do add a melancholy note to life, but such suffering may not typify our time on earth. And if we reject the idea that living entails misery, we could also reject the idea that the extinction of desire is worthwhile. At least some of the time, desire is followed by satisfaction. Furthermore, although time destroys some pleasures, it brings fresh ones, and change can mean relief from pain. The fact that experience is fleeting can be an encouraging thought when life is difficult.

As for reincarnation, that is an unproven notion. At various times, Western psychologists or psychics claim to have returned people to their previous lives, but none of these cases have been verified under scientific conditions. There simply is not sufficient proof to accept reincarnation as a reality; most academics think this is delusional, but people in the East treat it as fundamental.

We could also question the notion of the unreality of the self. To doubt our own individuality as persons runs counter to our deepest feelings. If we ourselves are not real, it is hard to believe that anything else is. Finally, the goal of extinction does not seem particularly attractive as the end of life. At least in the West, we want life after death in a conscious state, and annihilation is not appealing. The thought that our self will vanish is not our highest dream but our worst nightmare.

As for Christian and Muslim ideas of heaven and hell, to a desert people coolness and intense heat would be natural images of heaven and hell, respectively. Perhaps God revealed these ideas in a form that would be understandable to them, or perhaps the ideas were invented by Christians and Muslims because of their experience of living in a hot climate. We tend to conceive of the afterlife in terms of our own ideal, as Rupert Brooke parodies in his poem "Heaven":

> Fish (fly-replete, in depth of June,
> Dawdling away their wat'ry noon)
> Ponder deep wisdom, dark or clear,
> Each fishy secret hope or fear . . .
> We darkly know, by Faith we cry.
> The future is not Wholly Dry.
> Mud unto mud!—Death eddies near—
> Not here the appointed End, not here!
> But somewhere, beyond Space and Time,
> Is wetter water, slimier slime! . . .
> Oh! Never fly conceals a hook.
> Fish say, in the Eternal Brook,
> But more than mundane weeds are there,
> And mud, celestially fair;
> Fat caterpillars drift around,
> And Paradisal grubs are found . . .
> And in that heaven of all their wish,
> There shall be no more land, say fish.

The main philosophic criticisms, however, have to do with the nature of heaven and hell. As developed in theology, hell shows God's justice, heaven shows his love, but those two aspects of God can be in conflict. In particular, the "no escape thesis" of hell has been questioned. Would a God of love condemn people to hell for all eternity?

By comparison with our earthly system, we do temper justice with mercy, giving criminals second and third chances, and there is usually

the possibility of parole. That is, we assign different degrees of punishment (as in Dante). Moreover, we grade offenses, asking whether the
offender broke the law intentionally, whether there was coercion, di-
minished responsibility, or mitigating circumstances. We ask the age of
the offender, and whether he was mentally ill, and in the most heinous
cases, we do not sentence criminals to a long and tortuous prison term
but condemn them to execution in a painless way.

But the overall question is whether a perfectly good God would
consign people to hell forever as punishment for their sins. This creates
a fundamental paradox, if not a contradiction: if God grants all souls
admission to paradise, even those that do not deserve it, then there is no
justice. On the other hand, if he does not forgive all sinners, even those
who do not repent, then he is not wholly loving.

This is the problem that plagued Dostoyevsky, as expressed in *The
Brothers Karamazov*. In the "Grand Inquisitor" section of the novel,
Ivan Karamazov describes the random suffering of children to his
brother Alyosha: a child torn to pieces by dogs, another locked in an
outhouse during an icy, Russian night. He recounts these horrible experiences of children because "in their case what I mean is so unanswer-
ably clear."

The conflict is that for God to exact justice by punishing the torturers of the innocent does not do those children any good, and to establish some "eternal harmony" by forgiving them is morally repugnant:

> Listen! If all must suffer to pay for the eternal harmony, what have
> children to do with it, tell me please? It's beyond all comprehension
> that they should suffer, and why they should pay for the harmony . . .
> I understand, of course, what an upheaval of the universe it will be,
> when everything in heaven and earth blends in one hymn of praise
> and everything that lives and has lived cries aloud: "Thou art just, O
> Lord, for Thy ways are revealed." When the mother embraces the
> fiend who threw her child to the dogs, and all three cry aloud with
> tears, "Thou art just, O Lord!" but I don't want to cry aloud then.
> While there is still time, I hasten to protect myself and so I renounce
> the higher harmony altogether. It's not worth the tears of that one
> tortured child who beats itself on the breast with its little fist and
> prays in its stinking outhouse, with its unexpiated tears to "Dear,
> kind God"! It's not worth it, because those tears are unatoned for.
> They must be atoned for, or there can be no harmony. But how?

How are you going to atone for them? Is it possible? By their being avenged? But what do I care for avenging them? What do I care for a hell for oppressors? What good can hell do, since those children have already been tortured? And what becomes of harmony if there is hell?

Through Ivan Karamazov, Dostoyevsky asserts that to be wholly just and wholly loving are incompatible, yet a perfect God must be both. This sets up a logical tension. A loving God cannot apply a system of justice, especially eternal torture to the torturers, yet if God grants forgiveness to all, then the universe does not operate fairly.

Dostoyevsky leaves us with this problem, which he himself never resolved. As for Ivan, he refuses to worship an impossible God—but he will not reject him.

IS THERE LIFE AFTER DEATH OR DEATH AFTER LIFE?

Our main focus throughout the book has been on the Western concept of God, so we will examine the arguments for life after death in terms of this tradition. One distinction should be made at the outset: some theories treat the soul as the immortal part of the person, which can separate itself from the body. The flesh is the prison house of the soul, and at death it escapes these mortal coils to live on eternally. The other view is more holistic and regards immortality as including both body and soul, a dualistic view. It asks what would a person be like without a body, and whether a disembodied existence is possible. We want to examine both forms of belief.

Some thinkers have questioned the reality of the soul altogether, much less the soul as an enduring substance that survives bodily death. Behaviorists regard it as an illusion, and they define psychology not as the study of the mind or soul but of human behavior. Many philosophers, such as David Hume, reject the reality of the soul, and the Oxford philosopher Gilbert Ryle refers to mind as "the ghost in the machine." He sees it as a mythical entity that we postulate as the cause of action. We need a subject for our sentence, as when we say, "It is raining" or "It is 6 o'clock," and we are misled by the grammar into personifying rain or time. In the same way, we imagine a "homunculus" deep inside us that initiates our behavior.

Perhaps the soul is just a name for a series of mental events tied together by succession and memory. This is the "bundle theory" of the mind or soul that claims it is nothing more than a sequence of mental experiences occurring one after the other, such as seeing a flock of birds or remembering an embarrassing moment. There is no thread of continuity, no entity experiencing these moments—only beads without a chain. Of course, if the mind is nothing other than a series of mental events, we do have to account for how it can be aware of itself as a series, that is, how self-consciousness is possible.

For convenience sake, we can divide the arguments for immortality into three types: *theistic*, *philosophic*, and *psychic*.

Most theologians claim that belief in life after death follows as a corollary to belief in God, and the soul is the part of us that lives on. It is essential to the Christian dogma, or doctrine of faith. If we accept the resurrection of Christ, and the Second Coming described in the New Testament, we must believe that God's creatures will also be resurrected and have eternal life.

For example, St. Thomas Aquinas maintained that the soul continues to exist after the destruction of the body, until the two are reunited in the general resurrection. The soul has an "inclination" for the body, and when the two are joined again there will be "complete and full activity," but the soul is not dependent on the body and does not perish with it.

One specific argument used by Aquinas is that only corporeal things can be "corrupted," and since the soul is immaterial it is immune from decay: "God made man's soul of such a powerful nature, that from its fullness of beatitude, there redounds to the body a fullness of health, with the vigor of incorruption."

One key problem for Aquinas was to show that the resurrected soul, united to a particular body, is the same soul as in the earlier person. It is the problem of personal identity that usually requires a specific body. But to Aquinas, the soul is able to will and to understand, which might be sufficient to establish individuality.

An interesting question is, what part of yourself would you regard as your identity? Your body changes in all respects as your cells grow, decay, and are replaced regularly. Your outlook on life can change, your disposition, your personality, in fact, all of your mental attitudes, nevertheless you believe you are the same person. But what of yourself remains constant through time, that golden thread surviving all change? Aquinas may not have answered this question.

The *philosophic* defense of immortality begins with Plato's dialogue, the *Phaedo*, where he presents a formal argument attempting to establish the truth of this proposition. The *Phaedo* defense is highly abstract and worth noting, but it will not persuade anyone who is not already convinced.

In Plato's system, there are two worlds: that of Ideas (forms or universals), and that of Sense (matter), which is the realm of the senses. For every class of things that are sensed, there is some Idea that corresponds to it. Horses exist in the world but there is also the idea of Horse; human beings exist but also Humanness, just as there are beautiful objects but also Beauty itself. Interestingly enough, Plato treats Ideas as the fundamental reality, and things in the world of Sense are assigned a lesser reality; they are not unreal, but they have the mode of being of shadows.

Plato considers Ideas as more real because, unlike objects, they are eternal and perfect. First, they do not come into existence, then fade away. Horses may one day become extinct, but the idea of Horse will continue on, the way that the idea of Dinosaur does. Second, the idea of Horse is of an ideal horse, so that we judge all physical horses against the perfect mental model, saying this one has poor conformation, a sway back, that one has a choppy trot.

We know these Ideas, Plato declares, because they are present within our soul from birth. The soul has traveled through every realm of being and absorbed all knowledge, so that when we are born we already know the fundamental Ideas. We never learn anything new in life; all knowledge is recollection—remembering the Ideas buried deep within our soul. In Plato's dialogue *Meno*, he tries to prove this by having Socrates elicit the Pythagorean theorem out of an uneducated slave boy. (In fact, the questions were responsible for educing the theorem rather than innate knowledge.)

According to Plato, the human soul never dies because it contains immortal Ideas. He asserts this partly on the grounds that everything that dies is a composite thing, and death is a scattering of parts. Mortal things break down, shred into pieces, are smashed and scattered, but the soul is simple and indivisible, and for that reason it is indestructible.

It is beyond our scope to evaluate Plato's overall system of thought, but we can question the specific argument for the immortality of the soul. Does death only mean a scattering of parts?

Although Immanuel Kant rejects Plato's argument for immortality, he does have one of his own—a practical argument that involves ethics. It is very close to his argument for the existence of God, previously described. Kant claims that we recognize an obligation to behave morally, in fact, to attain the *summum bonum*, or "supremely good state of affairs." This obligation only makes sense if we could attain what we are obliged to seek, which means that we and our souls live forever. He writes, "Pure practical reason postulates the immortality of the soul, for reason in the pure and practical sense aims at the summum bonum, and this perfect good is only possible on the supposition of the soul's immortality."

As a coda, Kant adds that "ought implies can," which means that whatever ought to be, can be. Moral conduct ought to be rewarded with happiness, therefore it can be, not in this life where the good are not always happy, but in a life to come. Only the assumption of a God can bring about that correlation and ensure endless life. This argument resembles the Eastern one pivoting around the notion of karma, which is, roughly, that of just reward. Right actions do not always lead to happiness in a person's lifetime, therefore there must be another life where people can receive their proper rewards.

Like the Plato's argument, Kant's reasoning seems strained and unpersuasive, a "schoolish" argument. The premises in particular can be questioned. We do not always seek the highest good, so we do not need additional time to achieve it. Ordinary moral obligations are nevertheless meaningful. And we are not convinced that everything that ought to be can be in fact. Some of our longings remain unfulfilled, including ethical ones, yet it makes sense to have longings, even if our reach exceeds our grasp. For example, it is rational to want peace on earth, but we are not sure it will ever be achieved.

The pragmatic philosophers, such as William James, also offer arguments for immortality, but they are not very strong. The pragmatists hold that whatever "works" is true. That is, if a belief satisfies our inquiry or leads to comfort, reassurance, or peace of mind, then it should be accepted. Belief in life after death certainly qualifies: it makes life worthwhile and is a spur to moral living, therefore it is true.

But a claim is not true because it would be beneficial for our lives, and we cannot trust that we will live forever because it would be comforting to think so.

Besides Plato, Kant, and James, several philosophers have proposed arguments for immortality, including Benedict Spinoza and René Descartes, but none are conspicuously successful. In recent years, in fact, philosophers have shied away from involvement with this topic.

Finally, there is a class of arguments from *psychic experience*. These are the reports of individuals, usually based on mediums who claim to communicate with the dead. Excluded from this category is Ouija boards, ghosts, haunting, possession, resuscitation, near-death, and out-of-body experiences, with reports of a radiant light at the end of a tunnel. (The last could be due to the expectation of that image, or brain cells starved of oxygen.) Communication with the dead seized the public imagination, especially in the nineteenth century, and more recently the evidence has been investigated by psychologists at Duke University and elsewhere, allegedly under scientific conditions.

In almost all reported cases, a medium establishes contact with a departed spirit in a supernatural realm. The "sitter" requests the séance, which is conducted by the medium, while the "control" transmits the messages from the "communicator," who is the dead person. Usually a mental transmission is reported, but sometimes an apparition appears of the face, hand, or body of the deceased. The participants sit around a table in a dimly lit room, and there are sudden raps or the table floats or rotates. Occasionally a "spirit trumpet" amplifies the spirit whisperings, or "spirit slates" are used that are tied face to face, and when they are opened they reveal messages from the spirit world. The medium enters a trancelike condition in which the control takes over the person's body, and messages are relayed or "channeled" to the sitter; the session ends when the medium is exhausted.

Many cases have been reported, and the following may be representative. An inventor named Edgar Vandy died under mysterious circumstances, and his two brothers, George and Harold, consulted several mediums in order to establish the cause of death. According to the coroner, Edgar had died of drowning in an outdoor pool. There were bruises under his chin and his tongue had been bitten through, and the explanation was that he had struck his chin on the diving board, lost consciousness, and died. The brothers knew, however, that Edgar could not dive and could hardly swim.

In the ensuing séances, the mediums did not know anything about the identity of the victim or the circumstances of his death. Furthermore, they were not told the victim's occupation, and a proxy sitter was used in one case as a precaution against contamination. Nevertheless, they produced a remarkably accurate account. The mediums reported that the victim had accidentally drowned, after receiving a severe blow on the head. "There was a diving board . . . and he remembers going under . . . He could not come up, as he apparently lost consciousness under the water . . . It is an open-air pool, and he says he must have fallen forward, and crashed in, and knocked his head." One medium was also asked about the victim's occupation, and she replied, "He shows me a room, and I don't know if it has to do with wireless or radio, but it is like machinery and machines going very rapidly."

Many such remarkable accounts have come out of these séances with details that presumably only the departed person could know. They exhibit uncanny similarities, and with hundreds of such reports gathered at various times and places, the spiritualists believe it is more than coincidence. The claim is that the evidence of psychic experience proves there is life after death.

Furthermore, many prominent figures attended séances and believed in spiritualism, for example, Franklin Roosevelt, Arthur Conan Doyle, Alexander Graham Bell, and Mary Todd Lincoln; her husband attended séances with her.

Nevertheless, in the nineteenth and early twentieth centuries, many of the practitioners were exposed as charlatans. Magicians such as John Neville Maskelyne and Harry Houdini proved the demonstrations to be stage magic, and various societies revealed their trickery and fraud.

More contemporary researchers, for example at the Society for Psychical Research, note that the conditions under which occult phenomena occur are not conducive to scientific investigation, especially the darkened rooms. The channeling can be faked, the data can be misinterpreted, there are insufficient controls or blinds, and the experiences can be hallucinatory, reflecting the wishes of those around the table. The mediums are also skilled at picking up auditory or visual feedback from the participants. A nonphysical explanation has also been suggested: that a high level of extrasensory perception might be operating. This last explanation requires proof, of course, but it does offer an alternative to the theory of communication with the dead. In short, psychics have not provided hard evidence for life after death.

There are also theoretical problems, mainly that the soul or mind seems to depend on the body for survival. A disembodied existence appears impossible. As Bertrand Russell writes, "All the evidence goes to show that what we regard as our mental life is bound up with brain structure and organized bodily energy. Therefore it is rational to suppose that mental life ceases when bodily life ceases." Christianity assumes that the soul and body will be rejoined in the general resurrection, but that leaves the soul without a body for some time. The question is how does it persist without being incarnate?

None of the arguments for eternal life have traction, which leaves immortality highly questionable.

Theologians have sometimes asserted that our existence would not be worth living unless there were life after death; we hunger for another life. Human beings need a story to live by and a meaningful climax to their lives, a purpose that is fulfilled by a transformation to a higher state. We do not die but "pass away," which connotes a passage or transition, not an end.

But it seems that life still could have meaning even if humans were mortal. We could live well in the time that we have, lead a full existence on earth, and enrich others by our presence. Even if it isn't all that we want, it might be enough to make life meaningful.

14

RELIGION TODAY—ITS MULTIPLE FORMS

THE LORD HAS MANY NAMES

In our present age we are much more aware of other cultures, including the variety of religious beliefs across the world. Increased communication through television, films, radio, books, and the Internet have educated us about different ways of being in the world and of viewing reality. In addition, peoples are more disbursed across the globe and less confined to their native countries. Indians now live in Britain, Asians in Africa, Arabs in Europe, Hispanics in North America. Our food, dress, music, language, entertainment, and art have been globalized, along with our religious understanding.

As a result, we are somewhat uneasy about the beliefs we inherited from our culture, more accepting of other faiths where the worshipers seem equally devout. Of course, the majority of people will follow the religion of the country in which they were raised: most Americans will be Christians, most Iraqis Muslims, and converts are statistically insignificant. However, an increasing number of people have begun to question their received faith. In the light of the diversity of religious beliefs, we are more accepting of differences, more respectful of other views of God.

One manifestation of this tolerance has been the movement of *religious pluralism* in which we are asked to regard all major religions as equally valid. There are many paths, but they all lead to the same place. Each religion expresses a different point of view, another perspective, some aspect or facet of the divine, but no doctrine is superior to any other; they are all significant channels to God. As the Bible states, "In my father's house are many mansions (rooms, dwelling places)" (John 14:2), and the Koran says, "Wherever ye turn, there is the face of God" (2:115). In the light of the diversity of religions, we should be flexible and open-minded toward all faiths.

Sometimes the pluralist will argue that the various faiths overlap so that a syncretism is possible. That is, a synthesis of the world's religions can take place because of the common factors. This is a belief in one universal religion. When we point out some food to a dog, he will look at our finger, but what is indicated remains the same.

On the other hand, some religious pluralists will slip into a theory of relativism, which claims that truth is not an objective matter at all but a function of each individual's or culture's perspective. What is thought true is a question of tastes, attitudes, likes and dislikes, a society's unique history, obstacles, and challenges. This includes a nation's religion, which is a "social construct" created by custom and consensus. All religions are legitimate and valid to their adherents, and none are objectively true. The hard-core relativist regards all knowledge as subjective and would issue encyclopedias in loose-leaf form.

In other words, genuine pluralists wonder, "Which are the best ways to truth?" but relativists claim that whatever a society believes is true to that society; knowledge is not discovered but invented, and there is no external point of reference against which beliefs can be measured.

Obviously, pluralism and relativism are different, but it is an easy step from "all positions deserve respect" to "no position is really right"; from "we can all coexist" to "each culture is right according to itself."

Relativism, of course, is self-defeating because its followers cannot claim it is actually true but only relatively true. It is rather like saying that all generalizations are false, which would include that generalization, or there's an exception to every rule, which means that rule also has an exception. The relativist cuts off the limb on which he sits. In the same way, solipsism, the position that the solipsist alone exists, cannot be preached because no one else is there.

Inclusivism is the view that one religion is foremost but other religions contain important truths and should not be dismissed. Within Christianity, the inclusivist will believe that Jesus is the Christ but that other faiths can also have insights into God. The Lord reveals himself in various and mysterious ways. One's own religion is thought to be the final truth, but other groups possess portions or degrees of truth; salvation is open to all.

On this view, even Buddhists or Muslims who have not heard of Christ can be saved by upright conduct, by living an exemplary life in the footsteps of Christ. The German theologian Karl Rahner refers to such people as "anonymous Christians" who unknowingly have earned salvation. (This is a bit patronizing since we would not refer to "anonymous Hindus" or "anonymous Muslims.")

Exclusivism is the conservative view that a single religion is correct and all others mistaken, that there is a right road leading to the one true God, and numerous wrong ones leading to false gods. In an oft-quoted biblical passage, Jesus says, "I am the way, the truth and the life, no one comes to the Father but through Me" (John 14:6). The Bible also says, "strait [is] the gate and narrow the way which leadeth unto life, and few there are that find it" (Matt. 7:14). Both passages are taken to support exclusivism.

Unlike the inclusivist, the exclusivist denies that other religions contain partial truths, or that those who follow different religions can be saved. Instead, he asserts that other faiths are mistaken. Only one religion will deliver us to heaven, and the rest are heresies, perhaps forms of Satanism, where people are misled by demons. Sometimes this view is referred to by the euphemism of "particularism," but it still claims a monopoly on truth.

To the conservative Christian, we can only reach heaven by accepting Jesus as the incarnate son of God or, more specifically, by following a particular denomination, such as the Methodist or Episcopal faiths; otherwise we will never attain the Kingdom of God. To the Muslim, the final truth is Islam, and they believe that Jews and Christians have distorted the religion of Abraham; a Muslim must believe that Muhammad is the messenger of Allah. To Jews, the Messiah is yet to come, but Christians believe he has come and will come again. Each religion tends to hold their doctrine as exclusively correct, believing their way is the correct way.

Briefly put, the pluralist believes all religions are equal manifestations of God; the inclusivist holds that one religion is superior but other faiths can contribute to our understanding of God; and the exclusivist maintains there is only one correct religion that leads us to God. In a sense these divisions reflect the present "culture wars" in America. The left wing wants flexibility and openness to all points of view in order to build consensus, but the right wing wants to preserve our traditional Christian faith, regarding it as truth itself.

The principal advocate of the exclusivist position today is Alvin Plantinga, a Protestant theologian. Plantinga argues that we need not consider other beliefs because they are not on "an equal epistemic footing." In other words, Christianity has a higher mode of knowing. He regards it as perfectly warranted to have convictions in religion, just as we do in political, moral, or philosophic matters. To use Plantinga's example, we know that it is unjust to order the death of your lover's spouse, and to think that is wrong is not imperial, egotistical, or oppressive; it is not an "intellectual sin." In the same way, we can condemn child labor, slavery, genocide, and human sacrifice with a clear conscience and believe in the Christian God.

But the philosopher John Hick offers the following critique of Plantinga's position:

> The basic criticism of both Christian and Muslim exclusivism is that it denies by implication that God, the sole creator of the world and of all humanity, is loving, gracious, and merciful, and that His love and mercy extend to all humankind. If God is the creator of the entire human race, is it credible that God would set up a system by which hundreds of millions of men, women and children, the majority of the human race, are destined through no fault of their own to eternal torment in hell? I say "through no fault of their own" because it cannot be anyone's fault that they were born where they were instead of within what exclusivism regards as the one limited area of salvation.

Hick not only opposes exclusivism but is one of the leading exponents of pluralism. Despite his specific religious commitment, he affirms a multiplicity of ways to salvation. He writes:

> Do the people of one faith, taken as a whole, behave either better or worse than the people of the other? Or are virtues and vices, saints and sinners, to be found, so far as we can tell, equally within both? I think the latter. And what has made me, as a Christian, come to accept the assumption of the unique superiority of my own Christian faith is that these observable fruits are not specially concentrated in

the Christian church but, on the contrary, are spread more or less
evenly around the world among the different cultures and religions.

He further contends that the diversity of religions is due to God's
manifold revelations, speaking to people through their own cultural
forms. Salvation appeals to Christians, just as escape from suffering
resonates with Buddhists. As St. Thomas Aquinas remarked, "Things
known are in the knower according to the mode of the knower," and
this mode has been fashioned by various historical and cultural circumstances. Hick writes, "The world religions are oriented toward the same
Ultimate Reality, which is however manifested within their different
thought-worlds and forms of experience in different ways."

Hick's view is persuasive, but if we judge the validity of religion by
the fruits of moral action, then humanistic atheism would also have to
be judged correct. We would have to include altruistic people who do
not follow any religion. What's more, how do we know that the different
religions, with their separate revelations, all indicate the same reality?
This is the central question. Overtly, at least, the creeds of various
religions and their denominations seem to be not only different but also
incompatible.

Although Christianity, Judaism, and Islam claim that God is a personal being, that doctrine is denied in Hinayana (Theravada) Buddhism
and in Hinduism. Judaism and Christianity believe that God created the
world, but Buddhism rejects a creator God. Christianity is centered
round the divinity of Jesus, but Muslims regard Jesus as one of several
prophets. In Christianity, the soul is thought to be the essence of the
person, but Buddhism denies the reality of the soul altogether. The
Hindu trinity consists of Brahma, Vishnu, and Shiva, which cannot be
equated with Father, Son, and Holy Spirit. In the Hindu religion, the
goal is the extinction of the self as a conscious entity, but the Christian
and Muslim hope for an immortality of awareness.

The major split within Christianity is between Catholics and Protestants, and there is a further division between Eastern and Western
churches; within Islam it is Shiite versus Sunni versions of the faith,
each regarding the other as infidels. In Buddhism, there is a dispute
over whether the Buddha is divine, a bodhisattva. In Judaism, the Old
Testament is sacred scripture; in Christianity, it is both the Old and
New Testament; in Hinduism, the Vedas and the Upanishads; in Bud-

dhism, the Tripitaka and Sutras; in Islam, the Koran. To Christians, our existence on earth is a testing ground for the life to come, but to Hindus our mortal life is an illusion, "a flash of lightning in a summer cloud, a flickering lamp . . . a phantom—and a dream."

Although there are many similar beliefs, such as the Golden Rule, there are also numerous, deep-seated conflicts, so it may not be possible to meld the world's religions together, to claim we all worship the same God in different ways. In order to reconcile the various religions, we would have to ignore significant differences, and people have shed their blood over those differences.

It would seem that the exclusivist would be the most intolerant ("imperialist"), and that is usually the case, but pluralists can be equally intolerant—a tyranny of the left. That is, the pluralists charge that those who claim there is only one right way are wrong, that they are presumptuous and arrogant. But the same charge can be leveled against pluralists because they think the exclusivist is absolutely wrong and that the only correct position is to treat all religions equally.

The liberalism of the pluralist approach also can lead to logical problems. For if every position is right, the exclusivist is right in rejecting pluralism. This is the point made in Plato's dialogue *Theatetus*. In refuting the position of Protagoras that "man is the measure of all things," Socrates says, "and the best of the joke is that he acknowledges the truth of their opinion who believes his own opinion to be false for he admits that the opinions of all men are true."

Perhaps the answer is to have confidence that there are truths but not to be so arrogant as to claim that *we* know absolutely what they are. Our commitment to a position must be provisional and qualified, not uncompromising. Nevertheless, to maintain that there are truths to be known gives direction to our search, and although we cannot achieve certainty, we can reach sound conclusions.

Pluralism is a tempting option today in order to foster understanding and cooperation between faiths; it requires acknowledgment that we could be mistaken in our beliefs. Such openness is morally and socially necessary if we are to be sympathetic to other religions and receptive to interfaith dialogue. The current world has been riven with sectarian conflict, principally between Islam and Christianity, where fundamentalists on both sides seem absolute in their convictions. Violent jihads may be a distortion of Islam, but they produce suicide bombers and terrorists who attack targets both within the Arab world and in the West. On the other side of the coin, the protection of Israel and the wars in the Muslim world are sometimes framed by evangelists as a holy crusade. For pragmatic reasons, pluralism might be the healthiest option for peaceful coexistence.

Can we be confident that there are absolute truths that will never change? For example, will 2 + 2 always equal 4, for all time, in all worlds? Is there a universal mathematics? Will the speed of light always remain constant at 186,281 miles per second, and never be exceeded? Will salt always be composed of NaCl, or if it changed, would we would no longer call it salt? The same question can be asked about religious absolutes. Such truths may exist, but we should take the path of humility and not assert that we know what those truths are.

GODDESSES: THE ROLE OF WOMEN

The feminist movement claims quite rightly that goddesses have always held a prominent place in religious history, especially in polytheism. Here divine beings are assigned gender, and both gods and goddesses appear in the pantheon. Goddesses are especially prominent in agricultural societies, where they are responsible for generating crops and increasing herds. Ancient female statues usually depict women as fertility figures, and these goddesses preside over growing grain, gathering food, raising domesticated animals, and act as patronesses of the hunt.

There are goddesses of the earth and of the sea, mother goddesses and love goddesses. Female deities are depicted as symbols of healer, witch, mother, crone, and nurturer, as having wisdom, sexual power, and the gift of prophesy. The goddesses are images of purity and submission, and are seen in the maiden, prostitute, virgin, and temptress. The succubus appears to men at night and seduces them in their sleep, as Eve beguiled Adam to sin. There is women's magic and mother earth magic, and female reproduction in itself is something magical. The moon in its cycle is female, and time is measured by the lunar, not the solar calendar, waxing, waning, and full.

Aphrodite is the Greek ideal of love, lust, and beauty; Artemis represents the hunt, the moon, and childbirth; Demeter agriculture; Athena wisdom and weaving; Nike is the goddess of victory; and Psyche is where love and the soul come together. Nemesis is the goddess of righteous anger, and Mother Earth is Gaia. Ceres is the Roman goddess of the crops; Hera of family and marriage; Fides is trust; Invidia envy; and Aeternitas the personification of eternity. Hathor is the Egyptian goddess of music, dance, joy, and motherhood; Isis represents marriage, love, and sexuality; and Neith, with her cobra, is the Egyptian goddess of war and weaving. Devi is the Hindu mother goddess, and Lakshmi the gentle goddess of prosperity. Hina in Hawaii rules the ocean; Pele surfs the lava of volcanoes. There is also Anat, Aradia, Astarte, Brighid, Diana, Freya, Ishtar, Juno, Kali, Minerva, Ostare, Persephone, Venus, and Vesta.

There are approximately 188 Greek goddesses, 145 Roman ones. In addition, in Greek mythology there are three female Fates: the spinner, the unbending, and the caster of lots (who controls the thread of life); three Graces of splendor, mirth, and good cheer; the Furies (*Moirae*), of revenge, jealousy, and unrest; and the nine Muses of the arts.

In the monotheistic religions, many women are named in scripture but none attain divine status. Eve, of course, occupies a central place as the first woman, and the Old Testament mentions numerous other women as prominent, including Ruth, Sarah, Rebecca, Miriam, Rachel, Hannah, Judith, Naomi, Bathsheba, Delilah, and Jezebel. Lilith is an interesting Hebrew goddess-associate. She is listed in the Bible, the Talmud, and in Kabbalah folklore as the first wife of Adam. Lilith is banished as a demon (Isaiah 34:14) and replaced by Eve, but in her jealous rage she becomes a serpent and tricks Eve into eating the forbidden fruit. Lilith is strongly associated with reason and rebirth, the shedding of skin, with the screech owl and night demons; overall, she is a malevolent and sexual predator. The Dead Sea Scrolls state, "[there were] destroying angels, spirits of the bastards, demons, Liliths, howlers and desert dwellers, who fall upon men . . . and lead them astray."

Within Christianity, the Virgin Mary is the most important female figure, declared "the mother of God," *theotokos*, by the Council of Ephesus in 431. The New Testament describes the Annunciation by the angel Gabriel, proclaiming that she had been selected to give birth to God, which she does through the agency of the Holy Spirit. Another Mary, a woman of Bethany, is considered a disciple of Christ; Lydia offered hospitality to the apostle Paul. Priscilla was St. Paul's "partner." In Christian Gnosticism, there is the figure of Sophia, a female virgin spirit. Phoebe served as a deacon or servant to the Church, but the importance of her role is disputed. Mary Magdalene has traditionally been seen as a repentant prostitute, who wiped Jesus' feet with her hair, but recent biblical scholarship has rehabilitated her; she is now treated as an important disciple, the first to see the resurrected Christ.

Of course, hundreds of women have been canonized by the Catholic Church, some because they performed especially pious deeds, some because they were martyrs, and others because they were mothers of important saints. For example, St. Barbara is symbolized by chains as the patroness of miners and the military, and St. Elizabeth is always shown with an apron full of roses; she had a child in old age. St. Ursula appears with an arrow—presumably the one that killed her—and St. Lucy holds a dish with two eyes; the legend is that Lucy plucked out her eyes when they were admired by a suitor.

In monotheism, however, only males have divine status. God is definitely male, referred to as "father," "he," and "him." Although Judaism and Islam claim the Lord is not gendered, and the Catholic catechism states, "God is neither man nor woman: he is God," male imagery predominates in the Bible and in the Koran. In Judaism, Yahweh is treated as male, as is God the father in Christianity, with a son Jesus; even the Holy Spirit is male (John 14:16). In addition, the twelve disciples are all males. Muslims, in referring to Allah, say we should submit to his will, which is typical of Western religion in general in that the high god is the male god.

As might be expected in patriarchal society, women in the Bible are assigned a subordinate role and often carry a negative image. For example, "Wives, submit to your husbands as to the Lord. For the husband is the head of the wife as Christ is the head of the church . . . Now as the church submits to Christ, so also wives should submit to their husbands in everything" (Eph. 5:21–4); "I find more bitter than death the woman, whose heart is snares and nets, and her hands as bands: whoso pleaseth God shall escape from her, but the sinner shall be taken by her" (Eccles. 7:26); "From garments cometh a moth and from a woman the iniquities of a man" (Eccles. 42:13); and "A man shall choose . . . any wickedness, but the wickedness of a woman. Sin began with a woman and thanks to her we all must die" (Eccles. 25:33).

Major theologians have echoed these sentiments. St. Thomas Aquinas said:

A woman is deficient and unintentionally caused. For the active power of the semen always seeks to produce a thing completely like itself, something male. So if a female is produced, this must be because the semen is weak or because the material [provided by the mother] is unsuitable, or because of the action of some external factor such as the winds from the south that make the atmosphere humid.

The Reformation theologian John Calvin wrote, "The true order of nature, which proceedeth from the command of God, bears that women shall be subject . . . she should be at hand to render obedience to him." Martin Luther said, "Women are on earth to bear children. If they die in child-bearing, it matters not; that is all they are here to do."

Many of the men in the Bible were polygamous, but women were not. Jacob, Arthur, and Elkanah had 2 wives; Lamech and Rehoboam, 3; Abyah, 14; Solomon, 700; and Gideon, David, Jehoram, Joash, Ahab, Jeholachin, and Belshazzar had "many wives." In addition, there were concubines for Abraham, Jacob, Eliphaz, Caleb, Gideon, Manassah, and Saul. David had 10 concubines, Rehoboam 60, and Solomon 300.

For the woman's part, she had to be faithful, and there were awful tests to prove she was innocent of adultery. If she was raped while still a virgin, she had to marry her attacker, and if she was captured by a soldier, he could force her into marriage. What's more, a father could sell his daughter as a slave. One brutal passage states that if a woman is not a virgin on her wedding day, she could be killed: "The men of the city shall stone her with stones that she die" (Deut. 22:13–22).

Male superiority is sometimes justified in terms of the second creation story in Genesis. Man was created first, then woman from his rib to be his helper, which gives him primacy (Gen. 2:18). Moreover, Adam names her, saying, "She shall be called 'woman' for she was taken out of man." To name someone or something in biblical times implies having authority over it.

The feminists argue, however, that the first story of creation describes men and women as being formed at the same time: "So God created humankind in his image, in the image of God he created them; male and female he created them." Why not rely on this account, which gives men and women equal status? In an early work of feminist theology, *The Woman's Bible*, Elizabeth Cady Stanton wrote, "The first account dignifies woman as an important factor in the creation, equal in power and glory with man . . . [this] must prove more satisfactory to both sexes: created alike in the image of God—the Heavenly Mother and Father."

Male domination and female denigration also stem from the Fall, where Eve is blamed for persuading Adam to eat the forbidden fruit. It is "the curse" placed on women, when sin and death entered human life: "I will greatly increase your pains in childbearing; with pain you will give birth to children. Your desire shall be for your husband, but bringing the young into life will entail suffering" (Gen. 3:16).

Some feminists argue that the coming of Christ set women free, that Christ released all humanity from the burden of sin, and men would no longer "rule over" women. The two sexes can resume the equal relationship they enjoyed in the Garden of Eden. But one Southern Baptist minister has said the notion of equality "has been belched out of hell." It was the Southern Baptists who vigorously opposed the Equal Rights Amendment in the United States, just as they strongly supported slavery prior to the Civil War.

In general, feminists want to reinterpret scripture from a female perspective. The seminal work for this orientation was *The Church and the Second Sex*, by Mary Daly, which argued that key words and phrases were mistranslated and should have been rendered differently. For example, in the passage that reads "the husband is the head of the wife," the Greek meaning of head is "source." That is, women have their source in man but that has nothing to do with subordination. Or the apostle Paul declares that "women should remain silent in the churches. They are not allowed to speak, but must be in submission" (1 Cor. 14:34–35). This is sometimes taken to mean that women should not be ordained as priests or ministers. But the word "speak" may refer only to idle chatter and not to preaching or teaching.

The feminists also reject those passages that subordinate women on the grounds that they merely reflect the culture of the times. To refer to women as wicked and sinful, temptresses and harlots cannot be the inspired word of God but rather the work of scribes who projected their own prejudice onto scripture. As one theologian put it, such views are "distortions by the human instrument." Men have been in positions of power from the very beginning, often with sexist attitudes, so it is not surprising that this should be reflected in biblical writings.

As mentioned, exegesis, or the critical interpretation of scripture, tries to separate the authentic from the inauthentic parts. The Bible may be infallible, but it was written by fallible people, which means there can be mistakes. "To err is human." So even if scripture is inerrant, we can never be sure that the writers or readers are correct in their interpretations. In fact, the Bible was composed and transmitted over several generations, much of it orally, and errors were bound to occur.

This is evident by the numerous inconsistencies in the biblical text. For example, Adam was to die when he ate the forbidden fruit (Gen. 2:17), but we are also told that he lived 930 years (Gen. 5:15). According to Matthew, Christ's sermon took place on the mount (Matt. 5:1), but Luke says it was on the plain (Luke 6:17). Simon carried Jesus' cross (Mark 15:21), but Jesus carried his own cross (John 9:17). Then, of course, there is the major disparity with regard to aggression in the Old and the New Testaments, the first saying, "An eye for an eye," the second saying, "Turn the other cheek."

To feminists, the incorrect parts of the scripture include the portrayal of women as subservient to men. This may have been the view during biblical times, but today we know better. We understand there are differences between the sexes, and although we accept a certain division of labor, we regard men and women as having equal worth. As a society, we try to avoid sexism, which is treating a woman as inferior by virtue of her being a member of the female sex.

Most of the negative images of women occur in the Hebrew Bible. The New Testament, by contrast, treats women with greater equality, especially the gospel of Luke. Here Jesus is particularly solicitous toward widows, and he permits women to sit at his feet along with men. For this reason evangelical feminists maintain that Christ preached a liberation doctrine, which was not always followed by Christianity. One feminist, Virginia Mollenkot, writes, "We heralded the feminist movement because we were convinced that the church had strayed from a correct understanding of God's will for women." And although St. Paul has some harsh judgments on women, he also writes, "There is neither Jew nor Greek, slave nor free, male nor female, for you are all one in Christ Jesus." This is taken as the heart of the Christian message.

In brief, the feminists argue that we should pay greater attention to goddesses in the history of religion, note the contributions of women throughout the Bible, recognize that scripture has been misinterpreted because of male bias, understand that the New Testament, in particular, does not treat women as inferior to men, and ensure that today's society does not use the Bible as an excuse for subordinating women or limiting their roles.

NEOPAGANISM AND THE NEW ATHEISM

Part of the new landscape in religion includes the phenomenon of *neopaganism*, which harks back to the nature religions of ancient cultures, including the Celtic, Norse, Greek, Sumerian, and Egyptian. The word "pagan" comes from the Latin *paganus*, which can be translated as "rustic," "country dweller," "from the fields," or even "uneducated" or "uncivilized." In antiquity, it became a pejorative term for gentile, or infidel, and was later to designate someone who was not a Jew, Christian, or Muslim; in short, someone who practiced idolatry and worshipped a false god. Today, paganism has a growing number of adherents—an estimated 307,000 in North America and 250,000 in Great Britain.

Neopaganism is actually an umbrella term for numerous nature-oriented religions that have recently emerged, especially Wicca and Druidry. Although it has divergent forms, neopaganism can be characterized as revering nature as a manifestation of a divine spirit, a living system that should be worshipped through magic, mythology, and ritualistic sacrifice. It sometimes extends to astrology, astral projections, New Age healing systems, ecofeminism, green politics, and a generalized environmentalism. In neopagan belief, all of life is considered sacred, and human beings are caretakers of the land; we must be diligent stewards, and protect and celebrate the planet. It rejects Christianity and all forms of monotheism, thinking of the earth alone as worthy of veneration. We are not fallen creatures, weighed down with sin, but vital, life-affirming beings connected to the earth.

But for the most part, neopagans are also polytheistic, believing in gods and goddesses, and pantheistic, or, more accurately, panentheistic since they often separate divine beings from nature. Some regard the plurality of gods as aspects of a single divinity, or life force, but among genuine polytheists there are distinct deities, and their natures vary enormously. The goddesses have names such as Isis, Diana, Astarte, Cerridwen, Sekhmet, Kali, Innanna, Hecate, and the Lady; the gods are Anubis, Bacchus, Pan, Apollo. Zeus, Odin, Herne, and the Lord. The neopagans claim to follow the original religion of the Stone Age, a re-creation of the ancient rites of Britain and Europe; they feel we should all be initiated into a primordial and secret tradition.

Sometimes neopagans are accused of following a cult, but the worshipers respond, "A religion is only a cult with an army." In other words, when a set of beliefs becomes powerful, formalized, and widespread, it is institutionalized as a religion.

Ritual plays a large part in the worship, and there are seasonal festivals, especially around the winter and summer solstices, and the spring and summer equinoxes. At some sites, considered sacred shrines, candles, bowls of water, salt, feathers, stones, or statuary, branches, and vines may be placed on an altar. Magic may be practiced or other forms of occult rites, chanting and prayer take place, and sacrifices are made of food, drink, incense, jewelry, flowers, strands of hair, or handmade items. As in Lent, the worshipper must surrender something important to them. An animal might also be sacrificed and eaten by the group in a communal feast—an animal humanely raised and humanely slaughtered, with apologies to the species and the land spirit.

These celebrations are sometimes referred to as "Witches' Sabbaths," but that can be misleading. In fact, the most prevalent misconception is that neopagans are devil-worshippers. In point of fact, they reject Satanism and demonism, and believe in the bounty and goodness of nature. It is a positive faith of joy and abandonment, an alternative spirituality to today's institutional religions. Earth Day is also falsely identified by many people as a pagan holiday, but it is more a reminder that we are dependent on nature and should protect it, for its own sake and ours.

Wicca is the largest, best-known, and most distinctive form of paganism, and it emphasizes witchcraft and worship of the Goddess. It has been somewhat co-opted as part of the feminist consciousness movement, but it is much broader than that, attempting to establish communion with natural or supernatural forces, usually through white magic. Some of the leading books on Wicca are Margaret Murray's *The Witch-Cult in Western Europe*, Doreen Valiente's *The Rebirth of*

Witchcraft, Margaret Adler's *Dragging down the Moon*, Gerald Gardner's *Witchcraft Today*, and *The Alex Sanders Lectures*.

The ritual involves a certain amount of witchcraft, summoning the Goddess, who represents the fertility of nature. The worshippers meet in covens or small groups, and there are sacrifices, feasting and chanting, dances around a blazing fire, and sometimes ritualized sex. The Great Goddess is described by Doreen Valiente as "the beauty of the green earth, the white moon among the stars, the mystery of the waters . . . the soul of nature who gives life to the universe." She is also identified as Gaia, the earth mother. Her male counterpart has a variety of names: Lord of the Greenwood, the Sun King, the Corn King, Leader of the Wild Hunt, Lord of Death (and Rebirth), the Horned God, and the Green Man. Sometimes the godhead can be balanced between male and female, and the three phases of the moon.

Druidry can be traced back to the ancient Celtic culture, where the leaders functioned as religious practitioners, intermediaries with the gods. The Druids are best known for their meetings in "groves" to worship nature, especially their gatherings at Stonehenge and Glastonbury. As most people are aware, Stonehenge is a ring of massive, upright stones and lintels dating from 2500 b.c., a center of devotion in the Iron Age, a burial ground, and an astrological observatory. The Romans, who finally conquered the Druids at Anglesey, described them as seers, healers, and medicine men who foretold the future through divining. They are also described as a barbaric people who practiced human sacrifice and cannibalism. Such rituals were gifts to the gods and appeasement for success in battle.

In modern ceremonies at such sites, the worshippers arrange themselves in a circle, wearing white robes. They begin the ritual by extending greetings to the north, south, east, and west, and sometimes to the above, below, and within. The three vowels *A*, *I*, and *O* may be chanted, or the word "Awen," and this is repeated three times in a single breath. Another common chant pays tribute to the goddess or to the god and goddess, the fertile source of all creation. The ritual is meant to show respect to the powers of the earth and to express a love of all earthly things. A concern with justice is also a part of Druidry, for nature is unbalanced if injustice prevails.

Overall, neopaganism, whether as Wicca, Druidry, or some other form, offers personal and primal contact with supernatural forces. It offers communion with the divine outside of institutional worship, the way cults from the north functioned in ancient Greece. In our present world, many people feel disconnected from formal religion, especially Western religion, which they find unsatisfying. It does not speak to their spiritual needs, whereas nature seems to contain something worthy of reverence. And they can worship the divine essence in private ceremonies, using ancient rites that celebrate goddesses along with gods. They can seek the supernatural, not in a house of worship, but in the open air, through spells, chants, and dances rather than hymns, sermons, and sacraments. It is no wonder, then, that the number of neopagans is increasing as an alternative faith.

The problems that surround neopaganism are comparable to those of ancient and orthodox religion, chiefly the problem of verification. And the neopagans may be confusing the beauty of nature with its spirituality, the aesthetic with the religious. Nature seems to cleanse and restore us, to provide tranquility and balance but it may not rise to the level of the divine.

A movement called the *New Atheism* has also gained ground in recent years, not as an alternative religion but an alternative *to* religion. Five books, in particular, have appeared in this century extolling the New Atheism, and each has become a bestseller: Sam Harris's *The End of Faith*, Daniel Dennett's *Breaking the Spell*, Victor Stenger's *God: The Failed Hypotheses*, Richard Dawkins's *The God Delusion*, and Christopher Hitchens's *God Is Not Great*. Free Thought associations have sprung up that include agnostics, skeptics, and secular humanists, and in 2009 there was even a Blasphemer's Day celebration.

The movement is aggressive and argues that the time has come for atheists to be less polite in criticizing the superstition and fanaticism of religion. Atheists are no longer a thin, small voice but is now strong and strident. Instead of exercising tolerance toward the Abrahamic faiths of Judaism, Christianity, and Islam, rational argument should be used to expose their myths. Dawkins declares that faith is blind trust without justification; it is irrational and closed to all counterarguments. Harris believes that religion is founded on wishful thinking, and Stenger asserts that "faith is belief in something in the absence of empirical evidence or reason for that belief." Some atheists feel that religion is too silly to refute, but most say the time is ripe for rational judgments. In the twenty-first century, it is long overdue.

Stephen Gould and others have claimed that religion and science belong in separate spheres, but the New Atheists maintain that religious statements are not outside scientific investigation. Articles of faith, such as virgin birth, the resurrection of the dead, and the genesis of the world, must be tested like all scientific hypotheses. Religion is subject to confirmation by reason and empiricism, and it must be rejected if it is not supported by the evidence. "I dispute the claim that science has nothing to say about God," Stenger writes, and he argues that "absence of evidence is evidence of absence when evidence should be there and is not."

In point of fact, the New Atheists say, religion fails all tests, and therefore should be treated with "ridicule and contempt." The universe was created with the big bang and will probably end with the big crunch. It evolved through astronomical evolution, just as human beings evolved through biological evolution. Even religion itself can be explained by Darwin. As Harris declares in *The End of Faith*, there was a "selective advantage" to children who believed what adults told them; they then avoided harm. But religion today promotes irrational and harmful beliefs, and it promotes sectarian violence, especially in the Arab world. Dennett in his *Breaking the Spell* accounts for religion by postulating a "hyperactive agent detection device" that assigns invisible, personal, and supernatural powers to "anything complicated that moves."

Furthermore, the New Atheists argue that religion has done much more harm than good; it is "sinister, dangerous and ridiculous." Religion is responsible for the Inquisition, witch hunts, the Crusades, and numerous holy wars. Today the Christian evangelical right has unduly influenced U.S. politics, and fundamentalists oppose movements to legitimize abortion, euthanasia, and homosexuality. Muslim extremists are causing death and injury throughout the world. Harris, in fact, refers to Islam as "a cult of death." In the twenty-first century, the human race needs to embrace reason, science, and freedom from religious dogma or risk continued turbulence and misery. We do not need a refurbished creationism in the form of intelligent design but an acknowledgment of human evolution and an admission that all morality has a human source. As Victor Stenger writes:

Believers have been led to think that morality comes from God, [but] morality arises when humans, and even some animals, need to have rules of behavior in order to maintain the cooperative society necessary for survival . . . [Furthermore], atheists are at least as moral as believers.

Plato first pointed this out: either God decides what is good, in which case it is arbitrary, or God recognizes what is good, in which case ethics is independent of God. The latter seems preferable. Morality is therefore secular, and it concerns cruelty and kindness, that it is wrong to harm people and right to help them. Stenger writes further, "Any number of societies now exist where the majority has freely abandoned religion and God. Far from being dens of iniquity, these societies are the happiest, safest, and most successful in the world."

By contrast, reliance on the canonical Bible can produce horrors, terrors, and atrocities. Not only does it contain numerous factual errors, but it also contains a series of moral outrages, reported with approval. For example, "I will sing praise to your name, O Most High . . . The enemies have vanished in everlasting ruins; their cities you have rooted out; the very memory of them has perished . . . the Lord will swallow [up his enemies] in his wrath, and fire will consume them. [He] will destroy their offspring from the earth . . . their children from . . . humankind" (Ps. 9:2, 6; 21: 9–10). And "Joshua's army killed everyone in Jericho, both men and women, young and old, oxen, sheep, and donkeys . . . [He] left no one remaining, but utterly destroyed all that breathed, as the Lord God of Israel commanded" (Josh. 6:21; 10:40). In *The God Delusion* Dawkins writes, "The God of the Old Testament is arguably the most unpleasant character in all of fiction." One of his chapters is entitled "The New Testament Exceeds the Evil of the Old One." Bart Ehrman, the biblical scholar, states, "This is not the kind, loving, caring God of nursery rhymes and Sunday school booklets. God is a fierce animal who will rip his people to shreds for failing to worship him."

Philosophers have sometimes asked whether nonbelievers can ever be happy, but the New Atheists ask whether pious people can be happy with a judgmental God hovering over them and the possibility of hell before them. Christians are told they are born sinful and should feel shame, which is not a formula for happiness. The evangelical response to 9/11 was that it was the punishment of the Lord, which certainly was not comforting to the victims' families.

But don't we need to commit to something larger than ourselves? Perhaps, but the New Atheists point out that our family, our nation, humanity, and the physical world are larger than we are, and there are other, major sources of personal fulfillment outside of religion. For example, art, music, literature, the love of our spouses, partners, and children, participation in the political community, creative and productive work, and the beauty of nature can all provide satisfactions aside from any ultimate purpose.

The New Atheists have also had their critics—people such as Dinesh D'Souza, Paul Copan, Keith Ward, and William L. Craig. These individuals charge that the focus of the New Atheists has been on the social harm of religion; the good has been neglected—the charity work, providing educational opportunities, caring for the sick, and many other benefits throughout the centuries. What's more, a great deal of the world's suffering has been caused by two notorious atheists, Hitler and Stalin. It is also charged that the New Atheists slight the arguments for the existence of God, and when they do address them, a "straw God" is set up, a weak figure that is easily knocked down. Furthermore, as Paul Davies has argued, "Science has its own faith-based system."

The New Atheists counter by saying that religion has done a great deal of harm, then a little bit of good to make up for it. One would expect Christianity to generate more generosity and less vindictiveness. As Gandhi remarked, "Why aren't you Christians more like your Christ?" As for Hitler and Stalin, their monolithic systems were overtly atheist but in effect religions, with charismatic leaders, inspired writings, saints and ceremonies, devout followers, elaborate rituals, and a visionary ideal. They demanded the same kind of allegiance and threatened the same penalties as institutional religion.

Regarding arguments about God, the New Atheists argue that the burden of proof is always on the affirmative, and God's existence has not been proven. And with respect to science being "faith-based," Dennett says that confidence in science "is based on its practical success, not some logical deductions derived from dubious metaphysical assumptions." Furthermore, science is not closed to the possibility of the supernatural but simply "sees no evidence of anything beyond nature." Stenger reiterates the point: "Naturalism is sufficient to explain everything we observe in the universe from the most distant galaxies to the inner workings of the brain that result in the phenomenon of mind. Nowhere is it necessary to introduce God or the supernatural to understand the world."

All of the New Atheists maintain that the natural world is the entire world, and science is the means to access that reality. Truth-claims must be testable, observable, and falsifiable, and God does not meet the standard. The same can be said of the soul that "looks just like it should look if it does not exist." The "sword of science" must be wielded against all such unsupported beliefs, principally against the archaic, pernicious, and childish notion of a heavenly father. "Faith is absurd and dangerous," Stenger writes, "and we look forward to the day, no matter how distant, when the human race finally abandons it."

Are the atheists right? Is religion harmful and outmoded, or can we maintain the traditional beliefs even in a world of science and technology, of nuclear power and space exploration, of computers and cell phones? Do we need God more than ever, and do we naturally turn to him to help us solve our problems?

Perhaps belief has survived the rational assault and "gone into hiding under various aliases," as Terry Eagleton claims, some of which are morality, art, democracy, materialism, and the market, but traditional faith in a personal God is questioned today as never before.

The decision is now up to you, the reader, but at least it will be an informed decision. You are aware of the issues involved, the claims and options, the critical questions. Whatever conclusion you reach will have to be tentative because no one can be certain about these matters, but at least it will be based on sound reflection. It will be the most reasonable position you can find. Socrates said, "The unexamined life is not worth living"; in the same way, the unexamined faith is not worth holding. If you can affirm your belief after examining it, then you are justified in your faith. The risk is that you might be convinced to abandon your beliefs, but in that case it was never based on good reasons to begin with. An idea should only be accepted if it is acceptable, and now it is up to you to analyze the basis of religion. As the Buddha wrote, "Believe nothing, no matter where you read it, or who said it, no matter if I have said it, unless it agrees with your own reason and your common sense."

GLOSSARY

Agnosticism | in a religious context, the theory that knowledge of God is unattainable or insufficient to justify belief; therefore, we must suspend judgment, neither affirming nor denying his existence.

Ahimsa | Hindu doctrine of noninjury to any living creature. This implies a strict vegetarianism and a reverential attitude toward animals, especially the cow.

Altruism | extreme generosity to the point of selflessness; placing the good of others above one's own; the opposite of selfishness or self-interest.

Analytic statements | propositions that are necessarily true by the meaning of the concepts involved; a relation of ideas, as in "All circles are round."

Animism | doctrine that nature is inhabited by spirits; that souls are indwelling in all things, responsible for their activity.

Anselm of Canterbury (1033–1109) | bishop and saint of the Catholic Church best known in philosophy for his ontological argument for the existence of God.

Anthropomorphic	attributing human characteristics to a god or even an animal or object.
Apologetics	reasoned argument in support of a theory, usually a religious doctrine.
Aquinas, St. Thomas (1225–1274)	major theologian, whose most notable work is *Summa Theologica*, especially his "five ways"—arguments for God's existence. He remains the preeminent philosopher/theologian of the Catholic Church.
Aristotle (384–322 b.c.)	along with Plato, one of the two most important philosophers of ancient Greece. His prominent works include the *Physics, de Anima, Nicomachean Ethics,* and *Poetics*.
Atheism	denial of the existence of God, or, in popular terms, a belief that there isn't a God.
Atman	in Hinduism, the individual soul that contains karma and will be dissolved at death and reunited with the world soul, Brahma.
Atonement	reconciling with God after doing penance for one's sins. Ultimately, Christ's atonement as the savior and redeemer of humankind.
Attribute	quality or property that characterizes an object. God's attributes are thought to be known indirectly and are unique to him, e.g., omnipotence.
Barth, Karl (1886–1968)	Swiss theologian who maintained that God is wholly other than man and not accessible by human reason; Christianity is revealed.
Brahma(n)	in Hinduism, the impersonal world-soul, with which the individual soul (*atman*) seeks union.
Buddhism	religion founded in approximately 563 b.c. and based on the teachings of Gautama the

Buddha that stress the Four Noble Truths.
The last of the truths teaches worshippers
how to reach Nirvana through eight stages of
rightness.

Calvinism	belief within Protestantism emphasizing predestination, that the will of God is all-pervasive, governing cosmic and human events.
Christology	that part of theology that concentrates on the nature and personality of Christ, particularly his role as savior and redeemer of humankind.
Contingency	one object or event being dependent on another; a state of affairs that may or may not be. Used by St. Thomas to define God, by contrast, as a necessarily existent being.
Cosmological argument	one argument for the existence of God based on the impossibility of an infinite regress of causes, which suggests a primary cause behind all events, namely, God.
Creation myth	metaphorical account of the origin of a people or humanity.
Creationism	religious belief that human beings and everything in the universe have been created by a supernatural being; it is opposed to secular evolutionary theory.
Credo quia absurdum est ("I believe because it is absurd")	sometimes attributed to Tertullian (165–220) and taken to mean that faith stands above reason.
Darwin, Charles (1809–1882)	British biologist who, in *The Origin of Species*, expounded the theory of evolution. According to this doctrine, all organisms develop by natural selection according to the principle of survival of the fittest.

Deism	view that God is responsible for creating the world but does not have an immediate relation to it, including any interaction with human beings; he set natural laws in motion.
Deontological ethics	class of ethical theories that maintains actions are right or wrong by their very nature; also called formalism or intuitionism.
Destiny	belief that all events must occur as they do, inevitably, unavoidably, in accordance with fate. It is sometimes linked to God's foreordination or divine providence, or it can be connected to a secular, mechanical necessity.
Determinism	position that everything happens as the effect of prior causes in a universe governed by law. Psychologically, the denial of free will and the assertion that all thoughts are compelled by psychical or physical conditions.
Dewey, John (1859–1952)	leading American philosopher and a major exponent of pragmatism (or instrumentalism) along with C. S. Peirce (1893–1914) and William James (1842–1910).
Dogmatic	describes a broad pronouncement that is stated without empirical evidence or rational foundation.
Duns Scotus (1266/ 74–1308)	theologian of the high Middle Ages best known for his "univocity of being"—that existence is our most abstract concept. He also offered an argument for the existence of God and for the Immaculate Conception.
Durkheim, Émile (1858–1917)	French sociologist/philosopher who asserted the presence of a group-mind above that of individual minds that directs our behavior, including thoughts of religion and ethics.

Eckhart, Meister (1260–1327)	medieval theologian best known for affirming the validity of mystical experience.
Edwards, Jonathan (1703–1758)	American preacher and theologian renowned for his teachings on freedom and original sin, and for heading a spiritual revival. His sermon "Sinners in the Hands of an Angry God" is an American classic.
Empiricism	epistemological theory that knowledge is reducible to sensations or that sense perception is the most reliable means of knowing.
Enlightenment (Age of Reason)	eighteenth-century movement to reform knowledge and culture in the light of reason. Beginning in France, it quickly spread through Europe and to America, influencing Benjamin Franklin and Thomas Jefferson and the founding documents of the United States.
Epistemology	branch of philosophy dealing with the origin, structure, methods, and validity of knowledge.
Eschatology	that part of systematic theology that concerns death, judgment, heaven, hell, and the apocalypse.
Eternity	an infinite amount of time, everlastingness, or timelessness; without beginning or end.
Ethics	philosophic study of right and wrong conduct, good and bad ends in living, and praiseworthy and blameworthy persons.
Evil	events harmful or destructive to human beings, including the suffering men inflict on one another and the pain caused by natural occurrences, such as disasters, illness, and accidents.

Faith	strong belief in God or religious dogma based more on spiritual apprehension than empirical proof.
Feuerbach, Ludwig (1804–1872)	German materialist who defined religion as "the dream of the human spirit." He tried to reconcile the opposition between materialism and spiritualism, ultimately affirming a physical world.
France, Anatole (1844–1924)	French poet, novelist, journalist, and winner of the Nobel Prize, known for his irony and skepticism.
Frazer, Sir James (1854–1941)	British social anthropologist who investigated mythology and comparative religion; renowned for his multivolume *The Golden Bough*.
Free will	ability to reach decisions autonomously; personal self-determination without internal or external constraints.
Freedom	power to do what we choose, to carry out our wishes; in contrast to free will, which means the power to make independent choices.
Freud, Sigmund (1856–1941)	Austrian founder of the psychoanalytic movement that explained hysteria and neurosis in terms of the unconscious mind. He rejected religion in *Totem and Taboo*, *Moses and Monotheism*, and *Civilization and Its Discontents*.
Genetic fallacy	dismissing an idea because of its origins rather than its intrinsic worth, e.g., rejecting Nietzsche's philosophy because he was mentally ill at the end of his life.
God	in metaphysics, the supreme being, creator and ruler of the universe, accepted on the

	basis of authority, revelation, scripture, or religious experience.
God of the gaps	imputing to God whatever cannot be explained.
Hermeneutics	interpretation of authoritative writings, especially sacred scripture; it is equivalent to exegesis.
Homer	greatest of the Greek epic poets, author of *The Iliad* and *The Odyssey*.
Humanism	broadly speaking, any philosophy that places man rather than God as the central concern and endorses mutual compassion, honesty, forgiveness, and love. The virtues of social justice, equality, and freedom are also stressed.
Hume, David (1711–1776)	British empiricist best known for his *Enquiry Concerning the Human Understanding*. He maintained a skeptical view of religion and ethics, seeing no sensations, impressions, or proof that would establish them.
Huxley, T. H.	celebrated British scientist who staunchly defended evolutionism, most conspicuously in "A Piece of Chalk." He is credited with inventing the term "agnosticism."
Icarus	in Greek mythology, the son of Daedalus the image maker; best known for attempting to fly. He constructed wings of feathers and wax, but he flew too close to the sun, which melted the wax, causing him to fall to his death.
Immanent	state of being indwelling, inherent, or resident within; in theology, the presence of the divine spirit inside ourselves.

Immortality	doctrine that the soul, mind, or personality of a person survives the death of the body and lives on in a timeless mode of existence.
Immutable	fixed and unchanging, existing in the same state forever.
Infinite	endless extent of space, time, or any series; often predicated of God.
Intuition	direct and immediate apprehension of knowledge, unmediated by the senses or the intellect.
James, William (1842–1910)	influential American philosopher known for his *Principles of Psychology*, *The Will to Believe*, *Pragmatism*, and *Varieties of Religious Experience.* He emphasized the trustworthiness of our deepest yearnings.
Jansenism	founded by Cornelius Jansen (1585–1638), this movement taught the corruption of human nature through original sin and the impossibility of free will; it was eventually condemned by the Catholic Church.
Jefferson Bible	selected version of the New Testament by Thomas Jefferson (1743–1826), third president of the United States, deleting the alleged mistranslations and miracles, leaving a deistic interpretation.
Jesuit	member of a Catholic religious order known for its educational and missionary work. Jesuitism sometimes carries a negative connotation of craftiness and duplicity.
Kant, Immanuel (1724–1804)	extremely influential German philosopher best known for his *Critique of Pure Reason*, which explored the limits of rational thought;

religion, to him, was part of the "noumenal" not the "phenomenal" world.

Kierkegaard, Søren (1813–1855)
Danish theologian and founder of the theistic branch of existentialism. He criticized institutional religion, the reliance on reason, and systems of belief that protected people from a direct confrontation with God.

Law of similarity
within magic, the notion that whatever is alike is the same.

Law of contagion
within magic, the notion that things once in contact, remain connected.

Lewis, C. S. (1898–1963)
British author, Oxford don, and Christian apologist renowned for his *Chronicles of Narnia, The Screwtape Letters*, and *Surprised by Joy*.

Lightfoot, John (1602–1675)
British churchman and biblical scholar who was both praised and criticized for writing that the world started in 3929 b.c.

Locke, John (1632–1714)
first of the celebrated British empiricists, Locke denied innate ideas and moral principles, regarding the mind as a *tabula rasa*, or "blank tablet"; knowledge was acquired entirely through sense experience.

Magic
use of formulas, materials, and techniques, outside of empirical science, to gain supernatural control over nature. Black magic is harmful; white, beneficial.

Maimonides, Moses (1135–1204)
leading Jewish philosopher during the Middle Ages. His *Guide for the Perplexed* contains his main exegesis and a discussion of divine attributes, providence, evil, freedom, and God's existence.

Mana	notion originating in Polynesia of a supernatural power resident within objects or people that makes them excellent in their particular qualities.
Marxism	political philosophy expounded by Karl Marx (1818–1883), principal author of *The Communist Manifesto*, that stresses the owner–worker conflict, the inevitable overthrow of capitalism, the interim proletarian dictatorship, the ultimate classless society, and religion as an opiate.
Materialism	metaphysical belief that matter is the fundamental constituent of the universe.
Meliorism	view that the world is neither good nor evil, but human effort can increase the amount of good so that improvement in our condition is possible.
Metaphysics	branch of philosophy dealing with the structure, process, and nature of reality as such.
Misology	contempt for logic.
Monism	view that there is only one fundamental reality, as in the thought of Parmenides and Spinoza; in epistemology, the position that an object and our idea of it are one. This doctrine is opposed to multiplicity.
Moral argument for God	that our ethical awareness indicates a God who implanted a moral sense within us.
Mysticism	form of religion that emphasizes the direct experience of God, an intimate awareness of the divine presence.
Myth	figurative, metaphorical, or symbolic representation of reality, impossible to achieve through literal meaning. Later, a fiction presented as true.

Naturalism	view that the natural world constitutes the whole of reality. It is opposed to supernaturalism, which holds that the world requires a divine explanation.
Natural law	"higher law" theory, as distinct from the positive law of states, that argues there is an objective, cosmic law that is universally valid; God is sometimes postulated as the lawgiver.
Natural theology	theory that unaided human reason is capable of understanding the divine. It is opposed to "revealed theology," which depends on supernatural grace.
Nietzsche, Friedrich (1844–1900)	well-known German philosopher, founder of atheistic existentialism, who preached the "will to power" as fundamental to human progress. He famously said, "God is dead," and wanted people to assume personal responsibility rather than retreating into an imaginary world.
Nirvana	Buddhist ideal of the absence of individuality without loss of consciousness, the individual soul joining the world soul.
Occam's razor	logical principle articulated by William of Ockham (d. 1349) that explanations should not be compounded beyond what is required; the simplest hypothesis is best.
Omnipotence	attributed to God as being all powerful, almighty, without physical limitations but, perhaps, constrained by logic and his own nature.
Omniscience	attribute ascribed to God meaning complete and perfect knowledge of all things, past, present, and future.

Ontological argument	one "proof" for the existence of God, identified with St. Anselm (1033–1109), that claims "a being than which none greater can be conceived" must exist in reality and in the understanding; also associated with Duns Scotus, Descartes, and Leibniz.
Osirian fields	happy Egyptian paradise where the dead enjoy their just rewards, somewhere in the direction of the Milky Way, "the Great White Nile of the sky."
Paley, William (1743–1805)	British churchman famous for his watchmaker analogy in *Natural Theology* that supported the teleological argument: that if we found a watch we would assume a watchmaker, just as we must conclude the earth had a designer and creator.
Pantheism	religious belief that God is immanent in nature or identical with the natural world: "God is everything, and everything is God."
Pascal, Blaise (1623–1662)	French philosopher, scientist, and mathematician whose aphorisms are contained in his *Pensées* and *Provincial Letters*. Although he ultimately left the question unresolved, he felt that truth is found by faith, not reason.
Philosophy of religion	critical examination of religion, its foundations, mode of proof, implications to ethics, explanation for evil, relation to reason, and claims of immortality.
Plantinga, Alvin (1932–)	celebrated University of Notre Dame philosopher and devout Christian, best known for *Warranted Christian Belief* and *God and Other Minds*.

Polytheism	the belief in the reality of multiple gods; contrasted with monotheism, the belief in one god.
Post hoc ergo propter hoc ("after this, therefore because of this")	logical fallacy of assuming that because one event preceded another, the earlier event caused the later one; a confusion of subsequent with consequent.
Puritanism	movement to purify religion from corrupt beliefs and practices. The adherents stressed self-reliance, thrift, and industry, but it sometimes degenerated into severe living, a strict conscience, and rejection of all enjoyment.
Quiddity	essence of an object of thought or perception.
Reformation	short for the Protestant Reformation spearheaded by Martin Luther (1483–1546) that stressed the norm of man's conscience, scripture, and reason over the authority of the Vatican.
Renard, Jules (1864–1910)	French author best known for *Poil de Carotte* (*Carrot Top*), *Histoires naturelles* (*Nature Stories*), and his *Journal*.
Revelation	communication to humankind of the divine will through reflection, intuition, revelation, reason, dreams, visions, ecstatic experiences, sacred books, prophets, traditions, or authorities.
Rochefoucauld, François de La (1613–1680)	French nobleman and noted author celebrated for his cynicism and wit in works such as *Memoirs* and *Maximes*.
Russell, Bertrand (1872–1970)	British philosopher who contributed significantly to logic and methodology but popularly known for his social views,

especially his opposition to religion. His
works include *Principia Mathematica* (with A.
N. Whitehead), *Our Knowledge of the
External World*, and *Why I Am Not a
Christian*.

Schleiermacher, Friedrich (1768–1834)	German theologian, "The Father of Modern Liberal Theology," who tried to mystically harmonize the real and the ideal, and individual ego with human reason, especially in *The Christian Faith*.
Simplicity	concept descriptive of God signifying that his existence and his nature are one.
Sin	immoral or rebellious act regarded as transgressing divine law.
State of nature	original condition of man without social or political organization.
Taboo (*tapu*)	originating in Polynesia, something prohibited by virtue of an excess or imbalance of *mana*.
Talmud	encyclopedic Hebrew scripture written over an 800-year period expounding the civil law and religious ideas of Judaism and its ethics, science, and history.
Tauler, Johannes (1300–1361)	outstanding German preacher and mystic who trusted the insights of his private consciousness.
Teleological argument	one argument for the existence of God, associated with St. Thomas Aquinas and William Paley, that claims the order, harmony, and complexity of earthly forms reveal a divine purpose. Also called the "argument from design" and, more recently, "intelligent design."

Theism	generally, the belief in one God, the creator and ruler of the universe.
Theodicy	branch of theology that defends belief in God against objections that stem from the presence of evil.
Theology	study of the question of God and his relation to the world.
Theosophy	mystical belief that knowledge of God can only be achieved through religious ecstasy, individual intuition, or personal communion with the divine.
Tindale, Matthew (1657–1733)	Enlightenment thinker whose *Christianity as Old as the Creation* was considered the deist's "Bible."
Totemism	belief in a mystical kinship between a clan and an animal or plant.
Transcendent	wholly other, beyond human experience or comprehension, a higher spiritual realm.
Tyler, Sir Edward (1832–1917)	British cultural evolutionist who believed there was a functional basis for the development of society and religion, as argued in his *Primitive Culture*.
Unamuno, Miguel de (1864–1936)	Spanish writer and philosopher best known for emphasizing the individual man in his concrete situation rather than in the abstract. He struggled with issues of faith and reason, especially in his book *The Tragic Sense of Life*.
Voltaire (François-Marie Arouet) (1694–1778)	French writer best known for *Candide*, which lampooned the optimism of Leibniz and religion. Voltaire ultimately believed in a righteous God but criticized the intolerance of the Church.

Weltanschauung   German word for "worldview" or "perspective
                        on life."

Zoroastrianism   an Indo-Iranian religion, also known as
                        Mazdaism, founded by Zarathustra in the
                        eleventh or tenth century b.c. It preached a
                        dualistic cosmology of good and evil,
                        symbolized by the struggle between light and
                        darkness; man must ally himself with the one
                        or the other.

SELECTED BIBLIOGRAPHY

CHAPTER I
WHEN RELIGION FIRST TREMBLED INTO EXPRESSION

Boas, Franz. "The Origin of Totemism." *Journal of American Folklore* 23 (1910): 392–93.

Campbell, Joseph, ed. *Dreams and Religion*. New York: Dutton, 1970.

Cook, John W. "Magic, Witchcraft and Science." *Philosophical Investigations* 6 (1983): 37–52.

Durkheim, Émile, *The Elementary Forms of Religious Life*. London: Allen and Unwin, 1915.

Eliade, Mircea. *The Sacred and Profane: The Nature of Religion*. New York: Harcourt Brace,1959.

Evans-Pritchard, E. E. *Theories of Primitive Religion*. Oxford: Oxford University Press, 1965.

Frazer, James G. *The Golden Bough: A Study in Magic and Religion*. London: Macmillan, 1911–1915.

Harvey, Graham. *Animism*. Kent Town, Australia: Wakefield, 2005.

Hicks, David. *Ritual and Belief*. Lanham, MD: AltaMira, 2010.

Hodder, Ian. *Religion at Work in a Neolithic Society*. New York: Cambridge University Press, 2014.

Howells, W. W. *The Heathens: Primitive Man and His Religions*. Garden City, NY: Doubleday, 1948.

James, E. O. *Comparative Religion*. London: Methuen, 1938.

Jones, Robert A. *The Secret of the Totem*. New York: Columbia University Press, 2005.

Knox, John. *Myth and Truth*. Charlottesville: University Press of Virginia, 1964.

Land, Andrew. *The Making of Religion*. London: Longmans Green, 1898.

Levi-Straus, Claude. "The Structural Study of Myth." In *Structured Anthropology*. New York: Basic, 1963.

Praet, Islvan. *Animism and the Question of Life*. New York: Routledge, 2014.

Schmitz, Dennis. *Animism*. Oberlin, OH: Oberlin College Press, 2014.

Smith, Huston. *The World's Religions*. New York: HarperCollins, 1958.

Tylor, Edward B. *Primitive Culture: Researches into the Development of Mythology, Philosophy, Religion, Language, Art and Custom*. New York: Gordon, 1974.

CHAPTER 2
NATIONAL RELIGIONS OF THE ANCIENTS

Carlyon, Richard. *A Guide to the Gods*. New York: Morrow, 1982.
Cerny, Jaroslav. *Ancient Egyptian Religion*. Westport, CT: Greenwood, 1898.
Christensen, Lisbeth Bredholy. *The Handbook of Religions in Ancient Europe*. Bristol, CT: Acumen, 2013.
Freeman, Charles. *Egypt, Greece, and Rome*. Oxford: Oxford University Press, 2014.
Graziosi, Barbara. *The Gods of Olympus*. New York: Metropolitan, 2014.
Haydon, Albert. *Biography of the Gods*. New York: Macmillan, 1941.
Knust, Jennifer Wright, and Varheli Zsuzsanna. *Ancient Mediterranean Sacrifice*. Oxford: Oxford University Press, 2011.
Martin, Thomas R. *Ancient Rome: From Romulus to Justinian*. New Haven, CT: Yale University Press, 2012.
North, J. A. *Roman Religion*. New York: Cambridge University Press, 2000.
Quirke, Stephen. *Ancient Egyptian Religion*. New York: Dover, 1995.
Redford, Donald B. *The Ancient Gods Speak: A Guide to Egyptian Religion*. Oxford: Oxford University Press, 2012.
Salzman, Michele Renee, and Marvin A. Sweeney, eds. *The Cambridge History of Religions in the Ancient World*. New York: Cambridge University Press, 2013.
Schlesier, Renata. *A Different God? Dionysos and Ancient Polytheism*. Berlin: DeGruyter, 2011.
Shaw, Garry J. *Egyptian Myths: A Guide to the Ancient Gods and Legends*. New York: Thames and Hudson, 2014.
Woolf, Greg. *Rome: An Empire's Story*. Oxford: Oxford University Press, 2012.

CHAPTER 3
THE NATURE OF THE WESTERN GOD

Bennett, W. *Religion and Free Will*. Oxford: Clarendon, 1913.
Bergmann, Michael, and Michael C. Rea, eds. *Divine Evil? The Moral Character of the God of Abraham*. Oxford: Oxford University Press, 2011.
Davis, Stephen T. *Logic and the Nature of God*. Grand Rapids, MI: Eerdman, 1983.
———. "Divine Omniscience and Human Freedom." *Religious Studies* 15 (1979): 303–16.
Farnell, Lewis Richard. *The Attributes of God*. Durham: Acumen, 2010.
Flew, Anthony. *God and Philosophy*. London: Hutchison, 1966.
Flint, Thomas P., and Michael C. Rea, eds. *The Oxford Handbook of Philosophical Theology*. Oxford: Oxford University Press, 2009.
Geach, Peter. *Providence and Evil*. Cambridge: Cambridge University Press, 1977.
Hoffman, Joshua and Gary Rosenkrantz. *The Divine Attributes*. Oxford: Blackwell, 2002.
Khamara, Edward J. "In Defense of Omnipotence." *Philosophical Quarterly* 28 (1978): 215–28.
Lotufo, Zenon. *Cruel God, Kind God*. Santa Barbara, CA: Praeger, 2012.
Lucas, J. *The Freedom of the Will*. Oxford: Oxford University Press, 1970.
Mavrodes, George J. "Defending Omnipotence." *Philosophical Studies* 52 (1977): 191–202.
Morris, Thomas V. *Our Idea of God*. Notre Dame, IN: University of Notre Dame Press, 1991.
Palmer, George Herbert. *The Problem of Freedom*. New York: Houghton Mifflin, 1911.
Pike, Nelson. *God and Timelessness*. London: Routledge and Kegan Paul, 1970.
Plantinga, Alvin. *God Freedom and Evil*. New York: Harper and Row, 1974.
———. *Does God Have a Nature?* Milwaukee: University of Wisconsin Press, 1980.
Ross, Steven L. "Another Look at God and Morality." *Ethics* 94 (October 1983): 87–98.

Row, William L. *Can God Be Free?* Oxford: Oxford University Press, 2004.
Werenga, Edward R. *The Nature of God: An Inquiry Into Divine Attributes.* Ithaca, NY: Cornell University Press, 1989.
Wood, W. Jay. *God.* Durham: Acumen, 2010.

CHAPTER 4
AN ARRAY OF ALTERNATIVE BELIEFS

Bonansea, Bernardino M. *God and Atheism.* Washington, D.C.: Catholic University Press, 1979.
Bullivant, Stephen, and Michael Ruse. *The Oxford Handbook of Atheism.* Oxford: Oxford University Press, 2013.
Byrne, Peter. *Natural Religion and the Nature of Religion: The Legacy of Deism.* New York: Oxford University Press, 2014.
Botton, Alain de. *Religion for Atheists.* New York: Vintage, 2012.
DuBois, Page. *A Million and One Gods: The Persistence of Polytheism.* Cambridge, MA: Harvard University Press, 2014.
Evans, C. Stephen. *Philosophy of Religion: An Anthology.* Stamford, CT: InterVarsity, 2009.
Flint, Robert. *Agnosticism.* New York: Scribner, 1903.
Gildon, Charles. *The Deist's Manual.* New York: Garland, 1976.
Haldeman, Julius. *The Militant Agnostic.* Amherst, NY: Prometheus, 1995.
Hunt, John. *Pantheism and Christianity.* Port Washington, NY: Kennikat, 1970.
Joshi, S. T. *The Unbelievers: The Evolution of Modern Atheism.* Amherst, NY: Prometheus, 2011.
LePoidevin, Robin. *Agnosticism.* Oxford: Oxford University Press, 2010.
Levine, Michael. *Pantheism.* New York: Routledge, 1994.
Martin, Michael. *Atheism: A Philosophical Analysis.* Philadelphia: Temple University Press, 1990.
Miller, David LeRoy. *The New Polytheism: Rebirth of the Gods and Goddesses.* New York: Harper and Row, 1974.
Nielsen, Kai. *Philosophy and Atheism.* Amherst, NY: Prometheus, 1985.
Parker, Robert. *Polytheism and Society at Athens.* Oxford: Oxford University Press, 2005.
Ronaldo, Peter M. *Atheists, Agnostics, and Deists in America.* Briarcliff Manor, NY: Dor-Pete, 2000.
Schlesier, Renate. *A Different God? Dionysos and Ancient Polytheism.* Berlin: DeGruyter, 2011.
Sloterdijk, Peter. *God's Zeal: The Battle of the Monotheists.* Malden, MA: Polity, 2009.
Smart, J. J. C., and J. J. Haldane. *Atheism and Theism.* Oxford: Blackwell, 1996.
Stenger, Victor. *God: The Failed Hypothesis.* Amherst, NY: Prometheus, 2007.
Walters, Kerry S. *The American Deists.* Amherst, NY: Prometheus, 1992.

CHAPTER 5
CLASSIC ARGUMENTS FOR GOD'S EXISTENCE—AND THEIR CRITIQUES

Aczel. Amir D. *Why Science Does Not Disprove God.* New York: William Morrow, 2014.
Anselm, Saint. *Basic Writings.* LaSalle, IL: Open Court, 1962.
Barnes, Jonathan. *The Ontological Argument.* New York: St. Martin's, 1972.
Bauerschmidt, Frederick C. *Thomas Aquinas.* Oxford: Oxford University Press, 2013.

Bouwsma, O. K. "Anselm's Argument." In *The Nature of Philosophic Inquiry*, ed. by J. Bobik. Notre Dame, IN: University of Notre Dame Press, 1970.

Burrill, Donald R., ed. *The Cosmological Argument: A Spectrum of Opinion*. Garden City, NY: Doubleday/Anchor, 1967.

Copleston, F. C. *Aquinas*. Baltimore: Penguin, 1955.

Craig, William. *The Cosmological Argument from Plato to Leibniz*. New York: Barnes and Noble, 1980.

Delaney, C. F., ed. *Rationality and Religion*. Notre Dame, IN: Notre Dame University Press, 1966.

Evans, C. Stephen. *Philosophy of Religion: Thinking about Faith*. Downer's Grove, IL: IVP Academic, 2009.

Flemming, Arthur. "Omnibenevolence and Evil." *Ethics* 96 (January 1986): 261–81.

Ford, David. *Theology: A Very Short Introduction*. Oxford: Oxford University Press, 2013.

Geach, Peter. "Causality and Creation." *Sophia* 1 (1962): 43–61.

Hawkins, D. J. B. *The Essentials of Theism*. London: Sheed and Ward, 1949.

Keller, Timothy. *The Reason for God: Belief in an Age of Skepticism*. New York: Dutton, 2009.

Kenny, A. *The Five Ways*. London: Routledge and Kegan Paul, 1968.

———. *The God of the Philosophers*. Oxford: Clarendon, 1979.

LeMahieu, D. L. *The Mind of William Paley*. Lincoln: University of Nebraska Press, 1976.

Mawson, T. J. *Belief in God*. Oxford: Oxford University Press, 2005.

McPherson, Thomas. *The Argument from Design*. New York: St. Martin's, 1972.

Meister, Chad V. *Introducing Philosophy of Religion*. New York: Routledge, 2009.

Plantinga, Alvin. *The Ontological Argument*. Garden City, NY: Doubleday/Anchor, 1965.

Swinburne, Richard. "The Argument from Design." *Philosophy* 43 (1968): 199–212.

———. *The Cosmological Argument from Plato to Leibniz*. New York: Barnes and Noble, 1980.

CHAPTER 6
THE EVIDENCE OF COMMON SENSE

Baillie, D. M. *Faith in God*. Edinburgh: Clark, 1927.

Bennett, Charles A. *A Philosophical Study of Mysticism*. New Haven, CT: Yale University Press, 1923.

Bowman, Mary. *Western Mysticism: A Guide to the Basic Works*. Chicago: American Library Association, 1978.

Broad, C. D. *Religion, Philosophy and Psychical Research*. New York: Humanities, 1969.

Connor, James A. *Pascal's Wager: The Man Who Played Dice with God*. San Francisco: Harper, 2006.

Davies, Oliver. *God Within: The Mystical Tradition of Western Europe*. New York: Paulist, 1988.

Ewing, Alfred G. "Awareness of God." *Philosophy* 40 (1965): 1–17.

Flew, Antony. *God and Philosophy*. New York: Dell, 1966.

Hammond, Nicholas, ed. *The Cambridge Companion to Pascal*. New York: Cambridge University Press, 2003.

Hart, David Bentley. *The Experience of God*. New Haven, CT: Yale University Press, 2013.

Hick, John. *Faith and Knowledge*. Ithaca, NY: Cornell University Press, 1957.

Hook, Sydney. *Religious Experience and Truth*. New York: New York University Press, 1961.

Hunter, Graeme. *Pascal the Philosopher*. Toronto: University of Toronto Press, 2013.

James, William. *The Varieties of Religious Experience*. New York: Longmans Green, 1902.

Katz, Steven, ed. *Comparative Mysticism: An Anthology of Original Sources*. Oxford: Oxford University Press, 2013.

Lewis, H. D. *Our Experience of God*. New York: Macmillan, 1959.

Ludwin, Dawn M. *Blaise Pascal's Quest for the Ineffable*. New York: Peter Lang, 2001.
Matson, Wallace. *The Existence of God*. Ithaca, NY: Cornell University Press, 1965.
Otto, Rudolf. *Mysticism, East and West*. New York: Macmillan, 1932.
Penelhum, Terence. "Pascal's Wager." *Journal of Religion* 44 (July 1964): 201–9.
Rescher, Nicholas. *Pascal's Wager*. Notre Dame, IN: University of Notre Dame Press, 1985.

CHAPTER 7
IF GOD IS GOOD, WHY DO PEOPLE SUFFER?

Ahern, M. B. *The Problem of Evil*. New York: Schocken, 1971.
Allen, Diogenes. "Natural Evil and the Love of God." *Religious Studies* 16 (1980): 439–56.
Bowker, John. *Problems of Suffering in Religions of the West*. London: Cambridge University Press, 1970.
Chryssides, George D. "Evil and the Problem of God." *Religious Studies* 23 (1987): 467–75.
Clement, Dore. "An Examination of the 'Soul-Making' Theodicy." *American Philosophical Quarterly* 7 (1970): 119–30.
Cowburn, John. *The Problem of Suffering and Evil*. Milwaukee, WI: Marquette University Press, 2012.
Flescher, Andrew Michael. *Moral Evil*. Washington, D.C.: Georgetown University Press, 2013.
Hick, John. *Evil and the God of Love*. New York: Harper and Row, 1966.
Joad, Cyril E. *God and Evil*. New York: Philosophical Library, 1941.
Katz, Steven, ed. *Comparative Mysticism: An Anthology of Original Sources*. Oxford: Oxford University Press, 2013.
Knasas, John F. *Aquinas and the Cry of Rachel: Thomistic Reflections on the Problem of Evil*. Washington, D.C.: Catholic University Press, 2013.
Langtry, Bruce. *God, the Best, and Evil*. Oxford: Oxford University Press, 2008.
Lewis, C. S. *The Problem of Pain*. London: Bles, 1940.
Moser, Paul K. *The Severity of God*. Cambridge: Cambridge University Press, 2013.
Nadler, Steven M. *The Best of All Possible Worlds: A Story of Philosophers, God, and Evil*. Princeton, NJ: Princeton University Press, 2010.
Pike, N. ed. *God and Evil: Readings in the Theological Problem of Evil*. London: Prentice-Hall, 1964.
Plantinga, Alvin. *God, Freedom, and Evil*. Grand Rapids, MI: Eerdmans, 2001.
Surin, Kenneth. *Theology and the Problem of Evil*. Oxford: Blackwell, 1986.
Van Inwagen, Peter. *The Problem of Evil*. Oxford: Oxford University Press, 2006.

CHAPTER 8
OTHER EXPLANATIONS THAT HAVE BEEN PROPOSED

Beaty, Michael. "The Problem of Evil: The Unanswered Question Argument." *Southwestern Philosophic Review* 4 (1988): 57–64.
Bennett, Philip. "Evil, God and the Free Will Defense." *Australian Journal of Philosophy* 51 (1973): 39–50.
Booker, John ed. *Knowing the Unknowable*. London: I. B. Tauris, 2009.
Boyce, Mary. *Zoroastrians: Their Religious Beliefs and Practices*. London: Routledge, 1983.
Boyer, Steven D., and Christopher A. Hall. *The Mystery of God: Theology for Knowing the Unknowable*. Grand Rapids, MI: Baker Academic, 2012.
Cahn, Steven M. "The Book of Job: The Great Dissent." *The Reconstructionist* 31 (1965): 14–19.

Clark, Peter. *Zoroastrianism: An Introduction to an Ancient Faith*. Sussex, UK: Academy, 1998.

Hall, Douglas John. *God and Human Suffering*. Minneapolis, MN: Augsburg, 1986.

Journet, Charles. *The Meaning of Evil*. New York: Kennedy, 1963.

Mavrodes, George, ed. *The Rationality of Belief in God*. Englewood Cliffs, NJ: Prentice-Hall, 1970.

Omsby, Eric. *Theodicy in Islamic Thought*. Princeton, NJ: Princeton University Press, 1984.

Penelhum, Terrence. "Divine Goodness and the Problem of Evil." *Religious Studies* 2 (1966): 95–108.

Russell, Bruce. "The Persistent Problem of Evil." *Faith and Philosophy* 6 (1989): 121–39.

Swinburne, Richard. "Natural Evil." *American Philosophical Quarterly* 15 (1978): 295–301.

Walsh, James, and P. G. Walsh. *Divine Providence and Human Suffering*. Wilmington, DE: Glazier, 1985.

Zaehner, Robert Charles. *The Dawn and Twilight of Zoroastrianism*. London: Phoenix, 1961.

CHAPTER 9
HOW CAN RELIGIOUS CLAIMS BE ESTABLISHED?

Basinger, David, and Randall Basinger. *Philosophy and Miracle: The Contemporary Debate*. Lewiston, NY: Mellon, 1986.

Bergmann, Michal, and Patrick Kain, eds. *Challenges to Moral and Religious Belief*. Oxford: Oxford University Press, 2014.

Booker, John, ed. *Knowing the Unknowable*. London: I. B. Tauris, 2009.

Clark, Kelly James, and Raymond J. Van Arragon. *Evidence and Religious Belief*. Oxford: Oxford University Press, 2011.

Coakley, Sarah, ed. *Faith, Rationality, and the Passions*. Malden, MA: Wiley-Blackwell, 2012.

Drozdowicz, Zbigniew. *Standards of Religious Rationality*. Zurich: Lit, 2013.

Faber, M. D. *The Magic of Prayer*. Westport, CT: Praeger, 2002.

Geisler, Norman L. *Miracles and Modern Thought*. Grand Rapids, MI: Zondervan, 1982.

Giordan, Giuseppe, and Linda Woodhead, eds. *Prayer in Religion and Spirituality*. Leiden: Brill, 2013.

Gottlieb, Michah. *Faith, Reason, Politics*. Brighton, MA: Academic Studies, 2013.

Harvey, Michael G. *Skepticism, Relativism, and Religious Knowledge*. Eugene, OR: Pickwick, 2013.

Keener, Craig S. *Miracles: The Credibility of the New Testament Accounts*. Grand Rapids, MI: Baker Academic, 2011.

Kellenberger, J. "Miracles." *International Journal of Philosophy and Religion* 10 (1979): 145–62.

Larmer, Robert A. H. *The Legitimacy of Miracle*. Lanham, MD: Lexington, 2014.

Mangina, Joseph L. *Revelation*. Grand Rapids, MI: Brazos, 2010.

Miller, Corey, and Paul Gould, eds. *Is Faith in God Reasonable?* New York: Routledge, 2014

Moon, Beverly Ann. *The Role of Revelation in the World's Religions*. Jefferson, NC: McFarland, 2010.

Philips, D. Z. *The Concept of Prayer*. London: Routledge and Kegan Paul, 1965.

Schimmel, Solomon. *The Tenacity of Unreasonable Beliefs: Fundamentalism and the Fear of Truth*. Oxford: Oxford University Press, 2008.

Shorto, Russell. *Descartes' Bones: A Skeletal History of the Conflict between Faith and Reason*. New York: Doubleday, 2008.

Swinburne, Richard. *The Concept of Miracles*. London: Macmillan, 1970.

Woodman, Ross Greig. *Revelation and Knowledge*. Toronto: University of Toronto Press, 2011.

Wurthnow, Robert. *The God Problem: Expressing Faith and Being Reasonable*. Berkeley: University of California Press, 2012.

Zaleski, Philip, and Carol Zaleski. *Prayer: A History*. Boston: Houghton Mifflin, 2005.

CHAPTER 10
FAMOUS CHALLENGES TO FAITH

Benson, Bruce Ellis. *Pious Nietzsche: Decadence and Dionysian Faith*. Bloomington, IN: Indiana University Press, 2008.

Bettleheim, Bruno. *Freud and Man's Soul*. New York: Knopf, 1982.

Boer, Roland. *In the Vale of Tears: Marxism and Theology*. Leiden: Brill, 2014.

Fornari, Giuseppe. *A God Torn to Pieces: The Nietzsche Case*. East Lansing: Michigan State University Press, 2013.

Franck, Didier. *Nietzsche and the Shadow of God*. Evanston, IL: Northwestern University Press, 2012.

Freud, S. *The Future of an Illusion*. New York: Norton, 1975.

———. *Totem and Taboo*. New York: Norton, 1950.

Fritzsche, Peter, ed. *Nietzsche and the Death of God: Selected Writings*. Boston: Bedford/St. Martin's, 2007.

Gale, John, Michael Robson, and Georgia Rapsomatioti. *Insanity and Spirituality*. New York: Routledge, 2014.

Gay, Volemy Patrick. *Reading Freud: Psychology, Neurosis, and Religion*. Chico, CA: Scholars, 1983.

Guirdham, Arthur. *Christ and Freud*. London: Allen and Unwin, 1959.

Howard, Joan E., and David Hillman. *Marx and Freud*. London: Continuum, 2012.

Kovel, Joel. "Beyond the Future of an Illusion." *Psychoanalytic Review* 77 (1990): 68–87.

Marx, Karl. *K. Marx and F. Engels on Religion*. Moscow: Foreign Languages, 1957.

McGovern, Arthur. "Atheism: Is It Essential to Marxism?" *Journal of Ecumenical Studies* 22 (1985): 487–539.

McKown, Delos B. *The Classical Marxist Critiques of Religion*. The Hague: Nijhoff, 1975.

Mills, Jon. *Underworlds: Philosophies of the Unconscious*. New York: Routledge, 2014.

Parsons, William B. *Freud and Augustine in Dialogue*. Charlottesville: University of Virginia Press, 2013.

Raines, John, ed. *Marx on Religion*. Philadelphia: Temple University Press, 2012.

Raines, John C., and Thomas Dean. *Marxism and Radical Religion*. Philadelphia: Temple University Press, 1970.

Rice, Emanuel. *Freud and Moses*. Albany: SUNY Press, 1990.

Seed, John. *Marx: A Guide for the Perplexed*. London: Continuum, 2010.

Young, Julian. *Nietzsche's Philosophy of Religion*. New York: Cambridge University Press, 2006.

Zillboorg, Gregory. *Psychoanalysis and Religion*. London: Allen and Unwin, 1967.

CHAPTER 11
THE STORMY RELATIONS BETWEEN SCIENCE AND RELIGION

Banner, Michael C. *The Justification of Science and the Rationality of Religious Belief*. New York: Oxford University Press, 1990.

Barbour, Ian. *Science and Religion*. New York: Harper and Row, 1968.

Calloway, Katherine. *Natural Theology in the Scientific Revolution: God's Scientists*. London: Pickering and Chatto, 2014.

Clark, Kelly James. *Religion and the Science of Origins*. Basingstoke, UK: Palgrave Macmillan, 2014.

Dampier, William Cecil. *A History of Science and Its Relation with Philosophy and Religion*. Cambridge: Cambridge University Press, 1948.

Dennett, Daniel, and Alvin Plantinga. *Science and Religion: Are They Compatible?* Oxford: Oxford University Press, 2010.

Fuller, Michael, ed. *The Concept of the Soul: Scientific and Religious Perspectives*. Newcastle upon Tyne: Cambridge Scholars, 2014.

Gerengerich, Galen. *God Revised: How Religion Must Evolve in a Scientific Age*. New York: Palgrave Macmillan, 2013.

Gingerich, Owen. *God's Planet*. Cambridge: Harvard University Press, 2014.

Gonzalo, Julia A. *Intelligible Design*. Hackensack, NJ: World Scientific, 2014.

Henson, Shaun C. *God and Natural Order: Physics, Philosophy, and Theology*. New York: Routledge, 2014.

Jaki, Stanley L. *The Road of Science and the Ways to God*. Chicago: University of Chicago Press, 1978.

Johnston, Lucas F., and Whitney Bauman, eds. *Science and Religion: One Planet, Many Possibilities*. New York: Routledge, 2014.

Manning, Russell R., and Michael Byrne. *Science and Religion in the Twenty-First Century*. London: SCM, 2013.

Mayer, Thomas J. *The Trial of Galileo*. Guelph, Ont.: University of Toronto Press, 2012.

Michael, T. *The Routledge Companion to Religion and Science*. New York: Routledge, 2014.

Plantinga, Alvin. *Where the Conflict Really Lies: Science, Religion, and Naturalism*. Oxford: Oxford University Press, 2011.

Russell, Bertrand. *Religion and Science*. London: Oxford University Press, 1961.

Welker, Michael. *The Science and Religion Dialogue*. Frankfurt am Main: Peter Lang, 2014.

White, Andrew Dickson. *A History of the Warfare of Science with Theology*. New York: Braziller, 1955.

CHAPTER 12
HOW RELIGION RELATES TO SOCIETY

Audi, Robert, and William J. Wainwright, eds. *Rationality, Religious Belief, and Moral Commitment*. Ithaca, NY: Cornell University Press, 1986.

Began, Richard. *The American Constitution and Religion*. Washington D.C.: Catholic University Press, 2013.

Boer, Roland, and Christina Peterson. *Idols of Nations: Biblical Myth at the Origins of Capitalism*. Minneapolis, MN: Fortress, 2014.

Compton, John W. *The Evangelical Origins of the Living Constitution*. Cambridge: Harvard University Press, 2014.

Connolly, William E. *Capitalism and Christianity*. Durham, NC: Duke University Press, 2008.

Crossley, John P. "Theological Ethics and the Naturalistic Fallacy." *Journal of Religious Ethics* 6 (Spring 1978): 121–34.

Davis, Creston, J. Milbank, and Slavoj Zizak. *Theology and the Political*. Durham, NC: Duke University Press, 2005.

Dennett, Daniel, and Linda Lascola. *Caught in the Pulpit: Leaving Belief Behind*. Fishpond, NZ: Congruity, 2013.

Evans, C. Stephen. *God and Moral Obligation*. Oxford: Oxford University Press, 2013.

Fowler, Robert Booth. *Religion and Politics in America*. Boulder, CO: Westview, 2014.

Green, Ronald Michael. *Religion and Moral Reason*. New York: Oxford University Press, 1988.

Helm, Paul, ed. *The Divine Command Theory of Ethics*. Oxford: Oxford University Press, 1979.

Jenkins, Willis. *The Future of Ethics: Sustainability, Social Justice, and Religious Creativity*. Washington, D.C.: Georgetown University Press, 2013.

Lambert, Frank. *Separation of Church and State*. Macon, GA: Mercer University Press, 2014.

Langermann, Y. Tzvi, ed. *Monotheism and Ethics*. Boston: Brill, 2012.

Mitchell, Basil. *Morality: Religious and Secular*. Oxford: Clarendon, 1980.

Porter, Burton F. *Deity and Morality*. London: Routledge, 2013.

Quinn, Philip L. *Divine Commands and Moral Requirements*. Oxford: Clarendon, 1978.

Ward, Keith. *Morality, Autonomy and God*. London: Oneworld, 2013.

Yip, Francis Cing-Wah. *Capitalism as Religion*. Cambridge, MA: Harvard Divinity School, 2010.

CHAPTER 13
IMMORTALITY: A DIVERSITY OF BELIEFS

Bedham, Paul. *Making Sense of Death and Immortality*. London: SPCK, 2013.

Bedham, Paul, and Lina Bedham, eds. *Death and Immortality in the Religions of the World*. New York: Paragon House, 1987.

Belshaw, Christopher. *Annihilation: The Sense and Significance of Death*. Montreal: McGill-Queens University Press, 2009.

Benecke, Mark. *The Dream of Eternal Life: Biomedicine, Aging, and Immortality*. New York: Columbia University Press, 2002.

Cave, Stephen. *The Quest to Live Forever and How It Drives Civilization*. New York: Crown, 2012.

Dickinson, G. *Is Immortality Desirable?* Boston: Houghton Mifflin, 1909.

D'Souza, Dinesh. *Life after Death: The Evidence*. Washington, D.C.: Regnery, 2009.

Ducasse, C. J. *The Belief in Life after Death*. London: Blackwell, 1961.

Frazer, J. G. *The Belief in Immortality*. London: Macmillan, 1913.

Frohock, Fred M. *Beyond: On Life after Death*. Lawrence: University of Kansas Press, 2010.

Gollner, Adam. *Immortality: The Science, Belief, and Magic behind Living Forever*. New York: Scribner, 2013.

James, William. *Human Immortality*. Boston: Houghton Mifflin, 1898.

Kung, Hans. *Eternal Life*. New York: Doubleday, 1984.

Lamont, Corliss. *The Illusion of Immortality*. New York: Wisdom Library, 1959.

Leslie, John. *Immortality Defended*. Malden, MA: Blackwell, 2007.

Myers, F. W. H. *Human Personality and Its Survival of Bodily Death*. London: Longmans Green, 1903.

Penelhum, Terence. *Survival and Disembodied Existence*. London: Routledge and Kegan Paul, 1970.

Philips, D. Z. *Death and Immortality*. New York: St. Martin's, 1970.

Pieper, Josef. *Death and Immortality*. South Bend, IN: St. Augustine's, 2000.

Rouner, Leroy S. *If I Should Die*. Notre Dame, IN: Notre Dame University Press, 2001.

Spencer, Charlotte A. *Genes, Aging, and Immortality*. Upper Saddle River, NJ: Pearson, 2006.

Stein, Gordon. *Survival and Disembodied Existence*. New York: Humanities, 1970.

Walter, Tony. *The Eclipse of Eternity*. New York: St. Martin's, 1996.

CHAPTER 14
RELIGION TODAY—ITS MULTIPLE FORMS

Amarsingam, Amarnath. *Religion and the New Atheism*. Boston: Brill, 2010.

Brewster, Melanie E. *Atheists in America*. New York: Columbia University Press, 2004.

Dworkin, Ronald. *Religion without God*. Cambridge, MA: Harvard University Press, 2013.

Eagleton, Terry. *Culture and the Death of God*. New Haven, CT: Yale University Press, 2014.

Ehrlich, Stanislaw, and Graham Wooton, eds. *Three Faces of Pluralism*. Westmead, UK: Gower, 1980.

Flew, Antony. *The Presumption of Atheism*. New York: Harper and Row, 1976.

Fulkerson, Mary M., and Sheila Briggs, eds. *The Oxford Handbook of Feminist Theology*. Oxford: Oxford University Press, 2012.

Harris, Sam. *The End of Faith, Religion, Terror, and the Future of Reason*. New York: Norton, 2005.

Harvey, Graham. *Contemporary Paganism: Religions of the Earth*. New York: New York University Press, 2011.

Hick, John H. *God Has Many Names*. Philadelphia: Westminster John Knox, 1986.

Hitchens, Christopher. *God Is Not Great: How Religion Poisons Everything*. New York: Hachette, 2007.

Johnson, Elizabeth A. *She Who Is*. Danvers, MA: Crossroad, 2002.

Joshim S. T. *The Unbelievers: The Evolution of Modern Atheism*. Amherst, NY: Prometheus, 2011.

Keogh, Gary. *Reading Richard Dawkins: A Theological Dialogue with New Atheism*. Minneapolis, MN: Fortress, 2014.

MacLeod, Sharon Paice. *The Divine Feminine in Ancient Europe*. Jefferson, NC: McFarland, 2013.

Monoghan, Patricia, ed. *Goddesses in World Culture*. Santa Barbara, CA: Praeger, 2011.

Moser, Paul K., and Michael T. McFall, eds. *The Wisdom of the Christian Faith*. New York.: Cambridge University Press, 2012.

Newman, Jay. *Foundation of Religious Tolerance*. Toronto: University of Toronto Press, 1982.

Pike, Sarah M. *New Age and Neopagan Religion in America*. New York: Columbia University Press, 2004.

Sharpe, Eric. *Comparative Religion*. London: Duckworth, 2003.

Smith, George H. *Atheism: The Case against God*. New York: Prometheus, 1979.

Starhawk. *The Spiral Dance: A Rebirth of the Ancient Religion of the Goddess*. San Francisco: Harper, 1979.

Watson, Peter. *The Age of Atheists*. New York: Simon and Schuster, 2014.

INDEX

ABOUT THE AUTHOR

Including the present work, **Burton Porter** is the author of twelve books in print form: *What the Tortoise Taught Us* (Rowman and Littlefield), *The Head and the Heart, Philosophy through Fiction and Film, The Voice of Reason, The Good Life* (Rowman and Littlefield, 4th ed.), *Religion and Reason, Philosophy through Film, Personal Philosophy: Reasons for Living, Philosophy: A Literary and Conceptual Approach,* and *Deity and Morality.* He also has five books online: *The Moebius Strip, Lab Rats, The Gadfly, Forbidden Knowledge,* and *Black Swans and White Tigers,* and has published numerous book reviews and papers.

Dr. Porter received his bachelor's degree from the University of Maryland and his doctorate from St. Andrews University, Scotland, which included graduate study at Oxford University, England. He has been on the faculty of various institutions, including Russell Sage College, the University of Maryland (Europe), and Drexel University, and he has served as department chair and dean of Arts and Sciences. He taught at Mount Holyoke College as visiting professor of philosophy, and he is currently teaching at Western New England University in Springfield, Massachusetts. Porter received the award of Outstanding Educator of America. He lives in Amherst, Massachusetts, with his wife, Barbara, and indulges his interest in literature, music, running, and occasionally tennis. He has two children, Mark and Ana, and a stepdaughter, Sarah.